Building Programming Language Interpreters

A bottom-up approach to runtimes, execution, and implementation in C++

Daniel Ruoso

<packt>

Building Programming Language Interpreters

Portfolio Director: Kunal Chaudhari
Relationship Lead: Dhruv J. Kataria
Project Manager: K. Loganathan
Content Engineer: Richa Singh
Technical Editor: Irfa Ansari
Copy Editor: Safis Editing
Indexer: Hemangini Bari
Proofreader: Richa Singh
Production Designer: Prashant Ghare
Growth Lead: Vinishka Kalra

First published: January 2026

Production reference: 1130126

Published by Packt Publishing Ltd.

Grosvenor House

11 St Paul's Square

Birmingham

B3 1RB, UK.

ISBN 978-1-83763-807-9

www.packtpub.com

In the mid-2000s, I was fortunate enough to get involved in the development of the Perl 6 language. This was probably the steepest learning period in my life as a software developer. The long conversations on IRC with fantastic folks such as Audrey Tang, Flávio Glock, Jonathan Worthington, Larry Wall, Moritz Lenz, Nelson Ferraz, Paweł Murias, Yuval Kogman, and many others have given me the starting point of my understanding of programming languages and interpreter design. Without them, I would likely not have gotten interested in this area at all.

—Daniel Ruoso

Contributors

About the author

Daniel Ruoso has more than 20 years of experience in software development. He has contributed to various projects over the years, specializing in build tooling, static analysis, and automated code refactoring. He was a contributor to the early development of the Raku programming language and of the Debian project. More recently, he contributed to the tooling study group of the ISO C++ working group. Daniel has also presented talks at the LLVM Developers' Meeting, C++Now, and CppCon.

Thanks to my parents, Karin and Sérgio, who provided me with access to technology at an early age and the space to experiment at a time when this was not at all common in the small town of Iguatu; my older brother, Leonardo, who nudged me in all the right ways to kickstart my career; my wife, Arêtha, for supporting me in every risk I took in my journey to get where I am today; and my kids, Tito and Yann, for motivating me to keep learning.

About the reviewers

Tony Varghese is a compiler engineer and engineering tech lead with extensive hands-on experience in LLVM and MLIR frameworks. He has contributed multiple patches to the upstream LLVM project, including contributions to the PowerPC backend and optimization passes, and actively participates in the compiler development community through technical forums and mentoring. His work focuses on compiler optimizations, language tooling, and building robust infrastructure for complex systems. Tony is passionate about problem-solving and enjoys tackling challenging compiler and interpreter implementation issues. His open source contributions can be found at `https://github.com/tonykuttai/`. When not working on compilers, he enjoys spending time with his daughter and playing badminton.

I would like to thank my family for their support and encouragement during the technical review of this book.

Nikhil Kapoor has over 16 years of experience in the fields of AI and **machine learning (ML)**, where he has designed and implemented advanced models, intelligent platforms, and data-driven solutions at scale. His expertise extends to architecting end-to-end platforms and distributed applications at a leading cloud service provider, integrating AI/ML capabilities with cloud-native technologies to drive innovation. He has applied these skills across diverse sectors—including finance, investment management, audit, and telecom R&D—delivering intelligent, scalable, and production-ready systems. In addition to his technical depth, he has led teams through the full software development life cycle.

Join us on Discord!

Read this book alongside other users, developers, experts, and the author himself.

Ask questions, provide solutions to other readers, chat with the authors via Ask Me Anything sessions, and much more. Scan the QR or visit the link to join the community.

`https://packt.link/deep-engineering-cpp`

Table of Contents

Part 2: Modeling the Programming Language Syntax

Preface

I grew up experimenting with BASIC on an MSX computer in Brazil. That was a time when the computer would come with a printed manual that had little games and exercises with the code listings, and you would have to type it out to see what happened. When my family got a 486 PC, I transitioned to QBASIC. I still remember the first time I built an entire game with animations and everything from scratch.

Later, I transitioned to Delphi, where I would help my older brother in some of his projects, and eventually presented a small educational application at my school that I built with a colleague to explore the periodic table. At that time, I was also transitioning to using GNU/Linux and exploring with C programming.

I only became a "real" software developer once I learned Perl. This was 1998, and my older brother bought the *Learning Perl* and *Programming Perl* books. I still spoke "baby Perl," as Larry Wall would say, and it would be a few years until I was confident enough to ship my first module to CPAN.

I became an avid advocate for the Perl language and started publishing various CPAN modules and participating in conferences. I remember all the hours I spent on perlmonks.org, and the moment my name finally showed up on the *Saints in Our Book* page.

But while at the turn of the century, Perl was "the duct tape of the internet," by the turn of the 2010s, there was a very strong sentiment against it in the industry. I had to accept that I couldn't just be a Perl developer; I had to be an "anything developer."

This has led me to take a very different perspective when looking at programming language and interpreter design. To look beyond the *what* and start asking the *why*. Why did Python choose to use a Global Interpreter Lock? Why did Perl have a share-nothing approach for multi-threading? Why does the C++ language have entirely different systems for programming and meta-programming?

Meanwhile, my formal education was in social sciences, which made me look at all of this from an anthropological perspective. At the end of the day, we're talking about human communication; there's no stick we can use to measure whether one language is better than another. You have different languages and people with different levels of fluency. You have ecosystems and communities that build a specific culture around those languages.

It is with this perspective that I arrived at the premise of this book, which is that we will never stop creating new programming languages, for as long as we have to write code. But this doesn't need to be just a matter of aesthetic preference. Some niche problems require niche solutions, and building programming language interpreters is a way to introduce novel solutions to existing problems.

At the same time, a programming language is heavily influenced by the runtime environment it targets, but it's also possible to build custom runtime environments that target a specific programming language.

The existing literature tends to treat those areas as fundamentally independent, while I feel that there is a lot left behind by not considering the design and implementation of the programming language and of the runtime environment it targets as a coherent set.

That is why it was important to me to choose a bottom-up approach when working on this book. I want you to look at the entire problem of both programming language and interpreter design and implementation as a single unit.

By the end of this book, I hope that you find yourself as fascinated as I am by all the technical and non-technical aspects that are connected to programming language and interpreter design and implementation.

Who this book is for

This book is tailored for intermediate to advanced software developers, particularly those interested in language design and implementation. It's ideal for programmers seeking to expand their skill set and tackle complex problems efficiently. Professionals working in roles such as software engineers, language designers, or system architects will benefit from the practical insights and hands-on experience provided in the book. A good understanding of C++ programming and a basic grasp of language design concepts are recommended to fully grasp the content.

What this book covers

Chapter 1, Defining the Scope, starts with a reflection on why we keep introducing new programming languages and what benefits they can introduce, and then sets the problem statement for the programming language we will use for the exercise in this book, with the goals and acceptance criteria for the minimum viable product of that language.

Chapter 2, The Blurred Lines Between Native Code, Virtual Machines, and Interpreters, discusses how modern hardware architectures can no longer be thought of in the same way as historical architectures, and how an interpreter has a lot of similarities with hardware in terms of how we think about its capabilities.

Chapter 3, Instructions, Concurrency, Inputs, and Outputs, works through the decision of the general architecture of the interpreter that will be built in the book, discussing various alternative approaches used by other interpreters.

Chapter 4, Native Types, User Types, and Extension Points, explores how the choice of the type system of the runtime affects the programming language, how choices in the language affect the runtime, and how those choices come together to guide the design.

Chapter 5, Putting It All Together: Making Trade-Off Decisions, completes the overall design process for the interpreter and language runtime, contrasting the consequences of specific choices and how they affect the interpreter.

Chapter 6, Review of Programming Language Paradigms, goes over the various ways in which different programming languages make it easier or harder to solve specific problems, how some paradigms help in specific scenarios, and which approach makes the most sense for the language being designed and implemented in this book.

Chapter 7, Values, Containers, and the Language Meta-Model, discusses how various programming languages have different approaches for handling values, variables, and containers, and how they interact with runtime type information, copies, and references.

Chapter 8, Lexical Scopes, covers how the language handles names, how they get resolved to variables, how other languages approach that problem, and the trade-offs that we will focus on for our language.

Chapter 9, Putting It All Together and Creating a Coherent Vision, brings together all the various aspects discussed of how to make the programming language design into a coherent design.

Chapter 10, Initialization and Entry Point, covers the overall structure of the interpreter project, starting with the skeleton CMake project, then explaining how to drive development with tests, how the operation tree is implemented, and how the interpreter steps through it.

Chapter 11, Execution Frames, the Stack, and Continuations, covers how the programming language needs to handle higher-level concepts than the simple operation tree in the stack, including the execution of functions.

Chapter 12, Running and Testing Language Operators, brings together how operators are implemented, tested, and executed, getting to the point where the interpreter can parse and write an entire message.

Chapter 13, Lexing: Turning Text into a Stream of Tokens, starts the transition into the ability to actually run code in the programming language, starting with the lexer, which breaks down the characters in the source into a sequence of tokens.

Chapter 14, Parsing: Turning a Stream of Tokens into a Parse Tree, works through the definition of a grammar for the language, and how that is implemented in C++, including a custom grammar engine using modern C++ features.

Chapter 15, Analyzing: Turning a Parse Tree into an Abstract Syntax Tree, highlights how the parse tree is focused on the shape of the source code itself, while a language may have a different abstract structure, and how the abstract syntax tree needs to represent that higher-level structure.

Chapter 16, Generating: Turning an Abstract Syntax Tree into Instructions, closes the gap between the abstract syntax tree and the operations supported by the interpreter, concluding with a test that exercises the interpreter end to end.

Chapter 17, Proving That It Works, implements the code that a user of the interpreter would write to exercise the end-to-end experience and validate that we achieved the goals we set at the beginning of the exercise.

To get the most out of this book

The first two parts are mostly theoretical, but when we get to the implementation, you will benefit from being able to play along with the implementation.

Software/hardware covered in the book	Operating system requirements
CMake	Windows, macOS, or Linux
GCC, at least version 12, or Clang, at least version 17	

Make sure you are able to use an interactive debugger. Even better if it is integrated into your editor.

Download the example code files

The code bundle for the book is hosted on GitHub at `https://github.com/PacktPublishing/Building-Programming-Language-Interpreters`. We also have other code bundles from our rich catalog of books and videos available at `https://github.com/PacktPublishing`. Check them out!

Download the color images

We also provide a PDF file that has color images of the screenshots/diagrams used in this book. You can download it here: `https://packt.link/gbp/9781837638079`.

Conventions used

There are a number of text conventions used throughout this book.

`CodeInText`: Indicates code words in text, database table names, folder names, filenames, file extensions, pathnames, dummy URLs, user input, and Twitter handles. For example: "The C++ language offers a way to handle that case in a type-safe way by using `std::variant`."

A block of code is set as follows:

```
template <typename OT>
concept OperationConcept = requires(OT op, OT::Arguments args) {
    {
        std::tuple_size<typename OT::Arguments>::value
        } -> std::convertible_to<std::size_t>;
    { op(args) } -> std::convertible_to<Value>;
};
```

Any command-line input or output is written as follows:

```
Date is: 2024-12-31
```

Bold: Indicates a new term, an important word, or words that you see on the screen. For instance, words in menus or dialog boxes appear in the text like this. For example: "This is also known as the **actor model**."

Warnings or important notes appear like this.

Tips and tricks appear like this.

> *Quotes appear like this.*

Get in touch

Feedback from our readers is always welcome.

General feedback: If you have questions about any aspect of this book or have any general feedback, please email us at `customercare@packt.com` and mention the book's title in the subject of your message.

Errata: Although we have taken every care to ensure the accuracy of our content, mistakes do happen. If you have found a mistake in this book, we would be grateful if you reported this to us. Please visit `http://www.packt.com/submit-errata`, click **Submit Errata**, and fill in the form.

Piracy: If you come across any illegal copies of our works in any form on the internet, we would be grateful if you would provide us with the location address or website name. Please contact us at `copyright@packt.com` with a link to the material.

If you are interested in becoming an author: If there is a topic that you have expertise in and you are interested in either writing or contributing to a book, please visit `http://authors.packt.com/`.

Share your thoughts

Once you've read *Building Programming Language Interpreters*, we'd love to hear your thoughts! Scan the QR code below to go straight to the Amazon review page for this book and share your feedback.

https://packt.link/r/1837638071

Your review is important to us and the tech community and will help us make sure we're delivering excellent quality content.

Free Benefits with Your Book

This book comes with free benefits to support your learning. Activate them now for instant access (see the "*How to Unlock*" section for instructions).

Here's a quick overview of what you can instantly unlock with your purchase:

PDF and ePub Copies

- Access a DRM-free PDF copy of this book to read anywhere, on any device.
- Use a DRM-free ePub version with your favorite e-reader.

Next-Gen Web-Based Reader

- **Multi-device progress sync**: Pick up where you left off, on any device.
- **Highlighting and notetaking**: Capture ideas and turn reading into lasting knowledge.
- **Bookmarking**: Save and revisit key sections whenever you need them.
- **Dark mode:** Reduce eye strain by switching to dark or sepia themes.

How to Unlock

UNLOCK NOW

Scan the QR code (or go to `packtpub.com/unlock`). Search for this book by name, confirm the edition, and then follow the steps on the page.

Note: *Keep your invoice handy. Purchases made directly from Packt don't require one.*

Part 1

Modeling the Programming Language Runtime Environment

In this part, you will dive into the background for the design of programming language runtime environments and work through the specific trade-offs that I am committing to in the development of the interpreter presented in this book. To ground those design decisions, I'll begin with a broader look at the problem space and introduce the practical project that will guide you throughout the book. The goal is to navigate from the lowest to the highest levels of abstraction, giving you a broad perspective on how programming language runtimes work.

This part has the following chapters:

1

Defining the Scope

In this chapter, we will focus on defining the target programming language and interpreter that we will develop throughout this book. We will cover the following aspects:

- Reflecting on the continuing desire to refine the programming language landscape with new ideas
- Exploring how domain-specific languages help solve targeted problems
- Understanding how building an interpreter can help to iterate on language design
- Defining the use case that will serve as our exercise through this book
- Discussing how this new language needs to interact with existing ecosystems

By the end of this chapter, you will have a new appreciation for the diversity of programming languages in our ecosystem. You will also be more knowledgeable about the project that will be developed throughout this book.

Technical requirements

All the code for this book is available on GitHub: `https://github.com/PacktPublishing/Building-Programming-Language-Interpreters`.

Why do we keep creating new languages?

> *I suppose it is tempting, if the only tool you have is a hammer, to treat everything as if it were a nail.*
>
> —*Abraham Maslow, 1966, The Psychology of Science*

We tend to underestimate how the programming languages we use define the way we write code and the way we handle the problems that are presented to us as software developers. The shape of our solutions is influenced by the tools we have when we're working on them.

The environments and ecosystems of the programming languages we use shape us as developers. We can sometimes recognize the accent a developer has when they move from one programming language to another, and it takes a certain amount of effort and code review to become familiar with another language and to start *talking like a native*.

While it's true that you can solve any computable problem in any Turing-complete language, it's also true that some problem spaces are better addressed by certain languages, and those tend to become used persistently, even when they're no longer *in fashion*.

Fortran is a very good example of that. It has seen an important resurgence in the scientific computing community. It has straightforward semantics, very good support for numerical types, and a lot of efficiency when it comes to computing lots of numerical operations. Those characteristics make it extremely useful in that context, and it doesn't matter that Fortran is quite literally the oldest programming language still in use.

The ecosystem also defines a lot regarding how problems are solved. C++ has a significant deficiency in how code reuse is managed, particularly across projects. It still has no uniform package management, even though it is probably the language that needs the most amount of support from outside the language for its build to work properly. Header-only libraries in C++ were developers' response to this deficiency in the ecosystem, and it became a defining aspect of how libraries are made in the language.

Of course, sometimes we also just want to express aesthetic preferences on how we write our code. Programming is not a mathematical exercise; it is much closer to telling a story—a story you tell the computer, of course, but it's also a story you tell other developers. And it's easy to underestimate how strongly software developers feel about the choices that are made to solve programming problems.

Those choices are not always made based on empirical evidence—more often than not, they're derived from the culture that is built around a given community. The Perl community, for instance, was heavily informed by the *"There is more than one way to do it"* principle of the language itself. This could also be seen in how libraries were designed, with more flexible interfaces and the idea that the goal was to make it easier to solve problems.

This ended up becoming the fuel for a lot of the detraction from Perl, and opposition to it became a driving force in the design of Python, where *"There should be one—and preferably only one—obvious way to do it."*

You may have read the previous paragraphs thinking that I would present you with a definitive way to talk about the most important aspects of programming language design and give you the answer to the question: *"What is the best and worst programming language?"* But I'm going to go in quite the opposite direction.

Instead of trying to find the one ultimate language, our goal should be to use the programming language that best fits the specific problem we're trying to solve. Sometimes, we may have strong opinions regarding that programming language, but if it allows us to solve the problem more easily (maybe there's a library in that ecosystem that fits our problem), then we should prioritize solving the problem, independent of our opinions about that particular programming language.

Sometimes, disruption comes from unexpected places, and a language that takes a different approach will allow developers to create better solutions to existing problems. That can create a turning point and attract a lot of people to bootstrap an entirely new community. We've seen how fast Rust is gaining popularity, and how its memory management model changes the way people solve problems in that language.

Other times, disruptions occur without us having to replace any existing language. Focusing on niche use cases can create entirely new ways of solving problems. In the next section, we will focus on scenarios like that.

Domain-specific languages

Some use cases benefit from an entirely separate language focused on that particular problem. We call those **domain-specific languages (DSLs)**. They solve specific types of problems that don't fit well with the existing programming languages. They eliminate the need to express things that are not part of the problem and allow us to focus on the problem itself.

A great example of a language that is used a lot, but that most people wouldn't consider using in situations other than the one it's already used, is SQL. It is a language that focuses on expressing complicated relational algebra in a way that is intuitive and where you don't have to specify unrelated operations to the problem you're solving, meaning that there is less opportunity for bugs in the code.

A tool that is extremely powerful and that has become an integral feature of most programming languages is regular expressions. Specifying how to match a string against complex rules would be massively error prone if the developer didn't have access to that specific language.

The two examples provided happen to be languages that often belong to entirely different paradigms than the one the developer is using to write the broader application code, and this is not a coincidence. The declarative nature of regular expressions makes them very different from the imperative nature of the language usually surrounding their use. And it's that ability to easily go from being imperative to declarative that is the greatest power of DSLs. In *Chapter 6, Review of Programming Language Paradigms,* I will discuss the various programming language paradigms.

Before jumping into the programming language that we'll be designing in this book, it is important to take a step back and think about how our code will run.

Compilers and interpreters

Compilers and interpreters were roughly developed at the same time most programmers were expected to write native code for their target architecture. In general, a compiler will translate higher-level programming language code into native code that's executed by the CPU. On the other hand, an interpreter will translate the programming language into a series of abstract operations that will be executed by the interpreter indirectly. Some problem spaces required minimal overhead, something that a direct translation to native code could provide, while other spaces could afford that overhead and prioritized the easier iteration between writing code and having it executed.

In *Chapter 2, The Blurred Lines Between Native Code, Virtual Machines, and Interpreters,* I will discuss how this distinction has become increasingly fragile over time. However, the principle still stands: when we make the distinction between compiled and interpreted languages, we still think in terms of whether the execution is done directly, by the native architecture, or whether there is a user-level abstraction that will execute the code in terms of abstract operations.

One of the biggest advantages of working with an interpreter is that you get to define all the characteristics of the runtime for your programming language. This allows for much quicker iteration when developing the programming language since you don't need to worry about low-level machine behavior. And, more importantly, this does not prevent you from eventually generating native code from it.

Even if the problem space is one where the lower overhead of a compiler will be desirable in the end, the freedom afforded by starting with an interpreter will allow you to get to a working prototype faster.

In the next section, we will reflect on what we covered in the previous sections to define the use case that we will implement in this book.

The exercise we will complete in this book

This book will take you through the journey of creating a **custom programming language** and interpreter. This journey will be segmented into four parts:

- In the first part, I will discuss runtime environments, how they impact language design, and what trade-offs are available
- In the second part, I will discuss programming language design, and how that influences different kinds of problem-solving approaches
- In the third part, I will focus on the implementation of the interpreter runtime, getting it to a point where the interpreter can run a program
- In the fourth part, I will focus on processing the syntax of the language, leading to a functional interpreter

This bottom-up approach intends to give you a broad understanding of the entire problem space instead of just parsing code. I believe reflecting on these deeper aspects of how to build an interpreter will give you a stronger perspective when you start implementing your own interpreter and programming language.

To make this a fruitful exercise, we'll create a custom language that solves a real-world problem and can be used in future projects.

Note that whenever you are considering writing a custom language and interpreter, you should start from the same point I'm starting now and contemplate the following questions:

- What goal do you have for that language?
- What is going to be in the first release?
- What will be outside the scope at the start?

It's important to take these questions into account because writing a custom programming language and interpreter is easily something that gives way to scope creep and endless redesigning. My suggestion is that you resist that urge and stay focused on delivering what you set out to be your first release. Once you've done that, you will be able to use your custom language in the real world to inform the direction of its next releases—it's likely that the use case you've been thinking about won't be needed until much later.

With that said, let's start looking at the exercise we will complete in this book. I want to focus on the following problem space: writing code that interacts with a network protocol, which is very error prone. Bugs in managing the state machines required to implement more complex network protocols are common. This is because, in general, programming languages do not provide high-level enough abstractions to deal with those.

The challenge I'm putting forth for myself in writing this book is to come up with a DSL for specifying network protocols. The interpreter will perform the necessary operations and manage all the state machines required to implement the protocol correctly, whereas the language will specify in which parts of the protocol the control flow is meant to be transferred between the DSL and the native language.

I don't expect that the interpreter we'll create will be a complete solution that can handle any network protocol, as that would make it really difficult to finish this book. Instead, we will focus on a few basic requirements and specify acceptance criteria for a **minimum viable product (MVP)** for this new, custom programming language.

This interpreter will need to have the following characteristics:

- Be able to support synchronous request–response protocols, such as HTTP/1.1.
- Allow control to be transferred to the outside language at multiple points so that a request can be rejected before it's processed. As an example, a request could be rejected due to the path given in an HTTP request not existing.

- Allow values to be captured and communicated to the outside language.
- Allow captured values to be used to define aspects of the communication itself, such as the `Content-Length` header in HTTP, which specifies how long the body should be.

Likewise, some aspects will be intentionally left out:

- Support for protocols that utilize concurrent messages and asynchronous states, such as HTTP/2
- Support for continuation across network interruptions
- Support for general-purpose computation in the language
- Support for using more than one thread for each connection

This is not to say that those are never going to become features of the language and the interpreter, but the goal is to prevent scope creep from becoming part of the first release of the language.

The acceptance criteria for this first version of the language will be as follows:

- It must be able to start the interpreter by providing a source file when a daemon is initialized
- It must give a connected socket to the interpreter for it to drive the network protocol
- It must have the interpreter return control so that specific functions can be executed at the points defined in the interpreted program

In the next section, we will discuss how this interpreter will interact with existing ecosystems and how we can make it as useful as possible.

How will the interpreter be integrated?

A custom programming language that handles network protocols is not going to be very useful if you can't connect it to whatever code is already handling **input/output (I/O)** as you might be using different libraries and approaches to implement **concurrency**.

To make this custom language useful, the design for the interpreter needs to be considered with care. The way input and output are handled and the way concurrency needs to be supported will have a direct impact on the situations in which the interpreter can be used.

In our case, the crucial integration point is going to be the I/O layer since the language focuses on how a socket communicates. Other languages will likely have other, more dominant aspects. Here are some other scenarios that illustrate how different languages may have very different focus points for integration:

- A language focused on large mathematical computations would have to largely focus on concurrent processing and how to transfer values efficiently
- A language focused on message passing would need a fine-tuned scheduler that reduces the amount of time that's spent on managing message queues
- A language focused on real-time processing would need tight control over all the operations that could introduce unplanned latency to the execution

When you're starting the design process for your language, you must understand the runtime characteristics. This will be the dominating aspect, particularly if it is a DSL that is meant to be embedded into existing systems. This is because runtime characteristics will heavily influence how your interpreter needs to be designed and how it will be integrated.

Trying to cover more than one scenario would likely make this book much larger, so I will only focus on proposing one language. Following this design journey will give you a good perspective on the process and allow you to think about the important aspects of your language.

As I stated previously, the crucial aspect of the language we'll be developing is how it will integrate the I/O layer. At the time of writing, the ecosystem around processing I/O events is very fragmented. Many independent libraries and frameworks are used in different situations, and committing to just one would significantly limit where this interpreter could be used.

For instance, if you perform a plain read operation on a socket, that will block until bytes are received. On the other hand, if you use non-blocking reads, you still need to be able to know when something is there to be read.

Understanding I/O models—blocking, non-blocking, synchronous, and asynchronous

The interaction between programming languages and I/O operations is dominated by two main aspects:

- Whether the execution is going to wait until the operation is completed (**blocking**) or whether it will allow incomplete operations (**non-blocking**).
- Whether the control flow is managed by the program (**synchronous**) or whether it is controlled by the operation itself (**asynchronous**). In the former case, the program continues only after the operation is completed, while in the latter case, the program does not wait for the operation to complete and can execute other operations.

Different I/O libraries will make a specific set of choices regarding this that define how the program has to be written. Let's look at some examples:

- `libuv` uses an asynchronous and non-blocking mechanism, which means code that's integrated with that library will be defined by callback functions and external state management.
- Regular POSIX functions, such as `read()` and `write()`, are always synchronous, meaning your program manages the entire control flow. However, the functions can either wait until the requested number of bytes is read or written (blocking) or return immediately if the operation cannot be completed at that moment (non-blocking).

Another example we could consider is Node.js, which uses `libuv` to implement its I/O operations. If you try to embed Node.js into a process that primarily uses Boost.Asio, you will face a lot of challenges when integrating the two since their approaches to I/O are fundamentally different.

One way to bypass this problem is by utilizing the **sans I/O** approach. In this approach, instead of supporting a specific concurrency and set of I/O primitives, an API can be built that can be glued to any existing framework, maximizing code reuse.

In practice, this means that the interpreter will not perform any direct read or write operation and instead offer mechanisms so that the integration layer knows that the interpreter is trying to read or write.

Of course, anyone using `libuv`, for instance, will need to write the glue between it and the interpreter. However, the important point here is that the interpreter itself does not presume that a particular integration should be used; instead, it has an interface that allows any of those frameworks to be integrated.

The other aspect that I defined in the acceptance criteria is that the language will have callback points that will deliver control flow back to the outside language. This highlights an important aspect regarding concurrency and memory management for our interpreter.

There are two possibilities here: the first is that the callback is done entirely within the interpreter loop, meaning it will remain on the native call stack, while the second is that the callbacks are returned so that they can be started by an external scheduler.

This has a significant impact on how memory is managed. If the callback is executed from within the interpreter loop, then the interpreter can use the stack to store some of its state, which simplifies memory management. If the callback is executed outside the interpreter loop, the execution of the callback can be separated into a different thread from where the interpreter itself runs.

Figure 1.1 compares two different ways the callbacks can be integrated with the native code's call stack. The left-hand side of *Figure 1.1* demonstrates that if we just use the native stack to switch between the native code and the interpreter, each of those layers will be completely enclosed, which will limit how the native code can be integrated. On the other hand, the right-hand side of the figure demonstrates that we can execute each step, but instead of calling the next step internally, the system returns information about where the execution has to continue. This will allow the execution to be continued, interrupted, or reordered without constraints from the native stack:

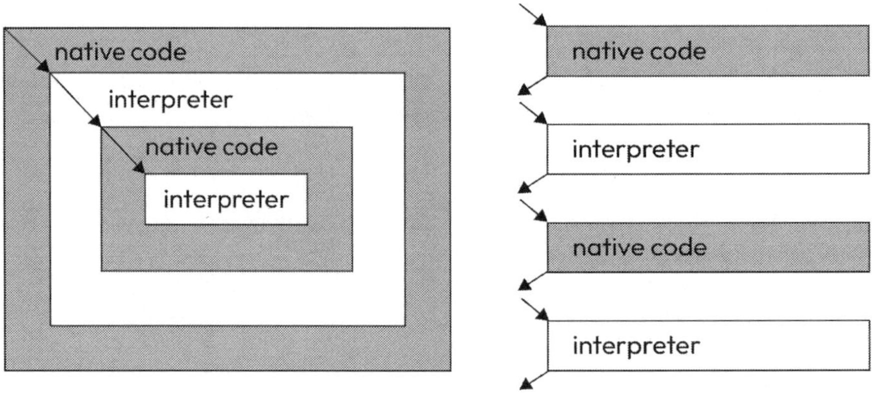

Figure 1.1: Comparing approaches on how to integrate with the native call stack

In this case, my goal is to maximize the flexibility of where this interpreter can be used, so our design will delegate to the outside language as much as possible. Making callbacks from within the interpreter will likely limit its usage, particularly if more complex operations are handled by code. Therefore, I will make the callbacks run from outside the frames processing the protocol itself.

Since I've limited our scope to a synchronous protocol for this first version, I only need to support one thread of execution for each socket. However, since we are executing callbacks from outside of the interpreter, they will be able to dispatch additional asynchronous work.

Additionally, there may be many sockets running different instances of the interpreter so that multiple concurrent requests can be handled. To avoid having to parse the code multiple times, we need to create a bootstrap environment that can only be initialized once and can be reused for each connection.

This is very far from a complete design of how the interpreter will work, but it gives us a good starting point regarding the constraints and requirements that must be set. This also illustrates how much complexity goes into building an interpreter.

Summary

Programming languages are an integral part of our culture as software engineers and developers—they define how we look at the problems we want to solve. Significant changes to that culture are sometimes driven by the introduction of entirely new general-purpose programming languages, but it's often the case that DSLs focused on very limited use cases have a much deeper impact on how problems are solved across a variety of programming languages.

Designing and implementing a new programming language requires careful consideration of what needs to be supported in the first version and what can be deferred to future implementations. In this book, we will be narrowing the focus to a DSL that focuses on implementing network protocols, with the first version limited to synchronous request–response protocols such as HTTP/1.1.

Beyond defining the scope, we also have to define some more concrete guidelines, such as how we're going to use the sans I/O approach to allow the programming language to be used in more scenarios.

Likewise, we will avoid coupling the execution of the interpreted code with the native stack, which will give whoever uses the interpreter various options regarding how to handle concurrency, callbacks, and execution.

In the next chapter, we will focus on the importance of the various levels of abstraction that programming languages use to make specific kinds of problems easier to solve.

2

The Blurred Lines Between Native Code, Virtual Machines, and Interpreters

In this chapter, we will explore how the distinction between programming language execution models—native code, virtual machines, and interpreters—driven by runtime modeling, is becoming increasingly blurred. Specifically, these are the topics we will cover:

- Modern computer **instruction set architectures** (**ISAs**) can no longer simply be mapped to concrete operations in hardware
- How interpreters also function as models of a specific virtual machine
- Reasoning about the effects of abstracting away complexity and the overhead those abstractions create
- How **just-in-time** (**JIT**) **compilers** change the way we think about the performance of interpreted languages
- And finally, how to think about those topics when designing your own language

By the end of this chapter, you will have enough context to help you think about what level of abstraction will make sense for a custom programming language, and how that abstraction can actually provide room for optimizations in the future.

Modern ISAs are virtual machines of sorts

Early microprocessors and microcontrollers had a very direct relationship between the instructions in the assembly code and actual hardware operations. This is still true of simpler architectures today, like some used in embedded environments. When we are targeting a modern **general-purpose architecture**, however, that picture changes significantly.

It's not my goal to use this chapter to give you a class on how a CPU works, but I think I do need to guarantee some baseline understanding, for those who might not have considered how code ends up actually being executed in the hardware. The naïve description is that *"In the end, it all needs to be zeros and ones."* While that is true, it's not a description that incites a deeper understanding of the problem.

Let's start with a very simple architecture and slowly add some of the complexities that arise in modern ISAs. This is in no way going to be exhaustive; this is just an illustration of how many layers of abstraction are hidden from you. *Figure 2.1* depicts the model for a simple hypothetical hardware architecture.

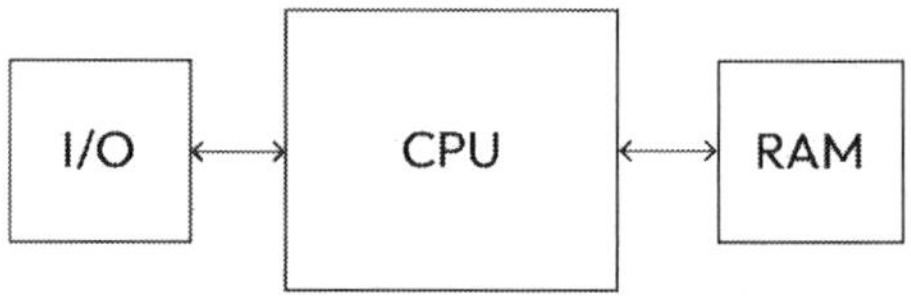

Figure 2.1: A simple hardware architecture

The figure seems simple enough. There is some executable code in the memory, the CPU will read it and execute it, and some of the operations of the CPU will read and/or write to the memory and/or the inputs and outputs. Some very simple microprocessors and microcontrollers still operate that way.

Here, the number of clock cycles required to fetch a word from memory is not necessarily the same as the number of clock cycles required to add two numbers together, which is faster since it happens inside the CPU. Adding to that complexity, the clock of the memory may be substantially different from the clock of the CPU.

In a simple architecture, this is solved by the vendor specifying that you have a minimum number of CPU operations between the instruction to interface with the memory and any other memory instruction, as well as any instruction that touches the registers being used on those operations. The compiler may be forced to add some **NOP** instructions (short for **no operation**) in your code to ensure those constraints are met.

As we add more complexity to the design of the system, that simple approach may not be sufficient anymore. Let's imagine that the hardware now supports an on-chip cache for memory access. *Figure 2.2* depicts that visually.

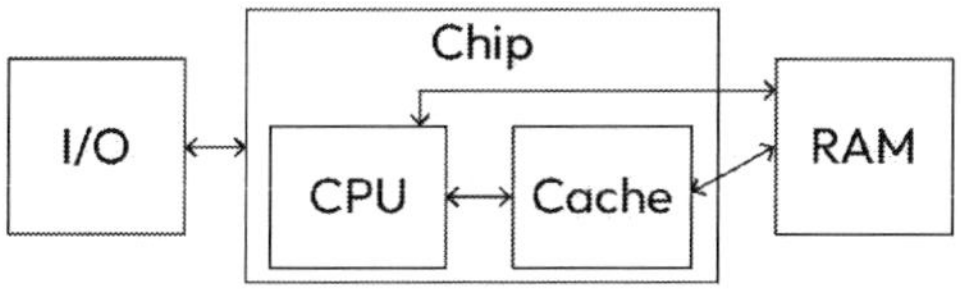

Figure 2.2: A simple hardware architecture, now with an on-chip cache

The difference between the model depicted in *Figure 2.1* and that in *Figure 2.2* is quite simple. We are simply adding a caching layer inside the CPU, such that if you're repeatedly fetching the same addresses from memory, we can use this faster access, and not have to wait for all the synchronization constraints that the memory requires. This is going to be a very small cache, compared to the overall memory, but the benefit for tight operations is undeniable.

It would be possible to just expose that cache in the instruction set. You could just add a few operations that manipulated the cache directly, such as the following:

- Check if page `0xDEADBEEF` is in the cache. If it is, return the cache address.
- Fetch `0xDEADBEEF` to the memory and report the cache address where it was stored.
- Store the value from register R1 in the cache address.
- Push the value in this cache address to its actual memory address.
- Evict the entry in this cache address.

Now let's add another piece. *Figure 2.3* depicts an architecture where we now have both an on-chip and an out-of-chip cache. The number of connections between those components should give a perspective on how much more complexity it introduces.

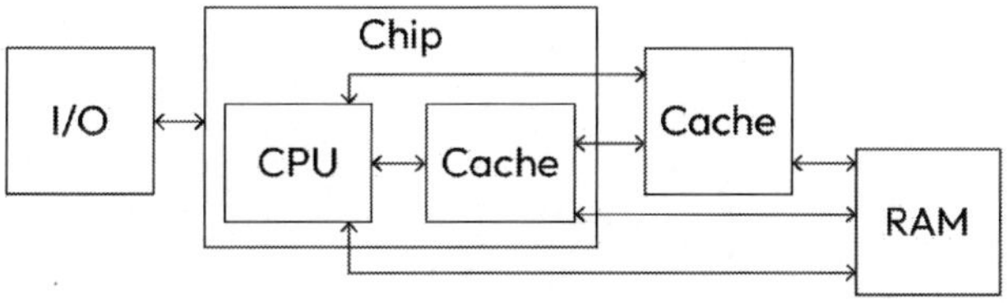

Figure 2.3: A simple hardware architecture, now with on-chip and out-of-chip caches

Let's imagine you just spent a lot of time optimizing your code when you upgraded from the architecture that didn't have that small cache inside the CPU to the one that has. You mapped out all your access patterns, to make sure you only used the cache when it was actually worth it, to avoid evicting memory that you knew you would need soon afterward.

Now the vendor sends you the specification for their next CPU, and they added a new caching layer, outside of the CPU, that is slower than the one inside, but still an order of magnitude better than going for the actual memory. That second layer of caching is also significantly larger than the first layer, although still nowhere near the actual memory capacity.

If that cache introduced a whole new set of instructions, it would mean that your program would need to be rewritten (if you were working directly in assembly) in order to take benefit of the new capabilities.

Before we wrap this discussion up, I want to *turn it up to 11* before concluding this section. In *Figure 2.4*, we can see a model that is closer to the complexity of modern architectures. It presents a different challenge, which is synchronization and cache invalidation, more broadly described as cache coherency.

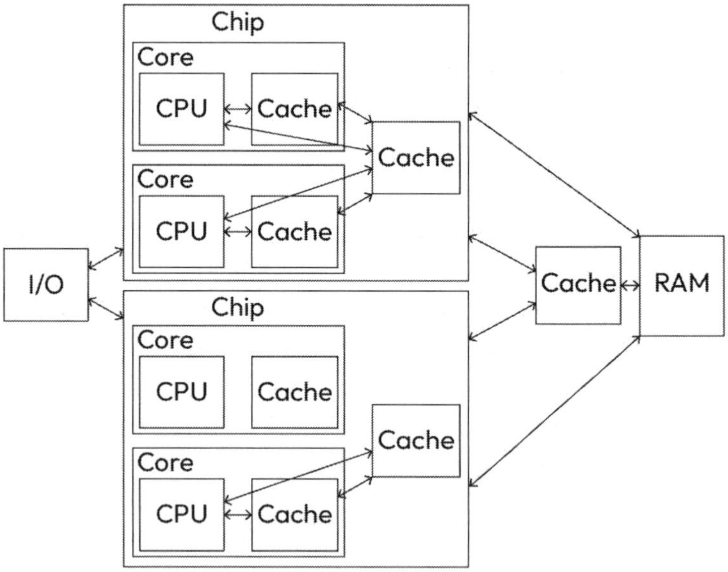

Figure 2.4: A diagram that is closer to what modern architectures look like, with different layers of caching and multi-processing capabilities

Suppose code running on different CPUs is reading from and writing to the same memory address. If the CPU accepted values from only its own cache, it could return stale values. Therefore, there needs to be a level of coordination to invalidate the value at every layer of the cache whenever the value gets changed.

Now imagine that the control of that cache invalidation was exposed as part of the ISA, with the expectation that the program would manage it itself. This would lead to an incredible amount of complexity, and it would be increasingly error prone. But, perhaps more importantly, it would mean that a new version of the CPU that offers new capabilities would not be accessible until the program is built targeting that new CPU. Every application would need to be built for the very specific model of the CPU being used.

With that being said, you will likely not be surprised when I say that modern ISAs, such as x86_64, do not expose the instructions to manipulate their various levels of caching and synchronization to the program, but instead offer only very high-level primitives to influence how the cache coherence is achieved.

The result is that the CPU will provide an abstraction of the sets of guarantees and expected behaviors. This abstraction, in a way, acts as a virtual machine model—not to be confused with software-based virtual machines like the **Java Virtual Machine (JVM)**. That virtual machine will, for instance, guarantee that when you read a value from memory, it actually results in the most up-to-date value (within certain constraints), regardless of what hardware operations will actually be performed.

Offering that abstraction, however, obscures the underlying performance characteristics of the hardware. If on simpler architectures you could predict how many clock cycles it would take for any given operation to be performed, on modern architectures that depends a lot more on the non-deterministic execution context, including factors such as cache hits, pipeline stalls, and concurrent access from other CPUs.

This is not the only area in which complexities are encapsulated by modern architectures. Here are some other examples:

- Memory mapping of different address spaces of different programs running in the same CPU
- Defining memory protections, such as areas where a program is allowed or disallowed to read, write, or execute
- Restricting which instructions should be allowed or disallowed on a given program

The end result is that the instructions in your program cannot be mapped directly to the execution in hardware. They are instead handled by the lower-level CPU instruction control logic, which sits between the ISA and the underlying circuitry.

The implementation of that control logic is handled differently depending on the approach in the design of the ISA and CPU. In x86_64, for instance, this is handled by microcode, which is an internal firmware of the CPU that will transform the ISA instruction into specific lower-level hardware operations. Those micro-operations are private to the CPU, which allows the vendor flexibility to change them without the need for programs to be recompiled.

Reduced instruction set computer (**RISC**) architectures, such as **Advanced RISC Machine** (**ARM**) or RISC-V, take a different approach. Because the instructions are significantly simpler, the CPU will use hardware circuitry that will manipulate the sequence of execution, the synchronization points, and other aspects of the execution without having to rely on microcode.

The takeaway is that, nowadays, it's not reasonable to use your intuition for the purposes of optimizing code. The only valid way to optimize performance is through measurement and experimentation.

It may not be entirely obvious the extent to which this applies to compiled languages today. Memory access patterns are, today, the most influential aspects affecting the performance of most applications running in modern architectures. Moreover, the diversity of execution models across various architectures also results in significantly different performance characteristics.

Native programming languages also have a virtual machine model

As is the case for the native code that runs in our modern architectures, native programming languages are also not a direct representation of the physical architecture of the computers the resulting code runs on. If that were the case, that programming language would not really work across multiple architectures. Or, perhaps even more importantly, there wouldn't be room for optimizations on newer architectures than the one the language was originally designed for.

If you take the C++ Language, for instance, the standard actually has a description of what that virtual machine is, what its capabilities are, what sorts of guarantees it needs to provide, and, more importantly, what guarantees it does not need to provide. The term used in the standard is **abstract machine**. A conforming C++ implementation needs to abide by those requirements and guarantees.

One example of the guarantees required of the implementations is that different memory locations should be accessible by independent threads such that a write to one location doesn't change the value of another.

This is similar to what I was describing in the concurrent access of memory locations that are in different layers of the cache and the management of the cache coherency requirements. But there's a significant distinction here, because while the physical architecture will implement caching in terms of physical addresses and cache lines, the C++ abstract machine specifies the behavior in terms of memory locations. This distinction is important because it gives the implementations room to optimize the memory access patterns to favor a particular caching strategy or another, depending on the target architecture.

Likewise, there are characteristics of that abstract machine that are specifically left unspecified, allowing freedom for the implementation of strategies for how to execute C++ code. As an example, the order of computations of expressions in the argument list of a function call is not defined. It means that if your code expects the side effect caused by the expression of one argument in another argument, you will not be guaranteed to have a specific behavior. That means the implementation is allowed to change the order in which the execution happens. Unless bounded by sequencing requirements, the user is not allowed to expect a specific behavior.

What I'm describing here may sound like complex details on how the C++ Standard was conceived. In reality, every programming language has an abstract model of what the requirements and guarantees are and where there is room for optimization for the implementation. It's just the case that because C++ has several implementations, those requirements need to be more carefully specified.

Understanding the abstract machine of the programming language you use will allow you to write code that fits better into that language, and will likely avoid lots of surprises in situations where you unintentionally rely on unspecified behaviors.

Likewise, when designing a programming language, you will benefit from designing the abstract machine for your language more intentionally.

Interpreters as virtual machines

As discussed earlier, modern ISAs are like virtual machines. Similarly, interpreters are an execution model that is distant from the executing hardware, because it introduces a layer of abstraction between the software and the hardware.

Understanding an interpreter such as Python or Perl as a virtual machine is not obvious. Historically, the distinction between native code and interpreted code was a lot clearer, until the JVM introduced an explicit compilation step to what was still interpreted code. The compilation step in Java made it clear that there was something between the higher-level language and the execution. However, anyone who has taken a deeper dive into any interpreter will know that the distinction has always existed.

What an interpreter does, ultimately, is to target a runtime environment that is still a few abstraction levels away from the native ISA. It is true that the constructs of the virtual machine of an interpreted language are much higher level than what a compiler targeting a native ISA needs to worry about. However, an interpreter needs to provide abstractions that encapsulate the native platform within its execution environment.

Whether it's the JVM, the .NET **Common Language Runtime** (**CLR**), or the bytecode interpreter at the core of languages such as Python or Perl, each interpreter defines an execution model that translates the semantics of a high-level programming language into runtime behavior within a managed environment.

In the next section I will highlight how, even if we are technically a few layers removed from the native machine, interpreters may actually be able to solve specific problems better than a native language.

Abstraction of complexity versus execution overhead

In an ideal world, we only need to solve any problem once, and then that solution will be available in whatever other contexts the same problem arises. In reality, however, this is a much more complicated problem. The main challenge is that every level of indirection also introduces an overhead in compute cost and memory usage, and the costs of those easily accumulate over a complex system.

Balancing abstraction and overhead has always been the biggest trade-off in the implementation of programming language interpreters. On one hand, you don't want to make your interpreter highly specialized to any given environment (be it the operating system or CPU architecture). On the other hand, every abstraction you introduce to make it more generic results in a potential overhead.

However, there are situations when an abstraction encapsulates so much complexity that executing it in the most optimized way possible could be the best choice. I mentioned regular expressions in the previous chapter, and few examples are as powerful as that in illustrating how the right abstraction can actually result in less overhead.

For the sake of illustration, and also to benefit those who haven't had a lot of experience writing regular expressions, I'll just use one scenario to walk through the way in which this abstraction can actually result in faster code. Don't worry—I'll break it down and explain:

```
\(([^()]+|(?R))*\)
```

This regular expression will match balanced parenthesis in a text. Suppose you have the following text:

```
This is text with (a balanced (but recursive)) set of parenthesis (maybe
more than one).
```

This will match any text surrounded by a balanced set of parentheses. The first match will be this:

```
(a balanced (but recursive))
```

The second match will be this:

```
(maybe more than one)
```

The way it works is as follows:

- The `\(` and `\)` at the beginning and end match the literal characters for opening and closing parenthesis
- The `(` and `)*` inside create a group that may repeat zero or more times
- Inside that group, there are two alternatives, indicated by the `|`:
    - `[^()]+` matches one or more characters that are not open or closed parentheses
    - `(?R)` recurses to try and match the entire regular expression again, when the character is an open or closed parenthesis

In that one single line, we have specified a complicated recursive state machine that will scan through the text and return fragments of the text with balanced parenthesis. I will leave it as an exercise for you to imagine how much code you would have to write in your favorite language to achieve the same thing.

This is not just a matter of expressiveness. The engine that executes the matching of the regular expression can be micro-optimized and fine-tuned to perfection because the inputs and outputs to it are much narrower. But, more importantly, those optimizations will be reusable anytime a regular expression is used.

The encapsulation of the abstraction of writing a complicated state machine that runs through a text to find matches is perhaps the most powerful example of when a higher-level abstraction can lead to significant gains in performance. This becomes even more relevant when the language itself has a higher execution overhead, such as is the case with interpreted languages.

But even when you consider a potential implementation in a native language, such as C++, it is very likely that the average engineer will not produce code as optimized as the regular expression engines are, at least not without a significant amount of effort.

Finding the right abstractions to present is, most definitely, the hardest part of this entire exercise. Just like I discussed earlier in the chapter, if the ISA architecture had included the primitives for the user to manage the cache, the microcode in the processor would have less room to optimize the code.

The abstract concept of uniform memory access doesn't really match how modern machine architectures work. A naïve analysis would say that it limits the performance because it means a lot of overhead. In reality, however, the abstraction creates very large avenues for optimizations that the original designers probably never considered.

I hope that, at this point, it has become clear why I've taken this somewhat contrived journey through this topic. What I want to frame to you as an exercise is to think about what kinds of abstractions your new programming language and runtime will introduce that could not only open important avenues for expressiveness but also create room for optimization in the implementation.

So far, I have shown that there are trade-offs between choosing a native runtime and an interpreted one, and that the calculation needs to take into consideration the fact that a higher-level concept may allow more optimized implementations by an interpreter. The use of JIT compilers makes those calculations even harder to evaluate. I will focus on that in the next section.

How JIT compilers change the performance calculation

While abstractions can lead to higher performance in very specific situations, the execution of straightforward imperative code by an interpreter will always introduce a significant amount of overhead. However, with the advent of JIT compilers, even that overhead becomes harder to predict. The interpreter now may generate native code for specific places in the code based on heuristics that are hidden from the programmer writing the code.

To illustrate this point, I will focus on an important characteristic of programming language design, which is whether it is statically or dynamically typed. One argument for dynamically typed languages is that it is a lot easier to write code that is more reusable, while in statically typed languages, that level of reusability depends on more advanced language features, such as templates in C++, since the compiler needs to know the exact binary representation of the value in order to generate code.

However, to achieve that flexibility, dynamically typed languages necessarily have an additional overhead, since as those decisions are deferred to runtime, the interpreter needs to keep the information about the entire type system at runtime, as well as wrap all values with the type annotations for each value. Not only does that result in additional memory usage, since you can't just store an integer as four bytes, but it also means that you have additional steps before you can perform any operation.

Let me provide a simple code snippet to illustrate that point. The following is a Python function that returns the next item in a Fibonacci sequence:

```
def next_fibonnaci(a, b):
    return a + b
```

As the Python interpreter cannot predict what the real underlying types of a and b are, or even what the + operator is meant to do with those types, the only option it has is to, at runtime, introspect what those types are and identify whether there is an operator overload that needs to be applied before it can sum the two numbers.

As you're thinking about evaluating the performance of your code, you know that this overhead is going to matter. What you don't necessarily know is that the Python interpreter may use heuristics to identify that your code very frequently calls this function with two integer arguments, and therefore it makes sense to generate a JIT-compiled version of that function that can be used in that case.

What the JIT compiler can do is achieve a limited version of the benefits of a statically typed language, as specific parts of the codebase can be transformed into much more efficient native code where, for instance, the numbers are just represented in four bytes, without the costs of a dynamic type system. The cost of the instrumentation required for the heuristics of deciding when to perform this optimization, as well as running the JIT compiler itself, needs to be considered in the overall performance picture, but experience shows that those frequently result in a good trade-off.

My goal here is not to give you a complete perspective on how JIT compilers work, and I do not plan on implementing one in the course of this book. However, I think this perspective shows how those calculations are really hard to predict. And that it's more important to focus on what makes your programming language useful instead of prematurely optimizing every overhead away.

In the next section, I will start working toward the trade-off decisions that I will make for the programming language I will develop.

Deciding which model our language will use

The starting point that I want to propose, whenever you are designing a custom programming language, is finding what the abstractions are that your language can introduce that will make that language more powerful to solve particular types of problems.

To illustrate better what I mean by that, I'll walk through some examples of what other languages do, and what abstractions they use, with the intention that it will serve as a starting point:

- Haskell completely abstracts away the imperative concept of scheduling the order of execution. This allows the compiler to implicitly split the computation across different threads of execution, including deciding how many different threads of execution will be launched, or even if the execution will happen at all.
- Perl abstracts the distinction between text, numbers, and boolean values. The operators coerce the values into the specific semantics they need, and the values don't have types at all. This allows the runtime to optimize by having those coercions calculated only once, instead of each conversion allowing arbitrary code to be run. Likewise, type-checking is vastly simplified.
- Regular expressions abstract the complex series of state machines and recursions necessary to evaluate complex matching rules. This allows the implementation to choose widely different strategies depending on the specifics of the given regular expression.

- SQL abstracts relational algebra into an intuitive language that represents the basic algebraic operations, without specifying the particular mechanisms that the database has to use in order to perform those. This allows databases to choose finely tailored execution plans that are informed by the contents of the database itself.
- Erlang abstracts the reliability mechanisms for a language based on message-passing as its main form of communication. This allows the runtime to implement different strategies, depending on whether the message is being sent across objects in the same address space or across different network entities.

The exercise I want to suggest here is that when you're thinking about your own programming language, you should try to identify what the abstractions are that would provide a unique capability. What is the thing that will be easier to do because of that abstraction?

For the language we're building as the exercise throughout this book, I want to focus on two specific abstractions:

- **Abstracting away input and output operations and scheduling**: This means the language will not offer an operation to manage those things, and instead the runtime will have complete control to optimize the execution depending on the specific context.
- **Abstracting away imperative control flow**: The language will describe network protocols and the control flow will be represented entirely by the relationship between the things being sent and received. This will limit how much complexity will be in the code written in the language itself, meaning the interpreter will be able to lower more of the execution into native operations.

What I want to bring to your attention is that this decision is made before deciding on any specifics about the syntax or before any code for the interpreter is written. The argument I'm trying to make is that this is probably the most influential aspect of your custom programming language, and this will guide many aspects of everything that will come later.

Summary

Modern architectures and modern programming languages have many different layers of abstraction. These allow the design of the hardware and the toolchain to take significant liberties with the implementation, and that is one of the most important ways in which optimizations are implemented.

The way in which memory is accessed and in which code execution is sequenced is an important part of the abstraction model, both for hardware and for programming languages.

More importantly, sometimes higher-level abstractions allow for much more powerful constructions, which can be a lot less error prone, and open up much more room for optimization. The regular expression language is a good example of when such abstractions have a significant impact.

For the exercise we will be working on in this book, we will focus on creating high-level abstractions for network communication, meaning all the state machines and interactions with partial reads and writes will be handled implicitly by the interpreter, creating a lot of room for optimizations.

In the next chapter, we will focus on discussing concurrency models, input/output, and the modeling of instructions.

3

Instructions, Concurrency, Inputs, and Outputs

In this chapter, we will look at how different programming languages approach how the instructions are executed. We will also work through the decision-making process for our custom programming language.

We will discuss the following aspects:

- What makes an instruction the fundamental abstraction building block of a programming language
- The difference between using operator stacks versus registers to process computation
- The distinction between the language stack versus the interpreter stack
- How interruptions to the control flow need to be taken into consideration in the design of an interpreter, both in the native language and in the interpreted language
- How the execution of native code is a different form of interruption for interpreted languages
- How different languages handle concurrent execution and how that impacts the interpreter design
- How to take all these aspects and guide the design of our interpreters

By the end of this chapter, you will have a nuanced understanding of how different design aspects of programming languages model the execution of instructions and how they should inform your design.

Instructions as building blocks

Following our discussion in the previous chapter, I want to dive a little bit beyond the basic abstraction to the specific concrete aspect of how programming languages work. In particular, I want to focus on the smallest unit of work for any execution environment: the instruction.

The boundary of an instruction is very easy to identify in the instruction set architecture for a particular hardware platform. The specific implementations of an instruction are abstracted away and the microcode will decode that instruction into an implementation-defined set of microinstructions, in what appears to any external observer as a single step.

Conceptualizing the instruction as a single step is a very useful abstraction that allows the hardware designer to evolve the microarchitecture without being bound to specific choices made on previous iterations of the hardware.

Likewise, in the C++ language, those instructions are defined in terms of particular operations, even when those operations consist of several steps that are required to fulfill them. For instance, when you call a virtual method, that operation is presented to the user as a single instruction, even if an implementation of the C++ specification will need to perform additional steps, such as the following:

1. Resolve the address of the virtual table for that particular object
2. Obtain the address of the actual function to be called from that virtual table
3. Set up exception unwinding information, the return point once the function has been executed, the arguments to the function, and the return value management, according to the local calling convention
4. Jump to the beginning of the concrete function being executed

Virtual table

A virtual table is also known as a vtable. It contains a pointer to all the virtual functions defined in the C++ code, with the value pointing to the correctly resolved member function for the class of the actual object that was created.

Being able to abstract all those operations into a single discrete unit provides a lot of room for optimization and being able to adapt to the implementation of the compiler. If a virtual method call was not specified as a single operation, the compiler would not be able to choose different strategies for the implementation.

In a way, designing an interpreter is like designing a new hardware platform. You are designing the specific abstraction points that will be seen as a single unbreakable step for the code being executed, regardless of how many underlying operations need to happen. This is similar to how storing a value in memory appears to the compiler like a single operation, while in reality, it involves managing many layers of the cache, as well as data synchronization requirements.

Next, we will focus on two different strategies to organize how those instructions can be handled.

Operator stack versus registers

Hardware instructions are usually organized as a linear sequence of operations that use local storage space as a scratch area to communicate data from one execution point to the next. Registers are the mechanisms by which intermediate values used in that sequence of operations are handled.

Let's consider the following statement in C++:

```
i = j % 5;
```

The hardware instruction set architecture will very likely not have a single instruction that reads the value from the address of one variable from memory, performs the modulo operator, and stores the result in the address of another variable.

Instead, it is much more likely the instructions will do the following:

1. Read the value of the `j` variable from memory and store it in register 1
2. Divide the value of register 1 by 5, and store the remainder in register 2
3. Store the value from register 2 into the address of the `i` variable

While this is not particularly complex, it illustrates the point I'm trying to make, which is that the registers are the mechanism by which data flows across the instructions that are being linearly executed. This is how most native instruction set architectures work.

When designing the execution model for an interpreter, it is possible to reproduce that same approach by creating virtual registers and offering a virtual instruction set architecture that operates on those registers. Some notable examples of this approach are as follows:

- Common Language Runtime, which powers the C# language
- LLVM **intermediate representation** (**IR**)
- The Lua language interpreter
- Dalvik Virtual Machine, which is part of Android

Also known as **register machines**, these are not the only way in which the execution of instructions can be modeled. The use of register machines in the context of programming language interpreters is a fairly recent development.

Most interpreted programming languages use a different model to represent the instructions and how values flow from one instruction to another. In **stack machines**, the operators are organized in a tree, where the inputs to a given operation are the result of one or more other operations.

If we were to look at the same code we used as an example previously, the code would be translated into a tree of operations, each taking the result of its children as input, something like this:

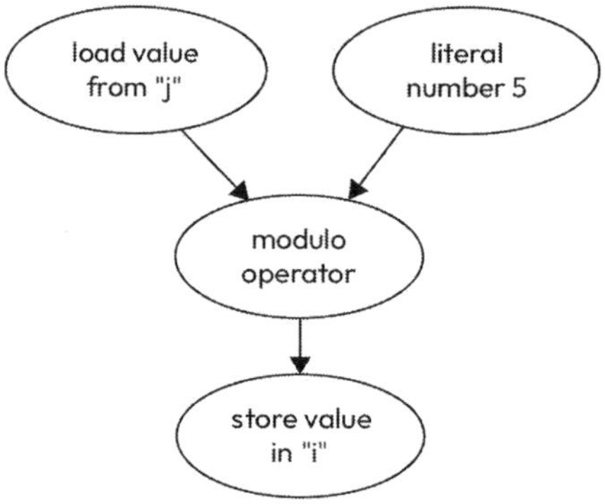

Figure 3.1: Representing i = j % 5 in a stack machine

The preceding figure demonstrates that each node in the tree represents an operation that takes zero or more values as input, in the form of other nodes, and itself produces a value that can be used as input for another operation.

The biggest advantage of modeling the execution as a stack of operations is the ease of transformation from the syntax of the language to the work to be done by the interpreter. There is no concern about the number of registers available, whether a given operation expects the values to be in specific types of registers, or saving the state of the registers as you enter and leave function calls. The interpreter just does a depth-first traversal of the operator tree, propagating the values down.

Here are some notable examples of interpreters that are implemented as stack machines:

- Java Virtual Machine
- Python
- Perl
- Ruby

Extensive research and literature compare the benefits and drawbacks of stack machines and register machines. It's not my goal to resolve this question or even dive into those comparisons. My goal here is to give you enough context so that you can do more detailed research if this topic interests you. Suffice it to say that successful interpreters and virtual machines have been created using both approaches.

For the language that's being created for this book, I will focus on building a stack machine. The reason for making this choice is that it will make it easier to focus on other elements of the design, particularly when we move on from parsing the text in the programming language to setting operations in the interpreter.

Next, I will go one level higher into the abstraction of our interpreter by moving from individual operations to how the language represents each frame of execution.

Interpreter stack versus language stack

In the context of interpreters and programming languages, the word *stack* can mean many different things. In the context of register machines, the stack is the saved state of the registers as you enter a new function. This is what allows the execution of one function to be able to use registers without knowing which registers are being used by the function calling it.

In the case of stack machines, however, the operators themselves form a stack, but in that case, the word has a different meaning because it doesn't represent the higher-level abstraction of stack frames in the language itself.

The distinction is between the function call stack as a feature of the language itself, how arguments are passed, and how return values are produced versus the implementation details of how the interpreter executes its instructions.

An interpreter that's implemented as a stack machine still needs to have a higher-level construct to represent execution scopes in the language itself. In this case, the stack frame will usually represent the state of execution of a single function. Calling a function is an operation that results in pushing the current frame down the stack to start the execution of a new context.

Let's consider the following example, which shows a simple recursive function to calculate factorials:

```
unsigned int factorial(unsigned int i) {
    if (i <= 1) {
        return i;
    } else {
        return i * factorial(i-1);
    }
}
```

If we were to translate this into the operators for a hypothetical stack machine, it would look something like what's shown in *Figure 3.2*:

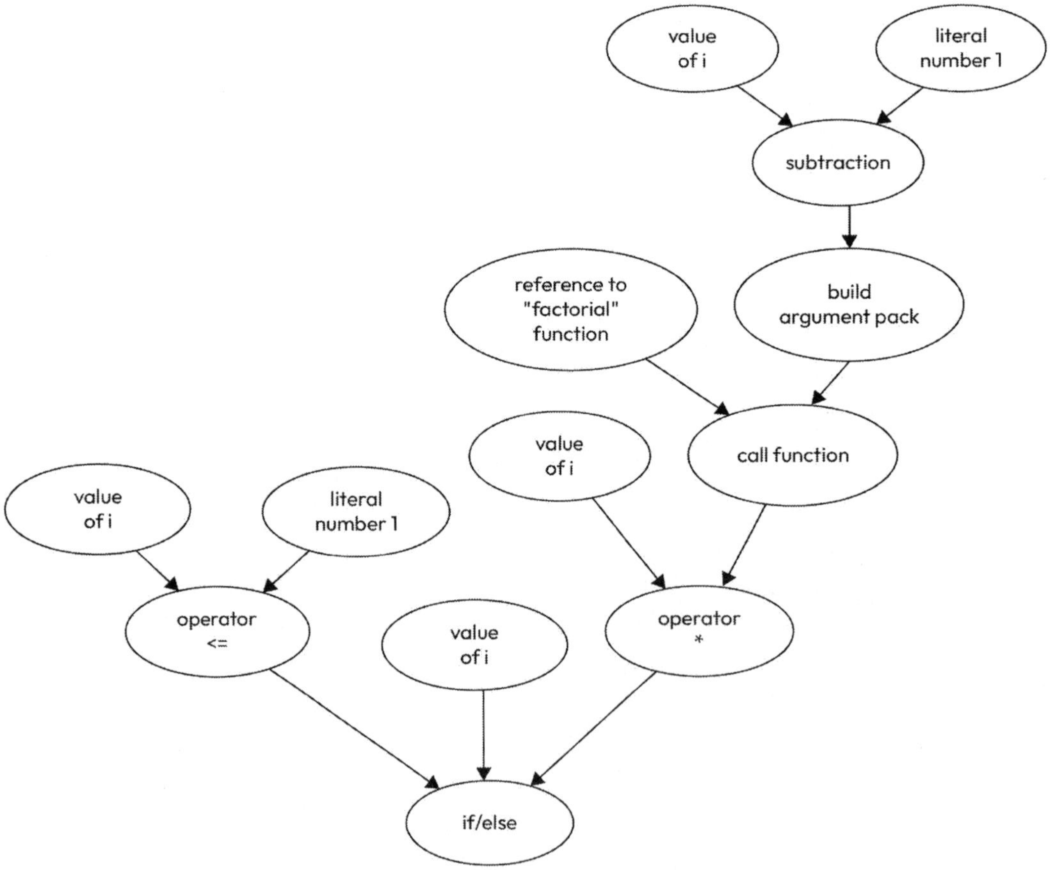

Figure 3.2: Stack representation of a recursive factorial function

The important thing to notice here is that we have operators fetching the value of the `i` variable, but there's no way to know which particular instance of the variable to fetch.

This is particularly relevant because this is a recursive function, so when the "call function" operator is executed, it needs to push the context of the current execution down and start a new execution context.

The execution context is the language stack frame, which is now defined in terms of the high-level abstraction of the programming language itself. The stack frame needs to hold local variables and the current state of execution.

The language stack frame, in turn, will hold information about where the execution context came from, allowing the interpreter to know what to return to once the execution of the current frame is finished.

Figure 3.3 illustrates the relationship between the language stack frames and hopefully provides enough contrast with the operations in the stack machine to make the distinction clear:

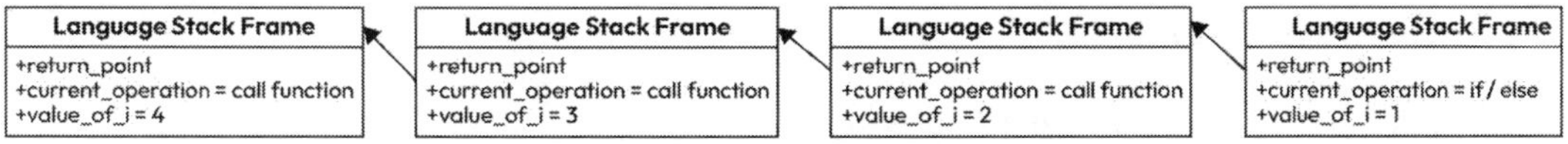

Figure 3.3: Function call stack for the execution of the recursive factorial function with the number 4 as an argument

In the preceding figure, we have the execution of the factorial function starting with the argument of 4. As the stack machine reaches the "call function" operation, it creates a new language stack frame. The new stack frame holds a reference to the return point and starts the execution process. In this particular state, the innermost frame is ready to return 1 when it was called with 1 as argument.

In the hypothetical stack machine described previously, the evaluation is purely functional, and the only way for the execution to be completed is for the operations in the tree to be completed. You may have noticed that even though the original sample code explicitly used the keyword `return`, the operations in the stack machine just had the values fall through the `if/else` operation.

In the next section, we will focus on the different ways in which the control flow is not always purely a pure traversal of the operator tree, and how to consider them when you're designing your interpreter.

Interruptions to the control flow

It's technically possible to always rewrite any control flow in terms of a stack machine. However, unless you have a specific technical reason to build your interpreter that way, it likely makes more sense to allow the control flow in the execution to be interrupted and moved around.

One simple example of this would be in situations where you have a return statement deeply nested in several conditionals. It would be possible to reorganize the operations so that the execution always flows back through the stack machine, but it would likely be simpler to simply allow a "return" operation that interrupts the evaluation of the stack machine and simply unwinds a language stack frame directly.

But return is just the simplest of the control flow interruptions that we see in most modern programming languages. Here are a few other cases:

- Breaking out from a loop
- Exception handling
- Short-circuit logical operators

A stack machine that supports such cases will need to stop evaluating a particular subset of the operation tree and jump to another one. In cases such as exception handling, it might need to traverse several language stack frames until the exception handling code can be invoked.

These are design aspects that are much harder to integrate into your interpreter after the fact. Trying to retrofit support for exception handling into a mature interpreter is going to be a lot more difficult than considering it from the start.

And, conversely, the capabilities of your programming language need to be aligned with the capabilities of your interpreter. Trying to add support for a programming language feature that doesn't have the machinery in the interpreter is also going to make things significantly more difficult.

The challenge I would like to put forward to you is to think about the different ways in which the control flow can be interrupted, and how that will change the design of your interpreter—particularly how the data that is stored in each language stack frame changes.

In the next section, I will focus on how the relationship with the native programming language affects the control flow mechanisms in your interpreter.

Continuations across native and interpreted code

Not everything that will be done by your interpreter is going to be mapped into interpreted instructions. As I described earlier, one of the most important tools for constructing new programming languages is the idea of creating powerful abstractions that will allow the interpreter to build different ways of addressing problems.

Interacting with inputs and outputs is something that will usually require your interpreter to interface the higher-level constructs of your language with lower-level concepts from the underlying native programming language and operating system.

For instance, your programming language may be dealing with encoded text, but the underlying operating system will usually operate in terms of octets. Therefore, your interpreter will have the responsibility of translating those different semantics.

One example of how this can happen is the idea that you may have a partial read that will give you half of a Unicode code point, and if your interpreter wants to present to the user with text, it needs to handle those partial reads transparently for the user.

> **Unicode code points**
>
> A Unicode code point is an abstract concept where any character in the entire database is assigned a unique number. Different text encodings will represent things in different ways, which often results in requiring more than one octet for a single character.

One way to think about this is that the execution of the interpreted code is blocked on the processing of the native call, and can only be resumed once those native calls are concluded.

Examples of reading to and writing from a network socket are the most obvious cases where the interpreter needs to be suspended for the processing of the native operations. There are other situations as well where that would be true:

- Transferring the control of the execution to extension points in native code
- Timers, such as the sleep system call
- Handling process signals

It's possible to implement these situations so that the interpreter just performs those operations in line with the execution. That is how Perl and Python handle those cases. The native stack trace of a Python program that interleaves interpreted and native calls directly represents that.

The alternative approach is to represent the execution of both native and interpreted code in terms of **continuations**. I mentioned this briefly in a previous chapter, but I would like to elaborate on this concept now.

The execution of a C++ program is represented by the native stack frame, which includes the state of a set of registers, among which is the pointer to the instruction to be executed. Suspending or resuming the execution of a program is typically under the control of the operating system.

While it is expected that a system call may block the execution, what happens while the call is blocked is entirely under the control of the operating system.

This is not to say that you can't write a C++ program that manages system calls in a non-blocking way, but the sequential execution of instructions is a basic characteristic of the abstract machine. Even if the operating system does a context switch, it won't be visible to the code being run and there are no mechanisms to control those context switches from the programming language.

While you can also manipulate the execution directly via calls such as `setjmp` and `longjmp`, they just redirect the sequential execution and don't prevent or interrupt a blocking system call.

An interpreter, however, can present a different abstraction. The sequential execution of the interpreted code can be seen as a managed task, meaning that the interpreter will schedule its execution much like the operating system schedules its processes. The interpreter, in that case, becomes responsible for scheduling and executing them.

The Node.js interpreter is an example of an interpreter that performs that scheduling on behalf of the interpreted code. I/O operations are represented in terms of callbacks, as are most calls that would block the native execution. The interpreter keeps track of all managed tasks, regardless of whether they are blocked on a specific event or scheduled and ready to be executed.

This does not regulate native code, however. Native code that's invoked by an interpreter performing that scheduling needs to follow the conventions of the interpreter; otherwise, it may block its execution since the native code is not managed.

Continuations are the abstractions that represent the state of execution to be scheduled by the interpreter:

- Interpreted continuations will reference the language stack frame being executed
- Native continuations will represent the delegation of execution to non-managed code

When the interpreter offers abstractions for the system calls that may block the execution as well as mechanisms to establish the information flow and readiness of execution of continuations, it will give room for the interpreter to schedule that execution in a way that decouples the native stack from the interpreter stack.

In the next section, I will focus on how the concept of continuations relates to the management of concurrency, and how that will allow the interpreter to produce a more robust execution model.

Concurrency model

Managing potentially blocking operations in a complex application is not a trivial task. In its simplest design, the code will just perform the system calls in a blocking way and the concurrent executions will be managed by the operating system. You create one thread for each task and perform the operations linearly.

However, this considerably increases the number of context switches that your application needs to do, and optimizing that execution becomes a non-portable game of operating system tuning:

- Affinity needs to be explicitly managed; otherwise, tasks that share information may end up on different CPUs, resulting in lots of synchronization requirements. At the same time, completely independent threads can end up in the same CPU, creating contention.
- Scheduling priority needs to be explicitly managed; otherwise, a thread that is responsible for latency-critical operations may end up with the same priority as the thread executing a single request. Often, the time of each request is less important than the latency to start processing a new request.
- The size of thread pools needs to be managed carefully; otherwise, you can create a deadlock condition where every thread is blocked while it's waiting for a slot in the pool before it can continue.

Perhaps unsurprisingly, this topic has been the subject of a lot of debate, research, and alternative implementations. There is, however, a consensus that just mapping processing tasks to threads in a 1:1 ratio is not the most effective way to handle I/O-bound operations.

To be able to decouple that ratio, you must ensure the following:

- All code that could result in I/O-bound operations yields execution to a central scheduler that's waiting for events without blocking
- The execution of CPU-bound not-latency-critical code yields to the scheduler regularly so that no execution gets starved

Combining these two characteristics allows scheduling to be performed in what is generally referenced as an N:M scheduler, where for a number of tasks, *N*, there is a number of threads, *M*, being used to schedule work. One of those threads will only focus on event processing, dispatching work for the other threads.

While this may seem like a very long tangent, how an interpreter performs I/O-bound work is perhaps one of its most fundamental characteristics. An interpreter that does not abstract away those operations will likely also be prevented from hiding the abstraction of threads of execution.

An interpreter that abstracts those away from the beginning will have a lot of room for optimizing and tuning the scheduler. This is particularly important for the interpreter of a domain-specific language that intends to be integrated into existing applications.

In that sense, the important decision is what approach you will use when designing your language. On the one hand, you can make your language expose the operating system threads and the mechanisms to use them directly on the programming language. Here are a few examples of languages that do this:

- C++
- Python
- Ruby

On the other hand, you can abstract away the management of the system threads and offer the abstraction of computation tasks, which will allow the language runtime to decide how the execution of those tasks is scheduled. Here are some examples of languages that follow that pattern:

- JavaScript
- Haskell
- Go

There are other alternatives when considering the execution of concurrent work. I will not dive into these here, particularly because I will not use them in the interpreter I'm building in this book. However, I do recommend doing further research on those topics when you're designing your language, as they may be a better fit for your particular problem spaces. Here's a non-exhaustive set of examples:

- **Actor model**: In this approach, instead of the execution being represented in terms of frames of execution, things that would normally be thought of in terms of method calls are instead represented as messages that are sent to the actor. Here, the actor runs in its home, potentially in a different node of the cluster. Erlang is the most prominent example of this approach.
- **Structured concurrency**: One of the challenges with the low-level threading model is that the programming language runtime doesn't have control over the scheduling and completion of independent threads. Those aspects have to be maintained by the programmer. Structured concurrency adds additional primitives such that the language itself is in control of the scope of when specific sets of tasks are expected to be completed. This was recently implemented in Swift and is also available as the Trio library in Python.
- **Choreographic programming**: The programming language itself describes the relationship between multiple concurrent entities and focuses on the flow of information, allowing the language runtime to schedule the synchronization points on behalf of the user. The Choral language for the Java Virtual Machine is an example of that approach.

All these approaches try to find a balance between the primitives offered by the language and what features can be implemented because of the limitations introduced by those primitives. Designing a programming language and an interpreter is primarily an exercise of deciding which trade-offs you will make between the flexibility for the user and the things that will be possible for the interpreter to do if that flexibility is not granted.

In the next section, I will focus on the decisions being made for the language being implemented in this book.

Deciding on the execution model

In the goals for the first version of the interpreter that I am implementing for this book, I defined that I was going to focus on network protocols with linear communication. Therefore, there is not going to be a significant need for concurrency within a single execution of the protocol.

However, that doesn't mean that the interpreter will only be capable of handling one connection at a time. Therefore, there's one layer of concurrency the interpreter will have to handle from the start, where the interpreted code is not concurrent but there are multiple instances of the interpreter running concurrently.

Future versions of the interpreter will need to support a more explicit level of concurrency, in cases where network protocols support different concurrent channels in the same connection, such as HTTP/2. So, I also need to make sure the current design doesn't hinder that development in the future.

With those requirements in mind, here are some of the design principles that I am defining for the interpreter and the language:

- The interpreter will initialize once, parse the code, and produce an immutable data structure that represents the entire execution in terms of stack machines.
- An execution instance will be initialized that points to that immutable data and only keeps the specific context for that execution. This can be done many times independently, where data from one execution is not shared with any other execution.
- Each execution instance will have a table of continuations, each with a status that allows the execution instance to schedule the continuation of the linear execution of code that is ready. In the first version, we expect this table to contain only one continuation at a time, but it will still track the status of whether that continuation is waiting for a read or write, for instance.
- When transferring control, such as when going from interpreted code to native code, this will be done using continuation-passing style, meaning that when the native code is invoked, it will be given the execution point where it should resume once the native code has finished executing. This allows for various forms of interruption to the execution, where the native code can divert the execution in a different direction and either discard that particular continuation or pass it along to be continued after the diversion. The end of the execution happens when there are no more continuations to run. Future versions will allow concurrent continuations to be created and managed in the execution instance.

- The language will not give access to the control of the concurrent execution of the continuations. Instead, it will represent points of concurrency in terms of the requirement of the network protocol, although this is not going to be implemented in the first version.

The interpreter and the language need to be designed with care to ensure the primitives required by the language are available to the interpreter. They must also ensure those primitives are high-level enough to allow the execution and concurrency models to be refined.

Summary

The instructions offered by an interpreter are the mechanisms by which abstractions are modeled, and they are powerful tools that allow the interpreter to refine how they are executed in the future.

Some languages and interpreters use a register machine, where instructions manipulate those registers since the execution of those instructions happens linearly. Other languages use a stack machine, where the instructions are represented as a tree of operations and the execution performs a traversal of that tree, with the output of nodes down the tree representing inputs for nodes they are connected to.

However, a stack machine will likely still need a language stack frame to represent higher-level states, such as recursive access to variables.

An interpreter also needs to consider how the execution can be interrupted, such as when you have a return statement or when you're dealing with calls that could block the execution of the code.

A continuation represents the state of the execution at any given point, and that abstraction should allow us to manage the relationship between the interpreted and native code.

Different languages and interpreters have different concurrency models, and the level of abstraction offered by the language will give the interpreter more or less control over how the code gets executed.

The language and interpreter I am writing for this book won't need to support significant concurrency in the interpreted code for the first version, although it should support multiple independent execution instances. However, I also need to make sure it doesn't hinder future development.

In the next chapter, I will focus on modeling the data types that are used by an interpreted language, how users specify types, and how that affects the relationship with the native language.

4

Native Types, User Types, and Extension Points

In this chapter, we will look at how different languages use different type systems, how users create their own types, and different approaches to modeling a type system for your own language. We will also look at how that relates to native code that needs to interact with the type system of an interpreted language.

We will discuss the following aspects:

- What types of type systems are used by different languages
- How native language types and user-defined types differ and how they interact
- How to think about modeling the type system
- How the type system interacts with the native language

By the end of this chapter, you will have a nuanced understanding of how type systems interact with the interpreter, how the language design informs and is informed by the type system, and how to develop a framework to help you think about the different characteristics of type systems in different languages.

Different types of type systems

As with the execution model, **type systems** are also diverse across different programming languages, and modeling the type system of your own language is as important as deciding on the execution model for the interpreter.

The type system encodes the way in which the language will understand the possible values that can be stored and retrieved from memory, as well as which kinds of operations can be performed on them. The specifics of the type system define a lot of the choices for the language in terms of what operations will be cheap or expensive, and these correlate with the level of abstraction that the language is able to present. The type system, in that sense, is the way in which the abstract machine for the language deals with values.

In order to make this explanation easier to navigate, I want you to think of a type as a representation of the set of all possible values that could be represented. The memory in your abstract machine will eventually have to encode everything in terms of bits in a region of memory. The type, therefore, describes how to interpret those regions of memory in a coherent way.

Static typing versus dynamic typing

In the C language, for instance, the `int` type represents all possible integer values between `INT_MIN` and `INT_MAX`, while the `unsigned int` type represents all possible integer values between `0` and `UINT_MAX`. Since the region in memory for those will have the same size, typically 32 bits, the same sequence of bits will be interpreted differently depending on the type.

While the compiler knows how a specific region of memory is meant to be interpreted, because the programmer specified it in the source code, that information is not encoded in the value itself. There is no meta-information about the value at runtime, which reduces how much memory is necessary to execute the program. But that also means that there's no way for that value to ever have a different type than the one that was specified in the source code. This enables a large number of optimizations because a lot more can be inferred from the runtime characteristics of the code.

This is what is called **static typing**. It means there is no other possible interpretation for how that specific region of memory can be interpreted. Let's look at the `factorial` function again to understand what it means:

```
unsigned int factorial(unsigned int input) {
    if (input <= 1) {
        return input;
    } else {
        return factorial(input-1) * input;
    }
}
```

The input argument is declared to be an `unsigned int`, the same type being returned. Because C is a statically typed language, it means there is only one way that the memory is given as input. Therefore, the language doesn't need to check whether this is an unsigned integer at runtime; it can directly accept the 32 bits and operate on them.

It also allows the calling convention to do an important optimization, where the inputs and outputs are transferred in registers rather than passed as a pointer to memory. The conditional in the first line can be generated into two simple instructions:

```
        cmp     edi, 1
        jbe     .L10
```

The first instruction will compare the value in the register with a constant value and set flags depending on the characteristics of the result. The second instruction jumps if the comparison says the value is smaller or equal.

Now let's compare this with an equivalent version of this function in the Python language:

```
def factorial(input):
    if input <= 1:
        return input
    else:
        return factorial(input-1) * factorial
```

In this case, there are no constraints on what set of values could be represented by the memory used by the input variable. That means the interpreter cannot just assume it knows how to perform the comparison.

Instead, the interpreter needs to carry a piece of meta-information about the variable that describes how to interpret the value stored inside of it and discover, at runtime, how to perform the comparison.

In **dynamic typing**, the execution will be dispatched conditionally on the specifics of the value being sent, and the interpreter will have to perform those meta-operations at runtime.

There is a clear cost to the choice of a dynamic type system. However, before we dismiss it, let's look a bit deeper. Let's first run the Python function:

```
print(factorial(13))
```

This will produce the value `6227020800`, which a calculator will confirm to be the correct value for the factorial of `13`. Now let's invoke the same code in C:

```
printf("%u\n", factorial(13));
```

When we run that code, we get the value `1932053504`, which is not correct. So what happened there? Let's look at what happens when we convert those numbers to binary:

6227020800	47	0	0	0	0		0	0	0	0		0	0	0	0		0	0	0	1	32
	31	0	1	1	1		0	0	1	1		0	0	1	0		1	0	0	0	16
	15	1	1	0	0		1	1	0	0		0	0	0	0		0	0	0	0	0
1932053504	47	0	0	0	0		0	0	0	0		0	0	0	0		0	0	0	0	32
	31	0	1	1	1		0	0	1	1		0	0	1	0		1	0	0	0	16
	15	1	1	0	0		1	1	0	0		0	0	0	0		0	0	0	0	0

The C compiler will accept the type's definition of what the set of possible values that can be represented by a 32-bit unsigned integer is, and it will keep performing its operations as intended. It would be possible to write code that checks for overflow; however, you would have to propagate the overflow checking for the factorial function itself, and the user would now have to deal with that error condition explicitly.

Meanwhile, a dynamically typed language will be able to detect the overflow and instead return a value of a different type that is capable of holding a larger integer, even if most numbers are stored in a more efficient way most of the time.

> When you design your own programming language, it's important to identify the trade-off that makes the most sense for your use case, as you are trading the power of the abstractions that dynamic languages can provide by the additional runtime cost and removed optimization opportunities.

Before we move on to more concrete aspects of the type system, I want to talk a little bit about another way in which dynamic type systems can differ from each other.

Strong typing versus weak typing

Let's continue using the factorial example from before, but now let's try to do something different, using the interactive prompt:

```
>>> print(factorial(sys.stdin.readline()))
10
Traceback (most recent call last):
    File "<stdin>", line 1, in <module>
    File "<stdin>", line 2, in factorial
TypeError: '<=' not supported between instances of 'str' and 'int'
```

The Python interpreter is complaining because the output of the `readline` method is of the `str` type, and the other argument to the <= operator is of the `int` type, and since it doesn't have a defined rule for how to apply that operator between those two values, it raises a runtime error. Hence, we can say the Python interpreter has a **strong typing** system.

Let's compare that output with the same thing in Perl:

```
use v5.36;
sub factorial($input) {
    if ($input <= 1) {
        return $input;
    } else {
        return factorial($input-1) * $input;
    }
}
say factorial(<STDIN>);
```

If you run this with `13` in the standard input, the output will produce `6227020800`. This is because Perl has a **weak typing** system and will transparently coerce the string into a number when it is used in a context where it needs to be considered as a number.

The spectrum between a weak typing system and a strong typing system is more nuanced, because it's possible that some weak characteristics exist in a language that is otherwise strongly typed. For instance, while the C language is strongly and statically typed, that can be trivially bypassed by explicitly casting.

> When designing the type system for your language, you will need to consider where your language sits on the axis of how strong the type system is. The type system trades convenience for the safety of intent.

There are also features a language may have that depend on a strong typing system. The Haskell language, for instance, has very powerful mechanisms for pattern matching on the types of its values, and that feature is entirely dependent on how strong its type system is.

In the next section, I will focus on the ways in which the user interacts with the type system to extend the definitions by creating their own definitions.

Language types versus user-defined types

The earliest programming languages had a fixed set of types. Functions and subroutines in Fortran 77 could only receive arguments and return results that were of one of the types supported by the language (e.g., `INTEGER*4` for a 4-byte integer or `CHARACTER*10` for text that is 10 bytes long).

This level of abstraction is far from complete, and as programming languages evolved, they introduced ways for the user to refer to more complex information. Just like with the example of `unsigned int` in the previous section, the language will need to understand what the set of all possible values that could be represented by that user-defined type is.

The way in which those user-defined types are supported by the language is also profoundly influential to how the execution of the code is handled. Let's look at another example in C:

```
#include <stdbool.h>
struct point {
    int x;
    int y;
};
bool is_same_point(struct point a, struct point b) {
    if (a.x == b.x && a.y == b.y) {
        return true;
    } else {
        return false;
    }
}
```

As with the simple case from the previous section, the compiler will use the static type information to access the specific regions of memory that store the values being passed to the function. There is no need to carry information about what `struct point` looks like to the runtime.

The type system of the C language, however, doesn't have support for a relationship other than composition. That is, you can have a struct that contains another, but there is no support in the language to create a type that extends it via inheritance, so you can't add new fields without altering the definition of the original type. This has a direct impact on how library design is done in the language.

Nominal typing versus structural typing

Let's look at how C++ also offers a "substitutes" relationship, where a type can be used in the place where another type was specified. Let's imagine a simplistic game engine:

```
struct entity2d {
    point center;
    rect bounding_box;
};
struct polygon : public entity2d {
    std::vector<point> vertices;
};
struct circle : public entity2d {
    unsigned int radius;
};
```

In this case, `polygon` and `circle` are extending the `entity2d` struct; the result is that if we have a function like the following, we are able to use `polygon` or `circle` whenever a function expects `entity2d`, and the same function is able to check whether `polygon` and `circle` have an overlap in their bounding boxes:

```
bool do_entities_overlap(entity2d &a, entity2d &b);
```

Most object-oriented languages implement this behavior.

This is what is called **nominal typing**, where the type is defined by its name, and substitutability depends on the relationship between types, rather than their attributes. If two types have different names, they are not substitutable by each other, even if they are otherwise identical.

The alternative is to consider the attributes of the type, rather than its identity. In **structural typing**, as used in the Go and OCaml languages, types can be substituted if they share enough of their structure, even if an inheritance relationship was not established.

Let's look at this example in Go:

```
type polygon struct {
    center point
    bounding_box rect
    vertices []point
}
func (p polygon) get_center() point {
    return p.center
}
func (p polygon) get_bounding_box() rect {
    return p.bounding_box
}

type circle struct {
    center point
    bounding_box rect
    radius int
}
func (c circle) get_center() point {
    return c.center
}
func (c circle) get_bounding_box() rect {
    return c.bounding_box
}

type entity2d interface {
    get_center() point
    get_bounding_box() rect
}
func do_entities_overlap(a entity2d, b entity2d) bool {
    …
}
```

In this case, there is nothing that ties the declaration of `polygon` and `circle` together. The identities of the types are completely disconnected from each other or from the definition of what `entity2d` is. However, the language will accept the substitution of any type that implements the requirements set by the `entity2d` interface as an argument to that function.

Experienced C++ developers will notice that these are exactly the same things that **concepts**, introduced in C++20, provides. It is a good illustration of how a language can navigate across different paradigms at the same time.

In fact, C++ templates also function mostly as structural typing, since the resolution of the template arguments is entirely based on the attributes of the argument, rather than the identity of its type.

Duck typing

When we take structural typing to a dynamically typed language, we often get what is described as **duck typing**, which is when the language doesn't perform any nominal type checking, and instead relies entirely on the type offering the required interfaces dynamically.

There is one very important distinction that needs to be made between a structurally, but statically, typed language and one that is performing duck typing. When we look at the Go example from earlier, the compiler can still perform the **method resolution order** at compile time, which is the order in which methods are called when there are multiple methods with the same name in the inheritance hierarchy, meaning there is no need to carry the information required for that resolution to the runtime.

In a dynamically typed language that allows duck typing, such as Python, the resolution of which method will be invoked needs to be carried to runtime.

For that to happen, the language needs to specify the way in which it will introspect the objects, the information about the classes, and the relationship between the types. When the code invokes a method in an object, there has to be a well-specified way to resolve it; we call that the **Meta-Object Protocol** (**MOP**) for that runtime, which allows introspecting the characteristics of the type at runtime in order to decide what needs to happen.

That is not something average users of your language will regularly interact with. Languages that offer reflection mechanisms, such as being able to obtain the names and types of the members of a class, enable a lot of very powerful coding patterns that are not at all implementable otherwise.

Some languages offer a read-only reflection mechanism. Others will allow the user to manipulate the type system as if it were just another value in the language.

The Raku language has one of the most powerful MOP definitions. Not only do you have a way to navigate and manipulate the classes that are used to create objects, but it actually introduces a second-order abstraction. Not only is the class of an object itself a value in the interpreter, but so is the implementation of how classes work, and it's possible to have alternative implementations for method resolution order living side by side in the same program.

In the Python language, the object and the class are dictionaries that carry an additional piece of metadata, but it is still all defined at runtime. To illustrate, let's look at the following code:

```
def create_accessors(classobj, name):
    def getter(self):
        return getattr(self, name)
    def setter(self, value):
        setattr(self, name, value)
    setattr(classobj, f"get_{name}", getter)
    setattr(classobj, f"set_{name}", setter)
class Foo:
    pass
o1 = Foo()
create_accessors(Foo, "a")
o1.set_a(1)
print(o1.get_a())
```

This demonstrates that we are able to treat the `Foo` class object as a runtime value, and that affects the runtime dispatch. Additionally, we can tell that the runtime lookup goes from the object to the class dynamically, since when we modify the `Foo` class, the objects that had already been created are also affected.

You may be wondering why I'm taking this strange detour into those implementation details. The reality is that when you are implementing a type system for your own language, those are all important questions that you're going to have to resolve.

Further, it should be encouraging to know that not everything needs to be object-oriented and that it is possible to implement the model the same way as other languages do. When you're developing your language, you have the opportunity to think about what kind of model makes sense for your use case.

In the next section, we will focus on approaches that could help you design the type system that best fits your intended language.

Approaches to modeling the type system

There is no definitive way to decide whether a given type system is better than another. In fact, it's mostly possible to translate the semantics of one type system into another, sometimes easily, sometimes with a lot of indirections.

The important thing to ask yourself, as you develop your own language, is what you want to make easier and what you want to make harder.

For instance, if you want to make a language that makes it easier to write high-performance parallel code, you may want to design a type system where all values are read-only and where you can only make changes by creating a copy. This will make it easier to write code that avoids cache invalidations across different CPUs, but it will make it harder to manage larger data structures.

The classic object-oriented model benefits the use cases where you want to model many different entities and their relationships, and where there are things in common across different types that can be abstracted and reused in abstract base classes. But it makes it harder to offer customization points. The C++ language, for instance, uses non-object-oriented concepts, such as templates and argument-dependent lookup, to make it easier for library owners to offer customization points in their APIs.

Pattern-matching function dispatch, as used by the Haskell language, makes it very easy to perform the traversal of complicated data structures and synthesize a complex output, but it makes it harder to have a global understanding of all the code related to a single type, since it will be grouped by the family of the function, rather than the family of the type.

The native types for your language

At the end of the day, it's all about aligning the objectives of your language. The type system will be a significant determinant of the capabilities of your interpreter and programming language. This benefits **domain-specific languages** in particular, since you can tailor the type system to the very narrow use case that you have.

If your goal is a general-purpose language, then you'll still be balancing flexibility with other runtime characteristics, such as memory usage and performance.

I will work through the exercise of what are the things that I want to make easier in the programming language that is the exercise for this book. My expectation is that this will inspire you about how to think about the requirements for your own language.

It's important to realize that I'm doing this design exercise even before I have a syntax for the language. This is intentional because I want to think about the capabilities of the language before I spend any time thinking about how it looks.

This being a domain-specific language, I don't need a type system that is very flexible, because the expectation is that any general-purpose code the user will write will be in another language anyway. But I need to be able to make the data from my language easily accessible through other languages.

The main interaction with the type system will be through matching the rules of the specific network protocol, the inputs that are given, as well as any literals that may be used as part of the protocol.

I'll start by identifying what types should be native to the language:

- Numbers:
    - Different sizes
    - Different encodings (network order, native order, represented as a string)
    - Integer or floating point
- Octets:
    - Different sizes or dynamic sizing
    - Representation (raw bytes, Base64-encoded, mime-encoding)
    - Streams or memory
- Text:
    - Different sizes or dynamic sizing
    - Different encodings (7bit-ascii utf8, utf16, utf32, iso8859-1, etc.)
    - Streams or memory

- Lists:
    - Dynamic sizing
    - Members of the same type
- Structures:
    - Fixed members
    - Values of different types
- Maps:
    - Keys of a fixed type
    - Values of a fixed type

The exercise of creating this list is mostly about imagining specific situations where the language will be used and trying to see what kinds of values we need to be able to represent.

For instance, you may notice that in the section for numbers, I included an aspect of the encoding for the number. This is because network protocols will specify how the number will be represented, and the conversion between the protocol specifications is a persistent source of bugs. Therefore, making that a fundamental part of the type system will allow the type checking to prevent them.

Likewise, I added maps when thinking about how HTTP headers work, meaning it should be easy to look up whether a header of a specific name is present and what was sent. Then I added lists because I remembered that it's valid to send the same header more than once, so you would need the lookup of a specific header to return a list of values.

The distinction between octets and text is also motivated by the desire to allow the type-checking to prevent mojibake bugs (text being corrupted because of mismatches in character encodings) where values come in as octets and they're assumed to be in a given encoding. Likewise, the representation of octets could just be the raw bytes, or it could be sent Base64-encoded.

This is a good time to transition to think about user types. As I was writing this list, I realized that it would profoundly limit the usefulness of my custom language if some protocol used an encoding that my language didn't support and there wasn't a way for the user to augment the language to support it.

How the users will declare their own types

So, my type system will be centered around the idea that sizes and encodings are parameters to the native types and that those should be customization points for the user of this interpreter.

This should be a good illustration of the power that you have as the designer of a new language and interpreter. You are free to look at the problem in an entirely unencumbered way and think about what kinds of decisions you can make to make the language useful in ways that you wouldn't easily be able to do by just writing a library in an existing language.

It's also important to find opportunities to avoid unnecessary complexities in your type system. This language will have types that are used when implementing specific network protocols. It is not very common for different protocols to be defined in terms of other protocols.

Therefore, code reuse is not a significant driving requirement for this language. It is likely more appropriate for similar protocols to have independent definitions of similar-looking types rather than them trying to establish common shared types.

This allows the type system of this language to take a simpler approach where we don't need to support polymorphism. We can do a simpler nominal type system where the user declares static structures and those are used to encode the data from the network session.

Being able to cut down complexities for the specific use case is one of the areas where domain-specific languages can deliver benefits that general-purpose languages can't.

I hope this is a good illustration of what kinds of decisions you need to make when designing the type system for your own language. Don't be too tied down by existing designs, and don't feel shy about removing complexity where it's not needed.

In the next section, I will focus on how your interpreter interacts with the native languages, either to build extensions or when the interpreter is embedded.

Interaction with native extensions

The way in which the interpreter represents the data becomes the bread and butter of folk implementing the integration with the interpreter, either when it's an embedded interpreter, as it is common in the Lua interpreter, or when you need to bind native libraries into a general-purpose interpreter, as happens with most general-purpose interpreters, such as Python.

The overhead of translating from the interpreter types to the native language types is a significant cost to take into consideration when designing your type system, particularly because someone writing code in the native language will not be able to use the types the same way that they are used in the language; instead, they will mostly have to operate with your MOP.

One way that can make your language easier to interoperate, if that is a possibility, is that you can generate code for the binding. That is, instead of translating the user types to interpreter types, the user types and the mechanisms by which they are accessed would instead be generated and built into the interpreter itself.

You will still have the challenge of the interpreter knowing how to interact with those types, but if you're already introducing code generation, it would be possible to solve that problem in the same way.

If you don't want to make the parsing of the custom code a build step for your native language, then you have two main avenues on how to interact with the language types:

- The first is to have a dynamic way to ask for specific values in the specific type of the native language with either coercion or error checking if the user makes an invalid request
- The second is to use a generic type that can represent any value the interpreter can handle, which in C++ could be represented as `std::variant` of all the different types the value could have

Since performance in accessing the data that was read from or that needs to be written to the network is a fundamental characteristic to make this language useful, I plan on opting to include code generation for both the user to access the data from our embedded DSL in C++, and also use code generation to allow the interpreter to access the data structures in the native language.

But since this would make the language not useful in fully dynamic environments, such as from Python, it is important that the bindings should be able to adapt to different types of data structures, as well as support representing all data structures dynamically.

The end result of those requirements is that my interpreter runtime needs to be able to do the following:

- Have the representation of the types customized for the specific integration
- Generate the data for the interpreter at build time if integrating with C++
- Generate the data dynamically if integrating with Python

I hope this illustrates just how much of the design of the interpreter runtime is informed by these early design questions, and why it's important to think about them before you write any line of code for it.

Summary

When designing the type system for your custom language, you will need to balance the trade-offs between static typing and dynamic typing, balancing optimization opportunities with flexibility on how the language can be used.

You also need to balance whether you want the language to follow a strong typing model or a weak typing model, balancing the ease of use of the language versus the correctness guarantees that type checking can provide.

Types can be defined by their identity, called nominal typing, or they can be defined by their attributes and where they can be used, called structural typing. The latter makes reusing functions easier, while the former will push the user toward making more shared types before code reuse is possible.

Regardless of those choices, you will need to design the MOP for your language, since that is what the interpreter will use internally. You can still decide how much of the MOP's reflection capabilities are exposed to the language users or keep them internal to the interpreter to manage objects and classes. This impacts the language's simplicity, flexibility, and security guarantees.

It is useful to think through use cases for your language when deciding the design of the type system, in order to allow you to accept required complexities and remove unneeded ones.

Finally, you also need to decide how the interpreter will interact with other languages, and the choices made there will also profoundly impact your design.

Going over all those questions before you start the first line of code in your interpreter will allow you to make sure you have the right set of requirements in place.

In the next chapter, we will put together the various aspects discussed so far into a coherent design for the interpreter and evaluate all the different trade-offs being made.

5

Putting It All Together: Making Trade-Off Decisions

In this chapter, we will focus on getting a final design for the interpreter for our custom programming language by pulling all the discussions from the previous chapters into a coherent vision.

We will look at the different trade-off decisions we have to make and the reasoning behind the specific choices being made. More specifically, we will focus on the following:

- The way in which the interpreter will integrate with existing code and allow the use of existing I/O libraries
- The specific choices to enable concurrency in the use of the interpreter
- Finalizing the memory model and the execution model of the interpreter into a coherent form

By the end of this chapter, you will be able to use the design decisions and trade-offs I walked through here when thinking about the design of your own interpreter.

Designing the execution model

In *Chapter 1, Defining the Scope*, I discussed the idea that for our DSL to be useful in multiple environments, I would design the interpreter with the approach called sans I/O. It is now time to dive a bit further into the specifics of this choice. The first aspect that I want to establish is the way in which the interpreter will execute the different types of operations.

I'll start by identifying the different parts of the work the interpreter will have to do:

- Interact with inputs and outputs
- Identify which interpreter threads are ready to execute
- Perform the next interpreted operation
- Perform the next native callback

Given my priority of making this interpreter easier to integrate into different systems and environments, I prefer to make these tasks as different entry points that the native code will call.

It is possible that your design will have different requirements. For instance, if your interpreter is going to use the native stack for the interpreter, the distinction I'm making may be entirely irrelevant.

Moreover, if your interpreter is meant to run the entire program, then that design will be completely different and you need to think about the entire life cycle of the interpreter program in a different way.

Further, the interpreter may also support being embedded into another program (as most interpreters support), at which point you need to consider what kinds of interfaces you want to support for that, and how you will make your interpreter available as a library.

I will focus on one specific design in this exercise. My expectation is that this will provide you with a practical example of the design process and that it will help you navigate your own design.

With that said, I want to dive a bit deeper into each of the aforementioned tasks that the interpreter will have to do.

Interacting with inputs and outputs

The main goal of the interpreter and programming language being designed is to abstract away the management of the state machines related to the implementation of network protocols. For that reason, handling inputs and outputs is completely separated from the interpreted operations.

The main outcome of this decision is that the interpreter will need to keep track of the state of the execution and be able to know whether the next operation depends on a read or a write to be completed.

An alternative approach would be to have the execution of the interpreter be managed by operating system threads and allow the operation to make a blocking system call when interacting with inputs and outputs. This is a very common approach. Let's look at an example in Python:

```
a = sys.stdin.readline()
```

When the Python interpreter executes this operation, it will actually perform the read system call during the evaluation of the operation itself. If you attach a debugger to the process as it is waiting for the data, you will be able to see in the native stack that the entire execution thread is blocked and the decision of when to resume is delegated to the operating system.

While it is possible to write non-blocking concurrent code in Python, the design decision of the language and the interpreter makes the blocking behavior the default, and you would need a recursive analysis of your entire codebase to make sure no blocking operations are performed in unexpected places.

The opposite approach would require a programming language that has set requirements from **real-time computing**, where the interpreter would have to avoid not only blocking system calls but also any system call that requires a **context switch**.

The requirements I'm placing for this project don't go that far. I just want to make sure that the interpreter can be used in an application that handles multiple connections in the same operating system thread. Therefore, it's important that the interpreter and the language don't have any operations that may block the execution in the thread.

The result is that the interpreter needs to know the state of the execution of each continuation in relationship with the I/O operations in the code, as discussed in *Chapter 3, Instructions, Concurrency, Inputs, and Outputs*. The interpreter needs to map the I/O handle and the continuation, keeping track of the state of both and the connection between them.

The way this is going to work is that whenever an interpreter operation requires an I/O operation, it will mark itself blocked and register the operation in the interpreter. The code will then be able to check the progress of all pending I/O operations and unblock the continuation that was waiting on the specific operation on a specific handle.

Identifying continuations that are ready to execute

Interpreters that directly expose the operating system threads, such as Python, don't have to consider this problem, but since I'm setting myself the goal of not blocking an operating system thread in the interpreter, it means I also need to manage how the interpreter decides which continuations to run at which point.

I already discussed that a **continuation** is associated with the information that describes whether it is waiting for an I/O operation or not, and that we most definitely know we shouldn't try to run a continuation that is blocked.

What is left, then, is to have a mechanism to decide which continuation to run at a point where multiple could be running. Considering I want to allow the interpreter to process the same connection in multiple threads, I need to be able to run continuations from the same interpreter in different operating system threads.

However, if I simply have multiple threads competing with the scheduler, it will likely generate undesirable contention on the access to the set of continuations.

Memory contention, particularly for data that is not read-only, is one of the biggest hindrances to performance in multi-threaded applications; therefore, instead of having every thread deciding which continuations they must execute, I'll put that in the hands of the user, and allow the user to schedule different continuations on different threads.

That way, a continuation will be assigned to a thread by the user, and the user will have the option of splitting them into separate executors, one in each thread, but once that configuration happens, there is no contention on the access to the set of continuations that need to be run.

I should point out that this is one possible solution to this problem. If your interpreter is meant to own the entire execution, you may decide on different approaches on how to divide the work across threads. One interesting example to investigate is how the **Glasgow Haskell Compiler (GHC)** manages the decision of when something is dispatched to a different thread.

An interpreter should be in a good position to measure how the code is running, identify that a given CPU is overworked, and move some of the work to a different CPU. However, this is significantly more than what I wanted to explore here, so I'll leave it as an exercise for you.

I will also not try to implement any prioritization system to the scheduler and, instead, will perform a simple round-robin across all the continuations that are ready to be executed at a given point. This is also a very broad topic that I will not cover here, but there is a lot of literature on different scheduling strategies with different benefits and drawbacks.

> If you're interested in learning more about task scheduling strategies, Andrew S. Tanenbaum's *Modern Operating Systems* is a great starting point.

Performing interpreted operations

At this point, we have a good understanding of how the interpreter will keep track of the continuations that it has waiting or blocked, and how it will decide which one to run. The next step is figuring out what actually happens when running a continuation.

This is an area where we converge back with existing interpreters, such as Python. Regardless of how we got to the point where we know the next interpreter operation to run, we now have to do it.

It is common for interpreters to use a technique called a **trampoline function**, which will essentially operate on the state of the interpreter without actually performing recursion on the stack. The basic concept is that the interpreted operation (be it a register machine or a stack machine) will be executed, manipulating the state in the interpreter, and return right away.

This is why, when you look at a native stack of a Python program, you will not see all the different Python function calls. The Python interpreter keeps that state entirely separate from the native stack, even if it uses the native stack when calling native code.

I have described before that I will use a stack machine. The unit of execution is naturally the node in the operation stack; the execution of a node produces the input to the next operation, which the interpreter can then execute.

It may be tempting to perform more operations in a single step, and if your interpreter is in complete control over the execution, you will be entirely free to decide how that happens. However, since I made it a requirement to more seamlessly integrate with existing environments, I need to make sure I yield as consistently as possible to the native code.

Making native callbacks

I realize I'm repeating myself, but I do think it's worth reiterating the point that this is entirely dependent on the design that you choose. If your interpreter, such as Python, just uses the native stack, this is mostly not a question you have (although you will need to adapt your interpreter to each operating system independently). However, you still probably want to figure out how to interleave interpreter functions with native functions. There are many examples to take from in that area.

As I have placed a requirement to make it easy to manage the difference between the interpreted code and the native code, it becomes a lot easier if I treat native callbacks as a distinct concept. This will allow the user of my interpreter to decide which operating system thread will run the native callback, and maybe avoid blocking the thread that is focused on I/O with the user code.

The concrete outcome is that I need to consider that a continuation may be blocked not only by the I/O operations but also by waiting for native callbacks to run. What I didn't talk about before is how we can correlate the operations happening on different threads back to the interpreter state. If we're not using the native stack to figure out how to return from a native call, we need to introduce a different mechanism.

Likewise, our interpreted language can't really resolve addresses to native functions at runtime (in a way that works everywhere), so we need to have a mechanism for the user to register which code to run when a native callback is initiated.

The approach I am taking here is that the interpreted language will need to specify identifiers for what the callbacks are, and then the user, in the native language, will need to fill those out at runtime so that the interpreter knows which native call to make.

This is a good example of how the design of the interpreter informs the design of the language. We have just set a requirement for the syntax based on how we want the interpreter to function. The language will need a mechanism to specify the identifier for a native callback.

The native operation will be sent to the native code, and part of the code to finish the execution will be to set the return value, which will unblock the continuation.

Since this is an entirely separate step in the interpreter API, it will be trivial for the user to move that to a different operating system thread, allowing other continuations of the interpreter to continue without having to wait for it.

I hope this gives you a good idea of what the general design process for the execution of the interpreter looks like. There are many avenues of design that I didn't explore, and many other influences you can take by looking at how other interpreters work.

I sincerely recommend investigating how different interpreters solve this particular challenge. Contrast that between languages designed primarily to be embedded (such as Lua) and those designed to be standalone (such as Python).

In the next section, we will explore how concurrency influences the design of the interpreter.

Concurrency in an embedded language

In an interpreter using the operating system-based model, concurrency is going to be mostly influenced by *how* the memory is managed. Different approaches to memory management come with vastly different trade-offs.

The Python interpreter, for instance, uses a **Global Interpreter Lock** to guarantee that the native Python structures are only manipulated in one thread at a time. This works because it's often the case that performance-sensitive code will be lowered to C or C++. Anyone writing concurrent code in Python is aware of this limitation and will design their applications accordingly.

The biggest benefit of that approach is in the simplicity and in the fact that significant parts of the interpreter don't need to be written with other concurrency controls. The result is that there are fewer operations that require the kernel to suspend the execution of a thread in order to satisfy a more fine-grained lock on a specific value.

The Perl interpreter, on the other hand, takes a radically different approach, by implementing a share-nothing approach. A thread in the Perl interpreter almost looks like a new process, with a complete **copy-on-write memory management model** (that is, if a thread modifies some memory, a copy is made first, and that copy becomes the version used in that thread, while the other threads continue seeing the original value). Then, any data that needs to be shared between threads is specially annotated as such, and concurrency control is implemented only in those cases.

The interpreter may also provide different levels of abstraction for concurrent execution. The Ruby interpreter has both **threads**, representing the operating system scheduling, and **fibers**, sometimes called **green threads**, that are managed by the interpreter. You can have multiple fibers in a single operating system thread, and it's the responsibility of the user to yield the execution such that different fibers get their chance to execute.

The **Java Virtual Machine** (**JVM**) sits on the other side of this space by using the operating system threads directly without a Global Interpreter Lock. Essentially, the internals of the JVM have to be implemented in a thread-safe way, such that the interpreter operations can run in parallel. The user code may still need to use concurrency controls, such as locks, for high-level consistency of the data, but the user doesn't have to worry about the interpreter itself getting into an incoherent state due to parallel work.

And finally, the last approach is to completely hide the imperative control of the scheduling of the work from the user, and instead have the interpreter itself (or the environment where the interpreter is embedded) control the concurrent execution of code.

This is the case for the interpreter I'm building. The interpreter will not offer any mechanism for the explicit control of concurrency and parallelism. Instead, the interpreter will presume that the environment where it will run will have control of splitting the execution across multiple threads.

Any given continuation will only ever be executed in a single thread at a time, which will allow the interpreter to limit which parts of the code need to be made thread-safe. The state of the interpreter in the execution of each operation can be implemented without any additional concurrency control.

The complementary topic to the concurrent execution of operations by the interpreter is the mechanism that it uses to manage the memory that is shared across multiple threads.

In the next section, I will focus on the memory model for the interpreter, keeping the concurrency requirements in mind.

Memory management

This is a topic that is the dedicated subject of several books, so I will not pretend to cover it extensively. However, there are a few aspects that I think are particularly relevant to the design process for an interpreter or language runtime. I want to briefly discuss those before jumping into the design decisions I will make here.

Memory access patterns

The access patterns to memory, particularly for write access, are currently one of the biggest drivers of the performance characteristics of any system. The coherency requirements for unified memory access across the execution of parallel threads in a program mean that if you try to read and write the same memory from more than one processor, it will result in several layers of cache invalidation, which will result in a slowdown in the execution of the code that is very hard to optimize after the fact.

Optimizing the memory access patterns is currently one of the most important activities when designing your application. The design of the language runtime and the features of the language itself inform how those applications are designed in a very profound way.

In C++, for instance, the object-oriented characteristics of the language can lead to the development of models where you design your data access based on an abstract representation of the concepts that you're trying to implement. This can lead to a design where data that is frequently modified is placed in the same location as data that is meant to be read concurrently by multiple threads, with severe consequences to performance.

In response to those challenges, a new paradigm of design for C++ applications has been gaining a lot of attention since the mid-2000s, which is the concept of **data-oriented design**. In this approach, you start your design by organizing the data based on how it needs to be accessed.

To illustrate this, let's look at `std::shared_ptr`. The concept being modeled is that you have a reference count to a pointer, which will allow you to manage the life cycle of that object based on whether it is still needed or not. If you start the design of this type from a conventional perspective, you'll be inclined to put the value of the reference count alongside the pointer being managed.

However, that means any time you change the reference count, you are also causing the cache for the pointer itself to be invalidated. This means that if you are using the same shared pointer across multiple threads, anytime you add a reference, you incur a penalty for any read-only access on every other thread.

A data-oriented design approach, instead, would consider that it's much more important to keep those two pieces of data as far apart as possible. With that constraint in mind, an implementation could prefer to maintain a pool of reference counters in a separate array and simply store the index to that array in the shared pointer itself. The result of this simple change is that threads just dereferencing the pointer will never have their cache invalidated when a new reference is created.

When designing an interpreter or language runtime, it's important to have in mind how the design decisions will inform the users in the design of their own code. If you design a runtime that provides incentives for data-oriented design, it is more likely that the code written by the users will follow that pattern. On the other hand, that may lead to additional complexity on how the code has to be written; after all, a C++ class that completely encapsulates all the required data in a single contiguous region of memory is easier to reason about than a data structure where the data is dispersed.

Managing mutability

Concurrent access to memory that may change presents additional challenges beyond the cache invalidation issues. While modern architectures offer some capabilities for atomic operations, it is not generally possible to manage an entire data structure in an atomic way. When you have a complex data structure, it's very likely that you need to perform multiple operations and that a read from another thread that sees an intermediate state would cause a bug in your program.

To illustrate this, let's imagine that you had a data structure for `Date` that stored the day, month, and year as independent integers. (Yes, I know there are better ways to design a date. This is just a toy example.) Let's imagine the following C++ class:

```
struct Date {
    int year;
    int month;
    int day;
    Date(y,m,d) :year(y), :month(m), :day(d) {}
    void increment_day() {
        day = day + 1;
        if (day > max_day_for_month(year, month)) {
```

```
            day = 1;
            month = month + 1;
        }
        if (month > 12) {
            month = 1;
            year = year + 1;
        }
    }
}
```

Now, let's imagine the following usage:

```
Date d(2024,12,31);
// in one thread
d.increment_day()
// in another thread:
std::cout << "Date is: "
  << d.year << "-" << d.month << "-" << d.day << std::endl;
```

There are two expected possible outputs in this case. The first is that you want the output to be the following:

```
Date is: 2024-12-31
```

The second is that it should be the following:

```
Date is: 2025-1-1
```

However, since the entire increment operation is not atomic and it doesn't have any concurrency control, you could end up with any of the following outputs:

```
Date is: 2024-12-31
Date is: 2024-12-32
Date is: 2024-12-1
Date is: 2024-13-1
Date is: 2024-1-1
Date is: 2025-1-1
```

Data races are a very frequent source of bugs in multi-threaded programs, and that's without even considering concurrent writes to the same data structure, which could easily result in the function producing an entirely invalid state.

Managing how shared data is mutated is, therefore, a profoundly important aspect of the correctness of the code. There are a few things the runtime can do to help the user:

- **Separating shared data from local data**: This can be implemented in various ways, including rigorous copy-on-write mechanisms such as what the Perl interpreter does, or by assigning data so that the local data is not entirely visible to other threads, such as by using thread-local storage.
- **Support for immutability**: The easiest way to solve data races is, of course, to never mutate the data. This has a significant impact on the cost whenever the data actually has to change, but it significantly simplifies a lot of optimizations that become easily accessible. The GHC is a prime example of taking extensive benefits from immutability.
- **Software transactional memory**: This is a somewhat exoteric approach, where the memory is managed with the same kinds of guarantees that a database would offer. The GHC also has an implementation of that approach.
- **Concurrency control primitives**: This is the simplest implementation, where you just support locking primitives and rely on the user setting the right boundaries to prevent data races.

This is not an exhaustive list. My goal here is to inspire you to do further research on what approaches will make the most sense for your particular situation. It is also important to note that the choice you make will have an impact on the accessibility of your interpreter to less experienced developers, which ultimately could impact how useful your interpreter becomes.

Data ownership

An entirely different way of handling this is to always have the data have an owner thread, either for reads or writes, and represent all operations in terms of messages. This is how Erlang is implemented, which allows its runtime to work not only across multiple threads but also across multiple hosts transparently. This is also known as the **actor model**.

However, there are other mechanisms to use data ownership to manage memory. The Rust language has used the concept of ownership as the cornerstone of how its memory is managed. This allows the runtime to assert that memory can only be mutated in one place at a time, and it also guarantees that you can't mutate a value when someone is reading it.

I won't go into details on how Rust works, or even why those design choices lead to specific important guarantees for the correctness of memory management. Many people have already written about that topic, and it is definitely a topic that should be interesting to someone designing an interpreter.

What I want to highlight, however, is that this is a choice that is so fundamental to the design that it is nearly impossible to retrofit it into existing systems. If this is an interesting approach for your use case, it's important to consider it as early as possible in the design.

Life cycle management

It is often the case that an interpreter will completely manage the life cycle of the memory on behalf of the user. This usually happens by the implementation of a garbage collector, which will automatically release the memory when it's no longer in use by the user code.

There are many different approaches to implementing a garbage collector, ranging from the simplest form of a simple reference count used by the Perl interpreter to much more complex infrastructures that the JVM or the **Common Language Runtime** (**CLR**) utilize.

It is also possible to design the language in such a way that the life cycle is known statically. Again, the Rust language is a good example of that. If the compiler can keep track of the references statically, it can statically know when the memory has to be released.

This is, once again, a topic that fundamentally informs a lot of what the programming language will look like, and it's very difficult to make radical changes later in the design process.

> There is plenty of literature if you want to dive deeper into this topic. I'd like to highlight *Garbage Collection: Algorithms for Automatic Dynamic Memory Management* by Richard Jones and Rafael D. Lins, and *The Implementation of Functional Programming Languages* by Simon Peyton Jones.

Finalizing my design

When dealing with network protocols, there are not a lot of situations where the result of processing a set of inputs should require a lot of mutability in the data. However, it's going to be important that the data is easily accessible from other threads since I don't want the response to the network message to be tied to the thread performing the I/O operations.

At the same time, not all the memory needed for handling the protocol needs to be made available for the code reacting to it, and that data doesn't need to be constrained that way. The approach I'll take, therefore, is to consider all data private to the continuation by default, except the data that is explicitly marked as shareable; the data that is shareable will be immutable.

In order to optimize the access pattern for the memory containing shareable data, it will be maintained in a separate location from the data that is private to the continuation.

The final big question is how to manage the life cycle of those values. The simplest implementation would be to simply add a reference count to all values. However, given the nature of the problem we're trying to solve, there's a specific simplification we can make.

I know the language will have to represent the state machine of the network protocol; therefore, it's possible to design the interpreter itself in terms of those discrete states.

The approach I'm taking is to make the memory life cycle be defined by those states, meaning that values will be allocated and deallocated depending on the state the protocol is currently in. Shareable values will only exist at the point where a state is complete. The transitional period when the execution is processing the I/O in order to determine what the state will be operates only in private memory and it can be released as soon as a stable state is achieved.

Finally, in order to ensure that the shareable data in a state is not released while it's still in use by user code in another thread, the data frame for the state will itself be managed under a reference count. Since we're doing a reference count for the entire frame, the overhead should be acceptable.

Summary

When designing an interpreter, you will need to keep in mind the specific use cases that should be prioritized, as the choices you make will result in important trade-offs that have a very wide impact on the final product.

One of the important aspects of the interpreter that will be heavily influenced by those trade-offs is how the interpreter interacts with system calls, such as I/O operations, or the execution of native callbacks. This includes trade-offs that make some use cases possible while making others impossible.

Likewise, the way your interpreter models parallel execution, either by using the operating system threads directly or with a more complex model, will narrow the areas where a language is more or less useful.

Putting all those constraints together early will allow you to build a more coherent vision for your interpreter, since changing those design aspects later will be significantly harder.

By this point, you should be able to start modeling the use cases that you are prioritizing for your own interpreter and making the decisions that guide the general architecture of your interpreter informed by those use cases.

In the next chapter, we will start focusing on the design of the programming language itself, with all the design choices for the interpreter being a major influence on the characteristics of the language.

Part 2

Modeling the Programming Language Syntax

In this part, you will focus on developing the syntax for the language while at the same time exercising the process of designing a programming language—from general programming language paradigms, through the type system of the language and naming of entities, and finally to a concrete syntax.

This part has the following chapters:

- *Chapter 6, Review of Programming Language Paradigms*
- *Chapter 7, Values, Containers, and the Language Meta-Model*
- *Chapter 8, Lexical Scopes*
- *Chapter 9, Putting It All Together and Creating a Coherent Vision*

6

Review of Programming Language Paradigms

In this chapter, I will do a brief review of the major programming language paradigms, contrasting them through examples. When designing a new language, you will have to make design decisions about how much each paradigm helps you solve the particular problems of your domain. We will work through the following concepts:

- How imperative programming allows the straightforward execution of instructions in a direct order
- How functional programming leaves a large space for the compiler to decide the best way to execute the program
- How declarative programming allows expressing complex state machines and rules in a way that abstracts away that complexity
- How logic programming allows specifying constraints and requirements without having to specify the instructions necessary to evaluate them
- The paradigm that works best for the use case we're focusing on

By the end of this chapter, you will have a framework to think about which aspects of programming language paradigms are going to be the most helpful to solve your particular use cases.

Imperative programming

When you consider the modern conceptualization of how computers work, such as the Turing machine and the von Neumann architecture, you will notice that they have *instructions* as the primary construct. The computer program will execute a sequence of instructions, altering the state of the machine as those instructions are executed.

This is the basic principle that drives the imperative programming paradigm, which evolved from the raw binary instructions that early processors supported into the assembly language, which is mostly a different encoding of the same structure, and finally to Fortran, the first programming language with an optimizing compiler.

The basic principle of the direct mapping of instructions in the high-level language to the instructions executed by the processor is still the fundamental driving principle of most imperative programming languages.

The C++ language is not an exception to that principle, even when you consider features such as generic programming. In the end, it is still a way of generating different sets of instructions based on the arguments of the template. The general expectation is that the code will roughly translate, even if in an extremely indirect way, to specific instructions to be executed by the processor in roughly the same order.

Of course, optimizers will do a lot of clever things that will make your sequence of instructions execute faster, such as taking into account the pipelining requirements of the specific target processor, but the amount of wording the C++ standard dedicates to the sequencing requirements is a good illustration of how much the language is defined by the principle of a sequence of instructions that manipulate the state, just like the original theoretical Turing machine.

As programming languages evolved, the relationship with native instructions became more abstract. Developers writing Python code are not likely to think about the number of instructions and registers involved in executing a particular piece of code. But the principle is preserved; just, instead of the native machine, we're now using the interpreter as a proxy for the native host.

That is not to say that everything that the program is doing has to be expressed in the programming language. For instance, it's frequently the case that interpreted languages will not expose access to raw memory management, abstracting it away.

The **Java Virtual Machine (JVM)**, for instance, uses a garbage collector that is mostly out of the control of the user. The programmer doesn't have a way to reason about the specifics of how the allocation and deallocation of memory happens. It is possible that a new value is using an area in an already allocated segment, as well as it likely being the case that the memory will not be reclaimed immediately when the scope is left.

However, it is important to acknowledge that there is a large spectrum in this space. As a point of illustration, the Perl interpreter also uses a garbage collector, but the end of the life cycle of the value is still deterministic based on the end of lexical scopes. The Perl interpreter provides stronger sequencing guarantees than the JVM, in that sense.

Perhaps the most important reason to prefer an imperative model is that it gives the user a significant amount of control over the execution of the code. High-performance computing, for instance, is an area where being able to reason about the specific execution of the code in order to more easily drive optimizations makes imperative programming particularly well-suited.

On the other hand, any higher-level abstraction will also have to be represented in terms of those same principles. This means that some classes of problems become significantly more complex to solve. Of course, it's still possible to abstract those complexities in terms of code reuse, but sometimes a different paradigm is just conceptually so much simpler that it makes more sense to just defer to a dedicated language, such as is the case with regular expressions.

In the following sections, we will look at the other three major programming paradigms, starting with the one closest to the way mathematics works.

Functional programming

The thing I hear the most when I introduce new engineers to functional programming is "*But how does anything happen?*". This question illustrates how diametrically opposed functional programming is to the imperative paradigm in its relationship with the actual instructions executed in the hardware.

But that is precisely the point, to defer the rendering of instructions to a point where the problem is comprehended in a more complete way by the compiler. The goal is that the user should be able to specify the problem in terms of the relationships between functions.

This drastically changes how the user is meant to specify the problem to be solved. Perhaps the easiest way to explain this distinction is through the concept of a *list of numbers* and how we think about sorting them.

In an imperative paradigm, the natural way to think about a list of numbers is by imagining a region of memory with discrete sub-regions representing each of the numbers. An algorithm to sort those numbers would be described in terms of how it reads values in specific indexes, compares them, and swaps them. You start with a state where the region in memory has unsorted numbers, you perform a number of instructions, and in the end, the state is a region in memory with sorted numbers.

The functional paradigm, on the other hand, will start by describing the list of numbers as the concept of the values. Sorting that list is then represented as the relationships between functions necessary to produce a function where the output is a sorted sequence.

To illustrate this point, let's take a look at how a merge sort is implemented in Haskell:

```
 -- Take a list of values that support ordering,
 -- return a sorted list using the "merge sort" algorithm
mergesort :: Ord a => [a] -> [a]

 -- A list with one element is already sorted
mergesort [a] = [a]

 -- A list with no elements is already sorted
mergesort [] = []

 -- Otherwise, split it in half, sort each half
 -- and then merge them into a single list
mergesort xs =
 mergesorted
    (mergesort (take halfway xs))
    (mergesort (drop halfway xs))
 where halfway = div (len xs) 2

 -- merge two already sorted lists into a single sorted
 -- list
mergesorted :: Ord a => [a] -> [a] -> [a]

 -- if one of the lists is empty return the other
mergesorted [] xs = xs
mergesorted xs [] = xs
```

```
  -- otherwise, recursively assemble a list by picking the
  -- smallest first element and recursing into the remainder
mergesorted (x:xs) (y:ys)
  | x <= y = x:mergesorted xs (y:ys)
  | x  > y = y:mergesorted (x:xs) y
```

I will not delve into the Haskell syntax, but I'm hoping that the comments are a good enough guide to what the syntax represents. If you read this from the perspective of comparing this code with an implementation in an imperative language, you will realize that there are no loops and no conditionals. There are just functions declared in relation to other functions.

Sure, in the end, the implementation has to transform this representation into a series of hardware instructions that will have to introspect the values and decide which version of the function is going to be invoked.

However, what this approach has given us is a way for the compiler to see the execution of the code in a way that is free from the sequencing constraints and the interaction with the state of the machine in between each of those instructions.

It is easy to underestimate just how much easier it is to reason about the assumptions you can make on the execution of the code that traverses a list when you describe it as a relationship between functions recursively splitting a list than it is to reason about a loop that increments a local state variable that represents the current index in the traversal of the list.

For instance, if the compiler can see that the function will split the list in half and operate on them independently, it becomes viable to transparently transform that execution in such a way that the sorting of the list happens in parallel. Not only that, the extent to which those operations are parallelized is something that can be fine-tuned at runtime depending on the characteristics of the input list and the specific hardware being used. All this without changing anything in the code itself.

Likewise, the approach of making values conceptually immutable also allows the compiler to decide whether it is better to change a value in place or it's better to copy the value. In an imperative language, that decision has to be represented in the source code, and the runtime environment has no control over it.

In the next section, we will explore the paradigm that turns the management of complex state machines into a simple series of statements.

Declarative programming

In previous chapters, I have already spent some time discussing how regular expressions, as a language, can represent problems that would otherwise be very difficult to express in other languages.

The root of that distinction is in the very nature of the language, where you are not specifying instructions to be executed in sequence, as is the case with imperative languages. But additionally, unlike functional languages, you're not specifying things in terms of functions being applied either.

Instead, you are specifying rules that describe the different states that the program may find itself in, and how to adapt to those states in order to complete the requested execution.

In the case of regular expressions, the language starts with the assumption that there is a string that is being operated on and a stack of cursors with associated captures, which store parts of the matched text. The final result is, unconditionally, a description of whether the expression finished successfully and whatever captures were performed. All of this without the user having to describe any of those operations.

Let's look at a simple expression as an illustration:

```
^a(bd)?be$
```

This will essentially only match the strings `abe` and `abdbe`. What is implicitly stated is that when you match the first `b`, it needs to start a capture in case the following character is a `d`, but be prepared to backtrack without doing the capture in case the following character is an `e`. The code for the regular expression specifies this behavior without any explicit description of it.

The more interesting aspect, however, is that the state machine I described previously is not the only way to implement it. An optimized implementation would bypass that entire process and simply start by checking the size of the string before looking at the contents, failing immediately if the size was not 3 or 5, and finally compare it to one of the two fixed strings, producing a static result of the capture if it matches.

As with the functional programming example in the previous section, the declarative code invariably has to be transformed into a series of hardware instructions, but an optimizer would have a significantly harder time detecting that possibility if we had described the pessimistic version in an imperative way.

That is to say, it would be possible to write code in an imperative way that is as optimized as the code generated by the compiler of a declarative language, but the point here is that the design of the language allows the compiler itself to perform those optimizations, rather than the programmer having to account for it.

Before we move on, I would like to use a different declarative language to illustrate the specialization of those languages. Let's look at the example of GNU Make:

```
%.c: %.c.in config.json
    generate-code --config config.json $< $@

    g++ -o $@ -c $^

myexecutable: foo.o bar.o baz.o
    g++ -o $@ $^
```

What these six lines have implicitly declared is that GNU Make will have to build a graph of rules that would look something like the diagram in *Figure 6.1*:

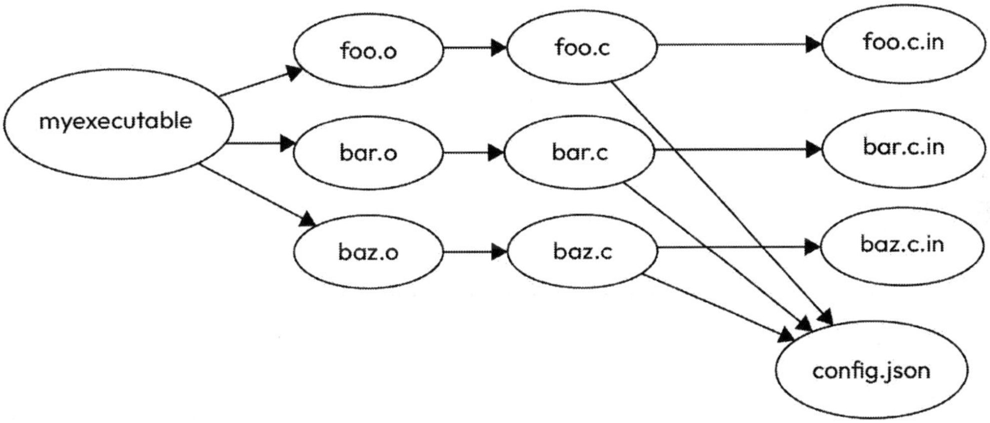

Figure 6.1: The dependency graph described in the makefile

And when you run `make myexecutable`, it will have to perform a graph traversal identifying which subgraph is relevant for that target, then start from the nodes with no dependencies and see if they are newer than the nodes that depend on them. Whenever a dependency is newer, it recursively invalidates all targets that depend on it.

As with regular expressions, the Make programming language is designed with a specific use case in mind. Because it can make assumptions about how it is going to be used, it can abstract away the graph operations and file operations on behalf of the user.

The choice of focusing on a specific use case allows the Make language to provide an extremely simple mechanism to address those use cases, as demonstrated in the earlier example, reducing the amount the user has to specify in order to achieve the desired outcome.

In the next section, I will focus on the last of the main categories of paradigms of programming languages.

Logic programming

This paradigm is the one that is usually the most exotic, particularly for those who come from an imperative programming background. It is probably fair to say that it is the most distant from actual instructions run in the hardware. My goal here is to give you a broad perspective of what is it that will make the most sense for your particular use case. I am hoping that this will give you a bit of a different perspective on what a programming language can look like.

Logic programming languages are the most useful when the use case can be described as a process of narrowing the possible solutions that satisfy all declared constraints. You can think of it as starting from the set of all possible values for a given solution and using constraints to reduce the space of possible answers to the ones that would be useful in that particular situation.

The solving of a Sudoku puzzle is a very good example of a situation where logic programming languages will shine. The process of writing code in that case becomes an exercise of formulating the rules that describe your particular situation.

Let's start by using human language to describe the rules of Sudoku:

- There is a 9x9 grid
- The grid is also divided into nine 3x3 square grids
- Each cell in the grid will contain an integer with values between 1 and 9
- Cells within a row of the grid must have distinct values
- Cells within a column of the grid must have distinct values
- Cells within a square must have distinct values

You would use a logic programming language when you want to find a set of answers that would satisfy all the constraints enunciated here, particularly when there are already some predetermined values in some of the cells.

The main difference in approach from other paradigms is that you presume that the runtime of your programming language knows how to evaluate those rules, rather than you implementing the search algorithm that would explore that space.

If you are experienced in imperative languages, you can probably come up with a set of operations that will iteratively and recursively narrow the search space until you have an answer that follows all the rules.

With a logic programming language, however, you delegate that searching to be performed by the language environment, and your goal is just to describe the rules in a precise enough way for the runtime to correctly find a solution.

I will present the code for the solution of Sudoku in Prolog, as supported by the SWI-Prolog interpreter:

```
% module that is used to solve constraints in
% finite domains
:- use_module(library(clpfd)).
% Describe the rules of a Sudoku puzzle
sudoku(Rows) :-
    % it must have 9 rows
    length(Rows, 9),
    % create a different view that represents the columns
    transpose(Rows, Columns),
    % the length of columns must also be 9
    length(Columns, 9),
    % all values must be integers between 1 and 9
    append(Rows, Vs), Vs ins 1..9,
    % all rows and columns must have distinct values
    maplist(all_distinct, Rows),
    maplist(all_distinct, Columns).
    % We use a recursion trick to declare
    % the squares, more later
    Rows = [As,Bs,Cs,Ds,Es,Fs,Gs,Hs,Is],
    square(As, Bs, Cs),
    square(Ds, Es, Fs),
    square(Gs, Hs, Is),
% A square is defined recursively.
% This allow us to reduce the amount of code we're writing,
```

```
% but you could specify this with a fully expanded grid.
% The definition is based on a group of three rows.
% It takes three columns from each and does recursion to
% define another square.  when we get to the end,
% it will be an empty list, which we'll set to a valid
% result.
square([], [], []).
square([N1,N2,N3|Ns1], [N4,N5,N6|Ns2], [N7,N8,N9|Ns3]) :-
    % all values in the square must be distinct
    all_distinct([N1,N2,N3,N4,N5,N6,N7,N8,N9]),
    % the remaining of the columns on those rows
    % must form another square, or it ran out of columns.
    square(Ns1, Ns2, Ns3).
```

If we ignore the part about defining the squares, it looks very similar to how we defined the rules in human language. The important point here is that we're not specifying the mechanism by which the search space is supposed to be narrowed. In fact, it would have been possible to declare the rules in terms of the fully expanded grid; it would have just been substantially more verbose.

I hope that you notice that this code doesn't specify how we're supposed to be applying the constraints. And that's the point. The runtime is able to use advanced algorithms to find a solution that satisfies all the constraints, and the programmer is able to focus entirely on how the rules and constraints are defined.

The capabilities of the specific Prolog implementations are the reasons why you will choose one or another. There are many ways in which one specific runtime will implement the constraint solving in one or another way, which will make it more suitable for the specific problem at hand.

In fact, those distinctions are the justification for someone to consider licensing a commercially licensed Prolog interpreter, as the set of constraints in a given problem may be complicated enough that a vendor may provide results with significantly better efficiency than another.

It is, hopefully, easy to see how the use case for logic programming languages is distinct from all other paradigms, and how problems that are really straightforward to specify in a logic programming language would require hundreds of lines to be specified in an imperative programming language. And that's before you consider that you can choose different solving strategies without having to rewrite anything about the code.

In the next section, I will go back to our use case for the exercise in this book and focus on what paradigm should inform us the most.

Choosing a paradigm for our language

Since we're focusing on solving the problem of how to specify networking protocols, the primary aspect that drives our decision is that it is mostly about managing the state machines to correctly represent where in the specified protocol the communication is.

For the sake of the design exercise, let's look at the ways in which each of the paradigms discussed here help solve this particular use case:

- The imperative paradigm would push us in the direction of having the user specify the operations that would lead to a specific transition between states. In reality, this is how most network protocols are implemented in imperative languages today. Therefore, choosing an imperative style would provide little benefit when compared with the protocol being implemented in the native language.
- The functional paradigm, particularly with strong pattern-matching semantics such as what Haskell offers, would allow you to specify the protocol in an interesting way. However, the transient nature of network protocols would force us into edge cases of the language as we would try to manage side effects, such as the data that is sent and received from a socket, as we try to interact with the remote host.
- The logical programming paradigm is the one where it would be the hardest to justify the adoption in this particular use case, as it works best with static constraints and values, which is not the reality of what interacting with network protocols looks like.
- Finally, that leaves us with the declarative paradigm. There is already a significant overlap with regular expressions as we will need to specify rules of what are acceptable inputs and outputs at any given point. But we also need to declare the relationships between different states of the program and allow the runtime to manage those transitions for the user.

Given what I just described, the most interesting approach for this exercise is to make our programming language design heavily influenced by the declarative paradigm.

It's important to notice that programming languages don't have to be fully committed to a single paradigm. Many languages, including C++ and Python, offer a mix of imperative and functional styles. Therefore, we should always be open to considering what aspects of a different paradigm would benefit our specific programming language.

Summary

Programming languages have designs that navigate through many different paradigms on how the code has to be specified. Some languages adhere more strictly to one style than another, but it is still useful to consider those broad categories.

The imperative paradigm focuses on describing the operations the computer will have to do in order to solve a particular problem. There is an expected mapping from the code to what the computer will actually do.

The functional paradigm pushes the problem into the space of how values are transformed by functions, rather than how the state is manipulated by specific operations. The runtime is then able to choose different execution strategies without changes being required in the code.

Declarative programming languages tend to focus on specific environments and make it significantly more straightforward to solve problems in that particular space. They allow the runtime to decide how to solve operational problems in order to achieve the expected outcome.

Logic programming languages, on the other hand, take a drastically different approach, where there's very little connection between what the code is describing and what will actually happen at runtime. They are particularly well-suited for problems that require choosing flexible approaches to constraint solving.

For the exercise in this book, the declarative paradigm is likely the most well-suited, as it will allow the user to declare the different states the network protocol goes through without requiring the user to implement the state machine themselves.

In the next chapter, we will focus on how programming languages look at values, how those values are carried through the logic of the code, as well as how values are managed throughout the life cycle of the program.

7

Values, Containers, and the Language Meta-Model

The way a programming language deals with variables, values, and complex data structures defines what the code written in that language looks like. In this chapter, we'll go through the following topics:

- How programming languages differentiate the abstract concept of a value from the transient states of a variable
- The distinction that programming languages make on containers that hold values
- How the mutability of values influences the design of the language
- The support for copies, references, and shared values in the design
- How to create a coherent design to address all those requirements

By the end of this chapter, you will have a nuanced understanding of how the aforementioned aspects affect the language design and the code written in that language.

Variables and values

It is common for the conversations around the implementation of an algorithm in an imperative language to talk about variables and values interchangeably. The distinction between these terms often doesn't make a significant impact on the reasoning of the code, particularly in languages with simpler semantics.

The Python language, for instance, has a simple model where variables just point to values, and the lifetime of those values is defined by whether they are reachable, directly or indirectly, through existing variables.

Some values, such as numbers and strings, are immutable. Other values, such as objects, lists, and dictionaries, are mutable. The distinction is made even clearer by the fact that the operations in the language are designed with that principle in mind.

Assigning a different value to a variable just means the old value is no longer reachable in that particular way since it now points to the new value. There are no special semantics attributed to the variable, beyond being the way to reach a specific value.

Languages with more complex semantics, such as C++, require the user to keep that distinction in mind. Advanced users of that language need to have a nuanced understanding of that distinction to avoid specific types of bugs.

For instance, variables in C++ represent more than just a reference to the value—they also represent the specification of the storage for the memory independently of the value and are much more directly responsible for the life cycle of that value.

As an example of how that complexity shows up in C++, we can look at variables of automatic duration, which have their storage created in the entry point of the function. However, when they are not initialized, they have an **indeterminate** value, meaning that even though a variable exists, the value for it doesn't exist yet.

Other languages take a diametrically opposite direction, such as Haskell, where talking about variables doesn't describe a storage location that can hold different values over time, as it does in Python or C++. The variable is just a symbolic way to reference the value that was given as input in a function. In a language like Haskell, where every value is immutable, the concept of separating the storage from the value is completely outside the user's control.

When designing a programming language, this trade-off is the thing you need to be balancing. If you want to make a language that is more imperative in how it allows the values, their storage, and their life cycle to be more explicitly managed by the user, then going in a direction closer to C++ makes sense. But if your intent is for the user to think about the values in a more abstract way and remove a certain amount of control on the specifics of the life cycle and storage in the context of the algorithms, then going for a solution closer to Haskell will bring a lot of benefits.

Finding the right balance between explicit control and abstraction is always challenging. It's also important to consider how the values will be utilized beyond their immediate creation and management—something particularly relevant in cases such as the embedded interpreter we are constructing in this language design exercise.

In the language I'm building, the main goal is to make it easy to extract information from the data stream that was sent from the remote end. I will avoid giving control to the user over the specific life cycle and storage decisions about the values. I intend to use the state machine of the protocol itself to manage that implicitly for the user.

Now that we've covered the distinction between values and variables, in the next section, I'll focus on the distinction between single values and containers, and how the language design is influenced by those requirements.

Values and containers

In addition to the distinction between the values and the variables, different types of values can be assigned to those variables. Some represent something straightforward, such as a number. Others represent how other values are stored and accessed. These are called **containers**.

This distinction is a lot more important in languages such as C++, where there is a lot of control over the life cycle of values. In contrast, it's a lot simpler when the only concern is efficiently accessing the values inside the container. Nevertheless, regardless of the type of language, the role of the container is to provide an efficient way of handling common use cases.

There is also a distinction regarding how much the user of the language is expected to construct their containers versus how much the language itself provides the features for most use cases. Contrasting Python and C++ is, again, an interesting way of demonstrating the different approaches language designers can take. If you look at the C++ language and the C++ Standard Library as two independent things, you will realize that the language offers arrays, structs, pointers, and templates for the user to manage complex data structures, but it doesn't go a lot beyond that.

The Standard Library offers powerful container abstractions and algorithms that can operate on those containers. If a language only offers a raw array, the Standard Library offers `std::array`, which provides most of the functionality that a user of the language would need. The language is built in such a way that the user should be able to construct custom containers and algorithms that are just as efficient as the Standard Library.

The Python language, on the other hand, offers high-level containers as part of the language itself. There's no expectation that the user should be able to produce a container as efficient as the one that comes with the interpreter, and the users of the language are much more focused on the higher-level applications and systems they're building. For instance, no Python programmer is expected to be able to create a custom implementation of a list that is as efficient as the native list. The same goes for dictionaries or other container types you would find in the C++ Standard Library.

The lesson to be taken from this discussion is that selecting specific use cases will also dictate how the language is going to be used and evolve. The C++ language was designed to offer full control to harness as much power from the underlying hardware as possible, where the user only pays for the cost of the abstractions that they are directly using. The Python language, on the other hand, was designed to solve higher-level problems, where performance was not the primary constraint on the design.

A language designer cannot cater to all use cases; they have to focus on the specific use cases that will make that particular language useful. If your goal is to enable the ability to build high-level systems and applications, then it's likely more useful to focus on providing the containers that most users will need, and then make those as efficient as possible with the knowledge that the users wouldn't be able to achieve the same performance by writing code in the interpreted language.

However, if your goal is to allow the user to optimize the data structures for their containers and fine-tune those to extract as much performance as possible, then you will probably want to align your language closer to what C++ does.

In the language I'm working on for this book, I will focus on providing the containers for the common use cases of the language. I won't even try to provide mechanisms to create custom containers in the language. I expect that the users of this language are going to be much more focused on the details of the specific network protocol they're implementing rather than trying to optimize the interpreted code.

The fact that the language will focus on a narrow use case will allow the interpreter to make specific choices that will make the performance characteristics appealing, even if the user doesn't have a lot of control over it.

Mutability

When you are designing a language that primarily focuses on a single thread of execution, the question of the mutability of the values and containers is reasonably easy to ignore. There are very few things that can get in the way of simply overwriting the value in memory and carrying on.

But there are nuances to be considered, even in the single-threaded use case. Consider, for example, a data structure such as a hash map. You could end up in a situation where a key and value that were added to a hash map become completely inaccessible because the key was inserted in one bucket, but as it mutated, it didn't get reassigned to a different bucket.

I want to explore a few different ways to address this particular problem. My goal is to use this as an illustration of the kinds of questions you'll have to ask yourself when you're designing your language, and explore ways to find a solution that matches your use case.

Perhaps the simplest of all approaches is the one used by the Perl interpreter, where the key to a hash table is conceptually a different kind of value—it is always an immutable string. Whenever something is used as a key, it gets coerced into a string before its hash value can be computed.

If you look at the internals of the interpreter, you will see that those strings are an entire special case throughout the code. This allows the interpreter to optimize the data structure in a way that would be impossible if arbitrary values could be used as keys.

The C++ language is the diametrical opposite of this since the language makes no specific choices and control over the data structure is left to the user, including the responsibility of making sure the objects that are used as keys remain immutable. There's nothing in the language that stops you from using a mutable value as the key, which could result in the key becoming unreachable. But since the hash value is also user-defined, the user has the flexibility to safely implement a type where only specific members that affect the hash calculation are immutable, while other members can be mutated. Once more, C++ focuses on giving the user full control over what the language is doing.

The Python language takes a middle-ground approach where you can use a data class as the key to a dictionary, but only if you make it immutable, producing a `TypeError` if you try to assign a mutable key to a dictionary. This still allows for some flexibility while still preventing the user from making a common mistake. This approach has its trade-offs as it can't be as optimized as the Perl hash tables since it allows user types, but it still places guardrails around common mistakes the user may make.

When you design a language, you need to figure out the right balance of providing flexibility, efficiency, and safety. It's often the case that you will have to compromise on at least one of those things. Those choices are going to have a deep impact on how useful the language is going to be in specific scenarios.

As I'm focusing on the use case of handling network protocols, I expect that the most important requirement is going to be transporting the information that was sent by the remote side to the native language that will process the events, as well as produce the required responses. I don't expect the user to need to perform a lot of mutations in the values.

With that in mind, the language will work with the principle that all values are immutable, and any data structures that need to contain other values will be able to be optimized with that assumption.

Copies, references, and shared values

The last aspect that I wanted to include in this discussion about how values and containers affect language design is the way the language values model operations such as copying, referencing, and sharing values. To explore this topic, I want to go back to a comparison between C++ and Python.

In Python, the lifetime of a value is managed by the interpreter based on its usefulness. This means that the value remains in memory as long as at least one reference points to it, directly or indirectly. Once the interpreter determines that a value is no longer reachable from any part of the program, it automatically reclaims the memory occupied by that value.

The Python language is designed in a way where there is very little ambiguity about what happens when you assign an object to a different variable or insert it into an existing container. This is also where the immutability of some of the values in Python gives room for the interpreter to optimize away copies when they point to the same contents.

In C++, the language explicitly gives the user control over what operation is being performed on the value, which means the language needs to expose different mechanisms to create a copy or pass a reference. This is important because the language runtime does not guarantee that if you make a reference to a value, the value will outlive the reference. That is, in fact, a frequent source of bugs in C++ code. On the other hand, very deliberate control over when copies and references are made, as well as when memory is allocated and deallocated, is also a very important feature for optimizing the performance of C++ code.

To give another example, the Perl interpreter has explicit support for references, but the existence of a reference is sufficient to keep the value alive. That means the interpreter is in full control of the allocation and deallocation of the memory. Garbage Collection, the runtime feature that manages memory allocation, can be implemented using various strategies, ranging from simple reference counting, as Perl does, to reachability-based rules, as Python does, or even more elaborate approaches, like those used in .Net CLR.

That doesn't mean that you can't write C++ code that has the memory managed at runtime. The C++ Standard Library has specific support for sharing the same value across different parts of the program using `std::shared_ptr`, where the Standard Library implements a memory management very similar to the Garbage Collector in Perl. The difference lies in the guarantees the language runtime can provide: once you give the user control, you lose the guarantees.

To complete this illustration, I want to highlight the way that Haskell inverts that picture. In Haskell, conceptually, all values are immutable. But since the user has no control over how those are managed, there are situations where the compiler can determine that the original value is no longer going to be used, and therefore it omits the copy and updates the value in place instead.

In the next section, I will bring all of these aspects together and provide a more complete description of how the design is impacted by the way values and containers are handled.

The language meta-model

Designing a programming language is an exercise in balancing various conflicting requirements, making the choices that align the best with the objectives of that particular language, and creating a coherent vision that guides the user into solving the problems most effectively.

Whenever the language has incoherencies in those design principles, it will lead to continued confusion among the users of the language. It is, of course, always possible to continuously guide the community around the language with documentation and linting tools. However, those are substantially less powerful than the natural direction that the language gives to its users on how to solve particular problems.

Here, the language meta-model represents the underlying principles—sometimes explicit, sometimes not—that drive how the language and the runtime manage the values the user is operating on.

I'll start by looking at the language that has one of the simplest of all meta-models: the POSIX shell. In this language, everything is a string and the values are sliced based on the input field separator. Numbers are stored and operated as strings in their decimal form.

Initially, this seems like a naïve way of handling values. However, when you consider the way the POSIX shell is used, it starts to make a lot more sense. The main use case of the language is to manipulate argument lists, inputs, and outputs across different processes, and those arguments are always strings. Likewise, the environment variables of a process are also defined in terms of a dictionary of strings.

If you consider this more carefully, you will realize that for simple scenarios where the shell language is expected to be used, having additional support for different types of values, copies, references, and containers would make the simpler use case harder to handle.

At the same time, whenever a shell script starts getting more complicated, the language nudges the user to realize that the shell is probably not the right tool for that job anymore.

Interestingly enough, that is the reason why the Perl language was created in the first place—to provide better tools for those use cases that were getting too complicated for shell, sed, and awk.

Perl's type system is also incredibly simplistic. The main distinction it introduced was the built-in array and hash containers. Before Perl 5, the language was not a lot more powerful than shell in its meta-model. It didn't support object orientation or even references. After Perl 5, with the support for packages and references, the language became a lot more powerful, but it still doesn't have distinct types for values that are numbers or strings, even if it stores both forms when it needs them to make the process cheaper.

Therefore, it is not an accident that Perl was incredibly popular with system administrators who needed to create more complex integrations in a Unix environment or the early web for creating dynamic interfaces using the **Common Gateway Interface (CGI)**. In the late 1990s, Perl was called "the duct tape of the internet."

Those are just two examples of relatively simple meta-models. Other languages have considerably more complexity. C++, for instance, has multiple categories of types and values to allow for the amount of flexibility the users have come to expect from the language.

The Raku language (formerly known as Perl 6) has a Meta-Object Protocol, meaning that the definition of what a class is and how it works can be specified directly within the language itself. This includes customizing algorithms for method resolution order within class hierarchies. It also allows explicit customization of where an object's data is stored, supports alternative ways of organizing code, and even lets users define their own storage and organization strategies.

In the language I am creating for this book, I don't want to incentivize complex operations to be specified in the language. The goal of the language is to have a simple way to specify the different parts of the state machine of a given network protocol, and offer a way for the inputs and outputs of that communication to be communicated to a different language where the actual operations will be performed.

I do, however, need to account for protocols that have intermediate calculations. In HTTP, for instance, some headers provide context for the body of the request, so I do need to allow values to be bound into named variables and be able to perform operations on those, but I don't need to support object orientation or a more complex paradigm. The goal of the language is to handle the state machine of the network protocol and delegate the complex logic to a different programming language.

The language will nudge the user to another language when they're doing anything beyond the intended use case.

This topic could easily be the subject of an entire book, but I am hoping that this brief introduction will give you a more nuanced understanding of aspects of language design that you had perhaps not thought about before.

Summary

Different languages have different ways to represent values and how those values are addressed by variables. In some languages, this is just a symbolic mechanism, while in other languages, this extends to managing the life cycle of the values.

When more complex data structures need to be represented, programming languages introduce a different category of value. A "container," for example, is a value that holds other values. In some languages, such as Python, containers are built into the language itself, and there's very little space for creating alternative implementations for those. In other languages, such as C++, containers are entirely implemented in the language itself, and the user has access to all the facilities necessary to make containers as efficient as the ones shipped by the Standard Library.

The mutability of values, however, can place significant constraints on how containers can operate. For instance, hash maps need the hash value for a given key to be immutable; otherwise, you may end up in a situation where a key is no longer reachable. Different languages take different approaches here. As a language designer, your role is to find the specific balance between flexibility, performance, and safety.

Copies, references, and shared values are yet another dimension of language design where languages take very distinct approaches, from giving almost no control to the user about the mechanisms used, such as what happens in Python, to giving the user complete control over how the values will exist through the life cycle of the program, as is the case in C++.

All of these aspects form what I call the language meta-model. Creating a coherent design in that area will allow your language to be better at guiding the user into solving the right problems the right way. Sometimes, it's important to make a specific type of problem hard to solve to make other problems easier. This is a very fine balancing act, and it is your role, as a language designer, to make it match your intended use case.

In the next chapter, I will focus on understanding how programming languages approach the naming of variables and other syntactic terms since those are the mechanisms users use to reference values and containers.

8

Lexical Scopes

Variables and values exist in different scopes, and different programming languages make different choices on which types of scopes are available to the user. In this chapter, we will cover the following:

- Introduce the concept of the **lexical pad**
- How different languages define the scope of names inside a given function
- The flexibility and complexity added by supporting **block lexical scopes**
- The **lexical scope** defined by a **closure**
- The way different languages handle names with a **global scope** and how it affects code reuse

By the end of this chapter, you will have a more nuanced understanding of how languages handle resolving names from various different scopes, and how that affects code reuse in those languages.

The lexical pad

In any specific expression in the code, a given name needs to be resolved to a specific variable at that point, and the compiler or interpreter needs to be able to unambiguously identify that.

In *Chapter 7, Values, Containers, and the Language Meta-Model*, I discussed the distinction between variables, values, and containers. Now, I have to clarify that a variable, at the end of the day, is a very special kind of container; one that only the compiler or interpreter has access to manipulate.

The mapping between the symbolic name the user writes in the expression and the container that holds the value associated with that variable is what we call the lexical pad. It can be implemented in multiple ways, but the end result is the same: when there is a name in the code, it needs to identify which particular container is being referenced.

The mechanism that is used to search the lexical pad, along with the internal data structures used by it, is usually not exposed to the user of the language. That choice allows the implementation to change over time or to make more tailored choices for each situation in order to optimize that resolution.

For interpreted languages, the entire lexical pad is usually completely available at runtime. However, in statically compiled languages, it's often the case that this information is no longer necessary, except for debugging. That's the reason why the compiler needs special instructions for C++ if you want to be able to debug the code and inspect the value of a given variable, so the compiler stashes that extra information in the debug section of your object.

It's usually the case that within a specific segment of code, all name resolutions will have the same results. The area where that is true is considered a lexical scope. Different programming languages make different choices on how to define the lexical scope for the language.

In the next sections, we will explore different approaches for defining the lexical scope for a language.

Function lexical scopes

In some languages, the name of a variable in a function is always scoped to the entire function. Let's look at the following Python code:

```
def do_something():
    for a in 1,2,3:
        print(a)
    print(a)
```

If Python is your primary language, the output here would be obvious, as the scope of the name is always defined by the function itself. The a variable, therefore, will have the value that it had in the last iteration of the loop. The output is as follows:

```
1
2
3
3
```

If you come from another language, such as Perl, you would have expected that code to be invalid, because the variable was defined inside the loop, and therefore it shouldn't be reachable after the loop is complete.

This, however, provides some simplification to the interpreter, because it only needs to initialize a single lexical pad to the entire function, and every variable defined within the function will be referenced directly from it.

There is also a matter of style in this choice, as there is no chance that the same variable could reference values of different types, for instance. When using type hinting in Python, you only need to annotate it once per name, and if you happen to use different types for the same variable, it will be considered an error.

In the next section, we will examine lexical scoping at the block level as an alternative to function-level scoping.

Block lexical scopes

The most common alternative to making the scope of variables tied to the entire function is to give a bigger meaning to individual blocks, regardless of their relationship with the given functions.

Let's use this C++ code as an example:

```
void foo() {
    {  int a = 1; }
    {  double a = 1; }
    {  short a = 1; }
}
```

In this case, the name a has an entirely different meaning in each of the blocks within the function. If you try to reference that name outside of those blocks, the compiler will give you an error.

Now let's look at the same idea using the example we previously discussed in Python, rewritten in C++:

```
#include <stdio.h>
int main() {
    for (int a = 1; a < 3; a++) {
        printf("%d\n", a);
    }
    printf("%d\n", a);
}
```

In this case, because the lexical scope is defined by the `for` block, the variable is not valid outside of it. Trying to compile that code with `gcc` will give you an output like the following:

```
/tmp/foo.cpp: In function 'int main()':
/tmp/foo.cpp:6:24: error: 'a' was not declared in this scope
    6 |       printf("%d\n", a);
      |                      ^
```

This is important for C++ because it means that the lifetime of a variable is also limited to the scope of the block in which it is declared. This has an important side effect because it means the compiler can reuse the memory space across different blocks.

In the example with three independent declarations of a variable with different types, the compiler will be free to use the same space in memory for all of them, since there's no code path that could lead to them being valid at the same time.

In the next section, I will explore a special case for both the function lexical scope and the block lexical scope, which is the creation of closures.

Closure lexical scopes

There is a special type of lexical scope that is created when a function is defined within another lexical scope, and that function definition outlives the scope of the variables being referenced. It is called a closure. Let's look at the following example in JavaScript:

```
function makeGreeter(greeting) {
    function doGreeting(who) {
        return greeting + ' ' + who + '!';
    }
    return doGreeting;
}
greet = makeGreeter('Hello');
console.log(greet('World'));
```

This is a common pattern in functional programming languages. The closure is created when the `doGreeting` function makes a reference to the `greeting` variable, which has its lifetime limited to the execution of the `makeGreeter` function, but the local function is returned, causing it to keep its own copy of the variable closed over the function definition.

The important distinction here is that the creation of the closure will require an additional level of management from the runtime of the storage of the variables. The life cycle of the variables that were closed over needs to be extended to the life cycle of the inner function itself, which keeps the references to the closed-over variables.

Implementing a language that supports closures will require the ability to extend the life cycle of variables and to keep a lexical pad alive for as long as a reference to that function still exists.

I will not try to justify why this feature is important, in case you're not familiar with it. I will leave it as an exercise for you to experiment using this functional pattern to solve problems that would otherwise become repetitive to implement.

But beyond the fact that this is a commonly supported feature in programming languages, closures highlight how complex the management of variables and variable names can become, and why it's important to do a thorough evaluation of what problems you're trying to solve in your particular programming language.

In the next section, I will look at a scope that depends on the call chain that has led to the current point in the code.

Global lexical scopes

In an ideal world, every single possible thing that could influence how a particular function operates would be given as an argument to that function. This would result in code that is a lot easier to test and customize to specific scenarios.

In reality, however, it's often the case that a function that has been in use for a long time suddenly has a new customization requirement. Changing the entire codebase such that this new parameter can be passed through every other layer of code is a very expensive approach to solving that problem.

The most common solution to that problem is to support the use of a global lexical scope, where a variable can be reached from any part of the code. That allows the creation of customization points that were not predicted beforehand, even if they're not explicit inputs to the functions being called.

The thing that is not as obvious, however, is that most languages have the global lexical scope as the default mechanism by which functions and types are discovered.

The name of a class in C++, for instance, is global for the entire program, regardless of call chains, function scopes, or block scopes. In fact, the language even allows a class to be used "in name only" by doing a forward declaration of the class, which means the name can be in scope even if the actual declaration for the class is never seen in that particular translation unit.

The same is true for packages and members of a package in Python. When your code specifies `import subprocess`, that name is global to the entire interpreter, and the members of that package are the same regardless of where in the code it happens.

This is particularly more relevant in a language such as Python, where it is possible to manipulate the lexical pad for a given name and replace it with something else. That is how the Python testing library is able to mock and patch various functions during the execution of the test. The global package is temporarily changed to replace a given member, and once the test is complete, it is restored to its original value.

The more important outcome of using a global scope for types and functions is that it becomes considerably easier for different parts of your codebase to use a unified vocabulary. You can assert by inspection that what one C++ translation unit calls `std::string` will be the same thing in a different translation unit.

Summary

The lexical pad is the name we give to the mechanism by which an interpreter or a compiler maps a name in the code to the container that holds the corresponding value.

Different programming languages put different requirements on the compiler or interpreter on what should be possible in terms of how the lexical pad can be queried and manipulated. There are areas of the code that have uniform visibility of names, which are called the lexical scopes for that particular programming language.

Some languages, such as Python, have the scope matching the body of a function. Any variable defined in a function is visible for the entire duration of the function. Other languages, such as C++, have the scope narrowed down to a particular block of code, meaning the language gives finer-grained control to the user of the life cycle of the variables.

In addition to those two choices, languages that support some functional idioms also support closure scopes, where a variable that is referenced from a function that outlives its own scope will be retained with the function itself. This places additional complexity requirements into the runtime but provides a very important tool for the end user.

The global scope is the most common form to create the identity of types and functions. Making these names global is actually a fundamental part of how to make code reuse easier since different parts of the codebase can easily share the same vocabulary.

This is the last chapter where I'll focus on various concepts related to the design of programming languages. In the next chapter, I will gather all those concepts into a complete design for the language.

9

Putting It All Together and Creating a Coherent Vision

Up to this point, I have been focusing on more abstract features in the design of a programming language. In this chapter, I will focus on the design of the syntax of the first version of the programming language itself, which will include the following topics:

- The general format of the language, based on the decision to follow a declarative programming paradigm
- How values and containers are going to be defined and used
- How variables are going to be declared and referenced
- A concrete use case of the HTTP/1.1 protocol to exercise the overall language design

By the end of this chapter, you will have a more nuanced appreciation of the minutiae involved in the design of a programming language and will have a blueprint for how to design your own.

The shape of a declarative language

The first step in the process of defining the final design for a programming language is figuring out how the overall shape of the code will look. In *Chapter 6, Review of Programming Language Paradigms,* I explained how a declarative paradigm would be well suited to describe the complicated state machine that is required for implementing a network protocol.

The first thing that I need to clarify is that there are two parties to the communication—the client and the server. Each software agent will play a specific role, but there's no reason for the specification of the protocol to be different. After all, both the client and the server are communicating using the same protocol, so there should be no reason for that description to be different between them. The interpreter will have to consider it from either the server's or the client's perspective, but the code in the **domain-specific language** (**DSL**) is the same regardless.

For the first version of this language, I will only implement support for straightforward client–server connections based on streams of data. This is an important limitation to reduce the scope of complexity I have to deal with. Some protocols, such as SSH, support creating multiple parallel streams of communication in the same connection, which would mean the interpreter would need to be able to branch the execution at those points, while simpler protocols, such as HTTP/1.1, have a single state machine for the entire protocol.

Practically speaking, this will cover protocols where a client initiates a connection with a server and they exchange data until one of them closes the connection. For that reason, I will adopt the terms *client* and *server* in the language itself. The server is always the one that is bound to a given address, and the client is always the one that initiates the connection with that address.

Since this language will not actually manage the sockets in any way, nor coordinate how the sockets get assigned to different native execution threads, the life cycle of the program in this language starts when the socket is connected on both sides. I will use the term *open* for the state that is the entry point for every program in this language.

When the connection is ended, the socket is considered closed on both sides. For that reason, I will use the term *closed* to represent the final state for every program, where the interpreter should exit.

At this point, I should be able to write the code for a network protocol where the server accepts the connection but immediately closes it without the client and server exchanging any information.

Specifying the empty program

This is the simplest possible case. I don't have to specify any data being transmitted; I just have to specify that I have the `Open` and `Closed` states, and that I need an unconditional transition from `Connected` to `Closed`.

There is, however, an important detail here, which is that the transition from `Open` to `Closed` is meant to be initiated by one of the parties. This is a good illustration of how important it is to guide the design using practical scenarios.

The empty program, therefore, needs to specify that there is a transition initiated by the server going from the predefined `Open` state to the predefined `Closed` state.

This is a good hint that the most important aspect of the program is not the description of the states, but rather the description of the transitions.

With all of that, I propose a syntax that describes just that:

```
transition "Server Automatically Closes" {
    agent: Server;
    from: Open;
    to: Closed;
}
```

Next, let's try to make this a little more complicated by making the server send a message before disconnecting.

Hello World!

Yes, this is the canonical first example in programming after all. But to make it more interesting, let's delegate to the native language to tell us what the greeting should be, and then describe the way by which the client should be able to capture the message.

This highlights another aspect of our problem, which is that the client and the server have independent but correlated state machines. It also highlights that I need to be able to specify what those variables are.

The way that I am envisioning this process is by having specific data associated with states and conditions associated with transitions. Let me try to mock up what the syntax for this example would be:

```
transition "Server Decides Greeting" {
    agent: Server;
    from: Open;
    to: DecidingGreeting;
}

state DecidingGreeting {
    greeting: str<Ascii7Bit>;
}
```

```
transition "Server Sends Greeting" {
    agent: Server;
    from: DecidingGreeting;
    to: Closed;
    tokens: {
        greeting, " World!"
    };
}
```

This looks like an interesting approach, and it works well for the server side. However, it's not clear how the client side is meant to be managed; there are no state transitions at all described for it, and it's not clear how it would collect the data sent from the server.

Maybe it would be better to express the transitions from both the client and the server side at the same time. But then the question is, how do I associate the data sent by the server with the state of the client?

Maybe instead of specifying transitions, I should specify them as messages, which also represent a change in state for both the server and the client; therefore, the data would be associated with the message instead of with the transition. Let me try a different approach:

```
message "Server Sends Greeting" {
    agent: Server;
    when: Open;
    then: Closed;
    data {
        greeting: str<Ascii7Bit>;
    }
    tokens {
        greeting, " World!";
    }
}
```

In this approach, I accept that the client and the server are working on a single state machine. Therefore, the language can focus on specifying the format of the messages and the overall shape of the state machine for the protocol, along with the specific data that is associated with each state.

However, that means I need to rework the first example to see whether it still fits. It may look a bit awkward, but you can understand that closing the connection is also a kind of message, so the empty program in this new approach looks like this:

```
message "Server Automatically Closes" {
    agent: Server;
    when: Open;
    then: Closed;
}
```

Being able to change my mind about the original idea I had for the design is an important part of this process, which is why I am walking you through failed designs as well. Next, let's try to include a bit more complexity by having a bit of a request response.

Hello who?

The natural expansion of the Hello World programming exercise is to allow a parameter that specifies *who* should be greeted. I will give the client the option of sending a message first to specify who should be greeted, and then the server will deliver its greeting:

```
message "Client specifies who" {
    agent: Client;
    when: Open;
    then: WaitingGreeting;
    data {
        who: str<Ascii7Bit>;
    }
    tokens: {
        who, "\n";
    }
}

message "Server sends greeting" {
    agent: Server;
    when: WaitingGreeting;
    then: Closed;
    data: {
        message: str<Ascii7Bit>;
    }
```

```
    tokens: {
        message, "\n";
    }
}
```

I think this design looks more promising. I can more clearly see how the user will reference data sent from either the client or the server, and when that data is expected.

The `tokens` property in the message works really well for the side sending the message, as it's clear that the message is concatenated with the newline character. However, on the other side, it is not clear whether a message itself could have a new line.

Now, in a general-purpose programming language, this would be much harder to solve, but since I am working on a DSL focused on networking protocols, I can make use of the fact that it is very common for those protocols to give specific characters the semantics of the terminator of the data. I'll change the `tokens` section and add a new section for the message terminator. I will not repeat the whole code, so here's just the part that is different:

```
    tokens: { message }
    terminator: { "\n" }
```

My goal with this section has been to illustrate the process of designing a language. You will have to explore alternatives, but don't be afraid to backtrack and change the overall shape of your language if it doesn't fit really well on your intended use case.

I will not narrate the entire design process for the entire language here, because it would mostly involve a continuous process of experimenting with different use cases and slowly refining the overall design until it fits well into the intended use cases.

In the next section, I will focus on how the language will deal with values and containers and how the user will interact with them.

Immutability, containers, and values

To explore these concepts, I will imagine a protocol where the client requests a number of messages, and the server will return exactly that number of messages.

This will require the language to encode the response in a container of values, informed by the client message. Let me try to write it down in code:

```
message "Quote Request" {
    agent: Client;
    when: Open;
    then: ExpectResponse;
    data: {
        number: int<8, AsciiInt>;
    }
    tokens: { number }
    terminator: { "\n" }
}

message "Quote Response" {
    agent: Server;
    when: ExpectResponse;
    then: Closed;
    data: {
        messages: array<str<Ascii7Bit>, "Quote Request".number >
    }
    parts: {
        for message in messages {
            tokens: { message }
            terminator: { "\n" }
        }
    }
}
```

This example allows us to investigate not only how the language treats individual values—for example, the number requested from the client and the individual messages from the server—but also how those are aggregated into containers, which, in this case, have the list of all the messages.

The fact that I make those values immutable means that it becomes straightforward to mention them in other parts of the code. The input number is given by the client, and it can then be used to identify the number of messages that the server will return without us having to worry about it changing over time.

This is also a good time to talk about how the language specifies the types of values and containers. I already used some type specifications in the examples so far, but I want to elaborate on the design, starting with the types of individual values.

Value types

I want to start by looking at strings, as that was one of the first examples I used, which looked like this:

```
greeting: str<Ascii7Bit>
```

I am borrowing the concept from C++ templates, in which I accept that types need to generically communicate a concept, while specific parameters drive implementation details.

In this particular case, the string has a parameter to specify what is the encoding that the value will have. While it is common for programming languages to have a runtime encoding, network protocols are often more specific, and forcing the conversion on every point is undesirable, not only because it is costly but also because the user may need to access the data as it was sent by the other agent.

However, there are other aspects of the type that may need to be parameterized as well, such as whether it has a dynamic or static size, and if it does have a dynamic size, whether it has a limit to how long it should be allowed to be. This is particularly relevant in network protocols, because it informs whether it's safe to attempt to read it at once, or whether it should be given to the user as a stream to be lazily consumed.

This is a good indication that using those parameters positionally is likely to become a problem over time as I discover new parameters or as parameters become dependent on other parameters.

With that in mind, I'll revise the design to make the parameters to the types be named rather than positional, so that the same string declaration would look like the following:

```
greeting: str<encoding=Ascii7Bit, sizing=Dynamic, max_length=255>
```

If, on the other hand, I had a string of a fixed size, it would look something like this:

```
greeting: str<encoding=Ascii7Bit, sizing=Static, length=10>
```

Next, I'll extend the same approach to the number from the `"Quote Request"` example. I'll start by rewriting it to include the named parameters:

```
number: int<encoding=AsciiInt, bits=8, unsigned=True>
```

The encoding parameter is also very specific to the use case of network protocols, as I want to offer an easy way to specify how the numbers will be encoded in transport, and allow unambiguous access to their actual numerical value.

To complement this example, I'll consider what it would look like if the number were instead represented in binary form:

```
number: int<encoding=NetworkByteOrder, bits=32>
```

This communicates that 4 bytes should be unconditionally read and that those should be interpreted in a specific way when extracting the actual numerical value.

Next, I will explore what container types look like.

Container types

I already had an example of an array in the "Quote Response" example. I'll start by revising it to include the named parameters and include the same reasoning I had about strings:

```
messages: array<element_type=str<encoding=Ascii7Bit, sizing=Dynamic,
max_length=255>, sizing=Static, length="Quote Request".number>
```

Likewise, if I had an array with a dynamic size, I would also want to allow specifying a maximum number of elements:

```
messages: array<element_type=str<encoding=Ascii7Bit, sizing=Dynamic,
max_length=255>, sizing=Dynamic, max_length=1024>
```

This works well for those scenarios, but it's also necessary to consider that I need to be able to represent values of different types in the same container, building a tuple.

Programming language design is, at the end of the day, a creative process, and you will need to come up with solutions that make sense for the specific use cases.

I was debating with myself whether it makes sense to introduce a dedicated syntax for tuples, since all the parameter names are essentially statically defined for the specific type, such as max_length for a string.

The use of a custom syntax may look something like the following:

```
header: tuple {
    key: str<encoding=Ascii7Bit, sizing=Dynamic, max_length=255>;
    value: str<encoding=Ascii7Bit, sizing=Dynamic, max_length=2048>
}
```

If, instead, I hijack the named parameters used in other types, it would end up looking like this:

```
header: tuple<key=str<encoding=Ascii7Bit, sizing=Dynamic, max_length=255>,
value=str<encoding=Ascii7Bit, sizing=Dynamic, max_length=2048>>
```

The reality is that there's nothing fundamentally better or worse about each of those approaches. Until the language has had a lot of usage, it is really hard to evaluate which option will lead to better outcomes.

And that is where you will just have to rely on your intuition at the start, make a decision, and be ready to change your mind in the future.

In this particular case, I will prefer to reuse the named parameter syntax, as I imagine this will likely make my life easier when parsing the code. But I just have to accept that once the language starts seeing some real use, it may be worth reconsidering.

In the next section, I will examine how to reference values and variables.

Variables and references

The main advantage of using immutable values in a programming language is that you don't need to make a distinction between using something *by value* or *by reference*. All uses point to a more abstract concept of the value itself, and the life cycle of the value is entirely managed by the language.

In the case of this particular language, I know that the life cycle of those can be tied to the specific messages and states of the network protocol itself.

In one of the examples, I had the following snippet:

```
messages: array<element_type=str<encoding=Ascii7Bit, sizing=Dynamic,
max_length=255>, sizing=Static, length="Quote Request".number>
```

The assumption here is that values are tied to specific messages, and that those messages can be called by name, and the parts of the data can be referenced directly. When the `"Quote Response"` message must be written or read, the value for this message has already been set.

This leads to an important complication, which is that references to previous messages need to be scoped to a specific history, and if the state machine is not a directed acyclic graph, it will not be straightforward to identify which particular instance of that message is being referenced.

An alternative approach, instead, is that every message lists the entire set of data that is allowed to be carried over between states; therefore, the lexical pad is always completely local to that one message. I will leave open the possibility of referencing previous messages, but I will not pursue that in the first version of the language.

Since the user of the interpreter will be the one deciding which messages to send, it becomes significantly simpler for that same code to also carry over the additional data across messages.

One benefit that was not immediately obvious to me when I made this decision is that this will limit a category of bugs in the handling of networking code, which is the leaking of out-of-order data, because there isn't a complete specification of which data should be available at any given point in time.

Once again, this illustrates how the design process should be iterative, allowing you to go back and revisit previous decisions. In the next section, I will specify the HTTP/1.1 protocol in this new language to validate the final design.

The final language design

Toy examples are really good to illustrate specific aspects of the design, but at the end of the day, it is only real usage that will demonstrate how useful the language actually is. From the beginning, I had set the goal of describing HTTP in that language, and now it is time to deliver on that.

HTTP is essentially comprised of a request and a response. It is possible for the client to request to send more than one request, which means I have a cyclic graph in the state machine.

I will work through the outermost elements, and then get into details for each of the inner elements:

```
message "HTTP Request" {
    when: Open;
    then: AwaitResponse;
    agent: Client;
    data { ... }
    parts { ... }
}
message "HTTP Response" {
    when: AwaitResponse;
    then: Open;
    agent: Server;
```

```
    data { ... }
    parts { ... }
}
message "Client Closes Connection" {
     when: Open;
     then: Closed;
     agent: Client;
}
```

The language describes a high-level state machine for the entire protocol, with the transitions being described in terms of messages sent by either the client or the server. In the case of HTTP, that high-level state machine can be described with the following diagram:

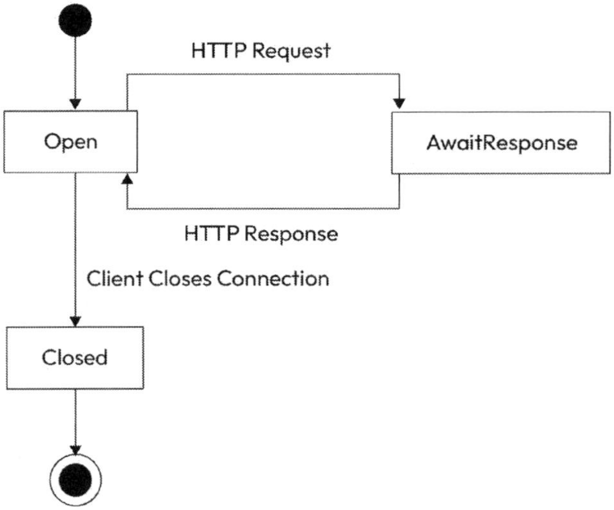

Figure 9.1: High-level state machine diagram for HTTP

The diagram communicates what messages are expected at which point, and what state the machine should move to once a given message is received.

Each one of those messages will have a set of data that is in scope for it. As discussed earlier, this means this is the only data available to the interpreter when writing a message, and it's the only data the interpreter will be allowed to read from the message.

That also means the point at which the execution is handed over to the user of the interpreter is at the end of the entire message, and the data transfer between the interpreter and the user of the interpreter happens at that point with well-defined, completed data elements.

Now, let me work through what the code for defining the data for the "HTTP Request" message looks like:

```
data {
    verb: str<
        encoding=Ascii7Bit,
        sizing=Dynamic,
        max_length=10
    >;

    request_target: str<
        encoding=Ascii7Bit,
        sizing=Dynamic,
        max_length=32768
    >;

    major_version: int<
        encoding=AsciiInt,
        unsigned=True,
        bits=8
    >;

    minor_version: int<
        encoding=AsciiInt,
        unsigned=True,
        bits=8
    >;

    headers: array<
        element_type=tuple<
            key=str<
                encoding=Ascii7Bit,
                sizing=Dynamic,
                max_length=32768
            >,
            value=str<
                encoding=Ascii7Bit,
                sizing=Dynamic,
```

```
                max_length=32768
            >
        >,
        sizing=Dynamic,
        max_length=100
    >;

    contents: stream;
}
```

I have mentioned most of the elements here before, except for the `stream` type. The `stream` type is required because HTTP does not specify a terminator for a message. Instead, the length is defined by the `Content-Length` header. And therefore, this type indicates that the user of the interpreter will need to deal with the connection.

I will not list the code for the data of the HTTP response, as it would be very similar to the preceding `"HTTP Request"` message. Instead, I will move on to the description of the `parts` section of the message:

```
parts {
    tokens { verb }
    terminator { " " }
    tokens { request_target }
    terminator { " " }
    tokens {
        "HTTP/" major_version "." minor_version
    }
    terminator { "\r\n" }
    for header in headers {
        tokens { header.key }
        terminator { ":" }
        tokens { header.value }
        terminator { "\r\n"}
    }
    terminator { "\r\n" }
    stream { contents }
}
```

For the agent sending the message, it just describes which sequence of octets has to be sent through the socket. However, for the agent receiving the message, it acts as a separate lower-level state machine, which tells how to match the stream with the expected message format.

Therefore, even though the client and the server run the same code, the interpreter will be able to specialize the execution based on the context. Also, for a particular message, it can determine whether it has the role of the one sending it or the role of the one receiving it.

To make it clear, I will translate the `"HTTP Request"` message, as received by the server, into the following state diagram:

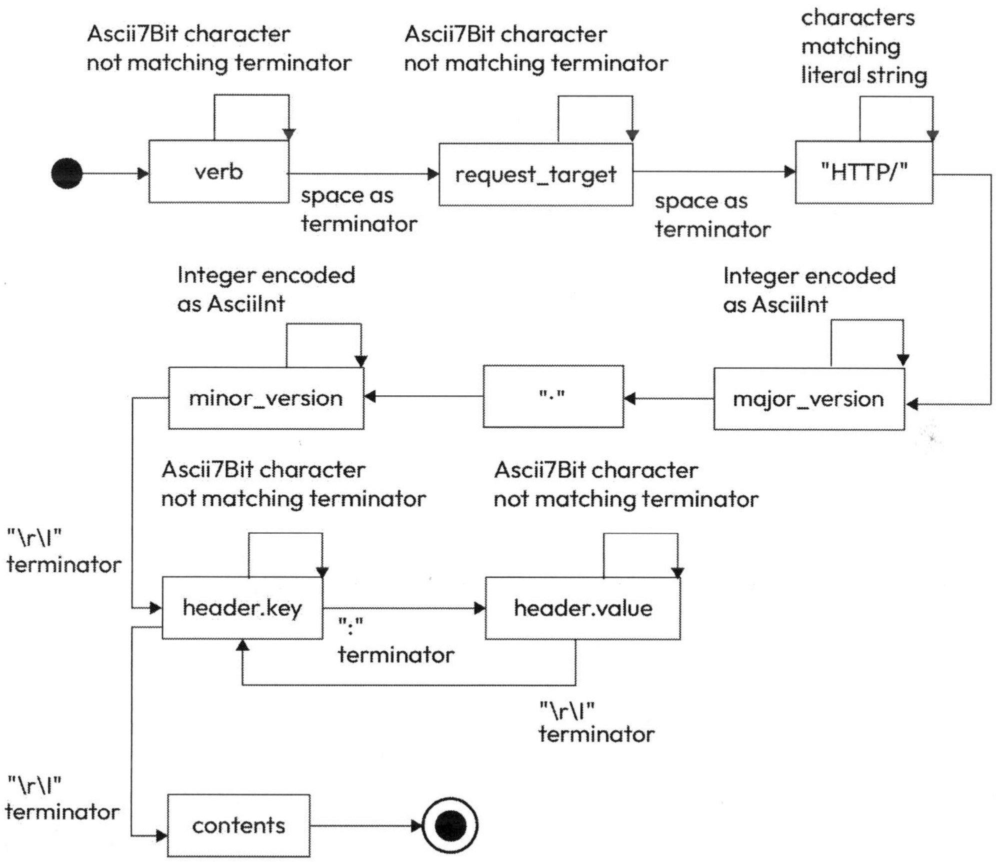

Figure 9.2: State diagram for the processing of the "HTTP Request" message

The state machine for the HTTP response message would look very much like this one, with just a few parts replaced, but I hope that, at this point, it's possible to visualize what the interpreter will actually have to do in order to execute this code.

It also illustrates the transformation the parser will have to do, since there is a significant difference in the structure of what the final state machine looks like and what the code actually says. And that was the reason why I chose a declarative programming paradigm, since it allows us to describe the protocol, and not the logic necessary to parse the message.

That brings me to a closure on the overall design of the programming language, with a fairly clear idea of how the language will result in operations being executed by the interpreter.

Summary

To finalize the programming language design, it is important to start with the overall shape of what the language will look like, using specific use cases to drive changes to that design. Then, the overall shape can be refined until all of the use cases can be satisfied in a coherent way.

Once the overall shape of the language is set, the interaction between the language design and the type system design needs to be taken into consideration. The ways in which the user will specify types being used need to be evaluated with specific use cases, just like the overall shape of the language.

The design also needs to build a clear definition of the life cycle of values and explain how references are taken and how the user is meant to use them.

Finally, it's only when the design is exercised with a complete use case that you can actually validate the design. It doesn't matter that you don't have a parser or an interpreter yet, but it's important to be able to visualize how the code will eventually be translated into actual operations by the interpreter.

This brings the language design to a close. In the next chapter, I will start the actual interpreter implementation.

Part 3

Implementing the Interpreter Runtime

In this part, I will start the implementation of the actual interpreter in C++. Starting from a skeleton CMake project, the implementation evolves through the basic interpreter interfaces, the interpreter loop, and the runtime stack, and concludes by introducing basic operations and testing them.

This part has the following chapters:

- *Chapter 10, Initialization and Entry Point*
- *Chapter 11, Execution Frames, the Stack, and Continuations*
- *Chapter 12, Running and Testing Language Operators*

10

Initialization and Entry Point

Up to this point, I have been working on design considerations for the interpreter and the programming language. Now, it is time to start on the actual code for the interpreter. In this chapter, I will work through the outermost layer of the interpreter, covering the following:

- The overall layout of the project
- The state of the interpreter that needs to be maintained throughout the execution
- How to make sure the interpreter can be easily embedded into existing systems
- Mechanisms to make the interpreter code more adaptable to growing needs
- How the interpreter will interact with I/O operations

By the end of this chapter, you will have a practical framework for thinking about the implementation of your own interpreter while being able to reference real working code.

The scaffolding

The first step in every project is to create the general scaffolding of the project, with the build system and the overall structure of how it will be developed. The code for the project can be seen in its entirety at `https://github.com/PacktPublishing/Building-Programming-Language-Interpreters`.

The book will not contain complete listings of the code being written. However, to make it easier to follow along, in case you need more context than what I explicitly reference here, for every section where I introduce more code on the project, I will reference a specific pull request where you can look at the code as it was at that particular point of the development.

The first step is to set up the build and continuous integration instructions for the repository.

This being a C++ project, I will use CMake as the build system. The main interpreter, meant to be embedded into other systems, will be delivered as a library. The tests in the project are going to exercise the interpreter. I also included a Dockerfile and a C/C++ workflow file for GitHub, both exercising the project.

As promised, the state of the code can be seen by inspecting the pull request at `https://github.com/PacktPublishing/Building-Programming-Language-Interpreters/pull/1/files`, which includes all the changes I have made up to this point, and allows you to inspect how the project looked at this point.

From this point forward, I will always have the changes introduced by a particular section submitted as a pull request to the GitHub repository, and I will reference them using the same convention that GitHub itself uses, which is the number of the pull request or issue.

In the next section, I will create the global interpreter state object and lay out what the life cycle of the interpreter itself looks like.

The global interpreter state

In *Chapter 5, Putting It All Together: Making Trade-Off Decisions*, I described the overall design of the interpreter. Now, it is time to put that into writing in the form of C++ code.

The interpreted program and the interpreter

I personally believe that it is best to design an API from the perspective of its usage, and test cases are the best tool I have to make that exercise as realistic as possible, so let me show what the usage for that API would look like:

```
std::string test_file =
  "data/002-empty-program.networkprotocoldsl";
networkprotocoldsl::InterpretedProgram program(test_file);
networkprotocoldsl::Interpreter interpreter =
  program.get_instance();
```

The main characteristic of this design approach is that I expect both objects—`InterpretedProgram` and `Interpreter`—to completely manage any memory they need by the object's life cycle itself.

Since I am considering `InterpretedProgram` and `Interpreter` to be independent objects with independent life cycles, it is likely that I will need to employ some additional memory management later, but from a usability perspective, I think it's best to allow such concerns to be internal to the interpreter instead of something the user has to care about. The state of the code at this point can be seen in pull request #2 (`https://github.com/PacktPublishing/Building-Programming-Language-Interpreters/pull/2/files`).

I don't have a parser yet, so giving the path to the source file is not that useful. Therefore, I will add a new constructor to `InterpretedProgram` that takes the already parsed operation tree, which will allow me to exercise the API more broadly at this point.

That leads to the question of how to represent the immutable instructions of what the program will do versus the mutable state of the execution of the operation tree, driven by dynamic parameters.

The operation tree and the mutable interpreter state

As discussed in *Chapter 3, Instructions, Concurrency, Inputs, and Outputs,* the execution happens in terms of an operation tree that needs to be traversed by the interpreter. Each operation takes a number of values as input and returns a value as output. Therefore, the first step is to define what a value looks like.

As discussed in *Chapter 4, Native Types, User Types, and Extension Points,* I need to be able to represent multiple types of values. The first step, therefore, is to create a type that represents any type the interpreter knows how to handle natively. The C++ language offers a way to handle that case in a type-safe way by using `std::variant`.

> Long-term users of the C and C++ languages will be familiar with the `union` specifier, which allows a specific memory region to be used by different types. However, using a `union` specifier requires the user to keep track of which specific value is realized at any point in the code.
>
> `variant` allows the language runtime itself to keep track of the actual type of the runtime value and handle navigation of the possibilities in a type-safe way.
>
> For instance, `std::variant<int, float>` is semantically equivalent to `union { int i; float f;}`, but it offers type-safe accessors such as `std::holds_alternative<int>(v)` and `std::get<int>(v)`, which validate the actual type of the value before use.

In this first step, I will not try to cover all types that will be needed. Instead, I will focus on supporting a single type, although I will do this with the type erasure mechanisms that will allow this to be extended later. The definition of a value, for now, looks like this:

```
using Value = std::variant<int32_t>;
```

This will be refactored later to have more complex definitions of the types supported by the interpreter, but for now, this should be good enough to exercise the basics of how the operations work.

Now that I have a definition of a value, I can start defining what operations look like. The basic mechanism is that an operation takes zero or more input values and resolves to an output value. Some of those values will be defined at parse time, and some will be defined at execution time.

To make this part of the exercise more complete, I will just have an operation that represents a literal value and an operation that performs an addition of two values. This should be enough to allow me to start the interpreter, execute some code, and check the resulting value.

As with `Value`, `Operation` is also going to be a `std::variant` type (I will define the specific operations later):

```
using Operation = std::variant<operation::Int32Literal, operation::Add>
```

To encode the requirements of what an operation interface needs to look like, I can use concepts, as introduced in C++20:

```
template <typename OT>
concept OperationConcept =
    requires(OT op, typename OT::Arguments args) {
        {
            std::tuple_size<typename OT::Arguments>::value
        } -> std::convertible_to<std::size_t>;

        { op(args) } -> std::convertible_to<Value>;
    };
```

While the goal of this book is not to offer an introduction to new C++ language features, I think it's worth briefly diving into **concepts**, as they are a language feature introduced in the C++20 version of the language.

Concepts allow you to easily define requirements that you expect from a template parameter. In this case, I am saying that if I ask for an `OperationConcept` template parameter, the template should only be instantiated if the requirements specified in the concept are fulfilled.

In this case, the `OT` type must have an `OT::Arguments` member type, where `std::tuple_size` returns `std::size_t`. It must also have `operator()`, which evaluates to something that can be converted to `Value`.

Before the introduction of concepts, this was still possible, but that would have to be implemented in terms of complex **substitution failure is not an error** (**SFINAE**), and concepts make this approach considerably simpler.

This particular concept will validate that all operations have a tuple template alias that describes the dynamic arguments, which will be sent as an argument when invoking the operation, which should return a value. Declaring this concept will allow me to simplify some of the visitor patterns in the `Operation` variant later.

Some operations will, however, define arguments in the source code itself, which means that they need to be constructed. It will be the responsibility of the parser to initialize them with the information from the source code, such as the operation that produces literal values:

```
class Int32Literal {
    int32_t int32_v;
public:
    using Arguments = std::tuple<>;
    Int32Literal(int32_t v) : int32_v(v) {}
    Value operator()(Arguments a) { return int32_v; }
};
static_assert(OperationConcept<Int32Literal>);
```

The `Arguments` inner type describes that this operation takes an empty tuple as dynamic arguments, and `operator()` describes that the operation will return the value provided to the constructor.

To make sure the operation type conforms to the concept, I also have `static_assert`, which will fail at that point if the operation fails to implement the expected interface.

The `Add` operation, on the other hand, takes no static arguments and takes two dynamic arguments:

```
class Add {
public:
    using Arguments = std::tuple<Value, Value>;
    Value operator()(Arguments a) {
        return std::visit(
            [&a](int32_t v1) -> Value {
```

```
            return std::visit([&v1](int32_t v2) -> Value {
                return v1 + v2; },
                std::get<1>(a));
        },
        std::get<0>(a));
    }
};
static_assert(OperationConcept<Add>);
```

This snippet starts to show some of the complexities that you need to handle when implementing code that handles dynamic types. The operation now needs to be implemented in terms of `std::visit`. The usage of the `Arguments` inner type lets me do that in a type-safe way, with the advantage that the compiler will identify all the places that need to adjust as new types of values are introduced.

> It would be possible to imperatively traverse all possible members of the variant by checking each type with `std::holds_alternative`. However, that results in a tight coupling of the types contained in the variant to the code that consumes the variant.
>
> `std::visit` provides a type-safe mechanism to make sure that you are handling all the alternatives. It achieves this by instantiating the visitor for each of the types of the variant at compile time.
>
> Combining variants with `std::visit`, argument-dependent lookup, and templated arguments will later allow me to significantly simplify the code as I add more alternatives to the `Value` type.

There are not a lot of programs I can write with those two operations alone, but it should be sufficient for exercising the instantiation of the operation tree and how that tree will be evaluated by the interpreter.

The operation tree is a simple data structure that represents a tree of nodes, where each node points at an operation and the children that are used as the dynamic inputs for each operation:

```
struct OpTreeNode {
    Operation op;
    std::vector<OpTreeNode> children;
}
```

```
class OpTree {
    OpTreeNode root;
public:
    OpTree(OpTreeNode r) :root(r) {};
};
```

Since I didn't want to force the user to manage the relationship between the life cycle of `InterpretedProgram` and the `Interpreter` objects, I actually need to store the operation tree in a shared pointer so that both objects can share the same data without the risk of one outliving the other.

Finally, as discussed in *Chapter 5*, I need the interpreter to be able to execute different continuations at the same time, so I need to introduce the `Continuation` class and make it a part of `Interpreter` itself. Before that, I need to explain how the execution of the operations will actually happen.

Since the operation tree is read-only, I need an additional data structure—modeled as the `ExecutionStackFrame` class—that represents the execution of the operation stack. The interpretation of the code actually happens in a two-way motion. First, you navigate down the tree up to a point that is ready to be executed, pushing all the operations that are waiting for input into the stack. Then, once you reach an operation that is ready to be executed, you can invoke that operation and accumulate the result of that operation as an input for the next item in the stack.

Executing the operations in the tree

I first need to set up the `ExecutionStackFrame` class, which will handle the execution of a single operation and the accumulation of the values that are used as input. The `ExecutionStackFrame` object is constructed with `OpTreeNode`, which describes what needs to be executed.

The `ExecutionStackFrame` class will have the following private members:

```
const OpTreeNode &optreenode;
std::vector<Value> accumulator;
```

This is where the earlier definition of `OperationConcept` becomes useful, because I will be able to make a type-safe execution of any operation fulfilling that concept.

The first operation I need to support in this class is identifying whether this operation is ready to be executed or whether the interpreter needs to traverse down to its children first. The `is_ready` method implements that using `std::visit`:

```
bool is_ready() {
    return std::visit(
        [this](auto &o) {
            return is_specific_operation_ready(o); },
                optreenode.operation);
}
```

There is a required bit of indirection here because I can't just use `OperationConcept` as a type directly in the argument to the lambda. Therefore, I use `auto`, which gets expanded for every member of the variant. I then invoke a `template` function that requires the concept:

```
template <OperationConcept O> bool is_specific_operation_ready(const O &o)
{
    if (accumulator.size() <
        std::tuple_size<typename O::Arguments>::value) {
    return false;
    } else {
        return true;
    }
}
```

This allows full type erasure on the `Operation` variant, and it will check whether enough input values have been accumulated before I can execute the operation.

Likewise, the execution of the operation, when it is ready, will use a similar technique:

```
Value execute() {
    return std::visit(
        [this](auto &o) {
            return execute_specific_operation(o);
        },
        optreenode.operation);
}
```

The definition of `execute_specific_operation` looks like this:

```
template <std::size_t... Indices>
auto make_argument_tuple(const std::vector<Value> &v,
                         std::index_sequence<Indices...>) {
     return std::make_tuple(v[Indices]...);
}
template <OperationConcept O>
Value execute_specific_operation(const O &o) {
    typename O::Arguments args(make_argument_tuple(
        accumulator, std::make_index_sequence<
            std::tuple_size<typename O::Arguments>::value>()));
    return o(args);
}
```

The thing that is different in this snippet is that I also need to transform the `accumulator` vector into the tuple that is used to execute the actual operation. The `make_argument_tuple` template will unroll as many elements from the vector as are needed to assemble the input tuple.

Finally, the last operation of the frame is returning the next operation when an input is missing:

```
const OpTreeNode &next_op() {
    assert(!is_ready());
    return optreenode.children[accumulator.size()];
}
```

Now, I can define `Continuation` itself, with a stack of `ExecutionStackFrame` objects, which is initialized with `OpTreeNode`:

```
class Continuation {
    std::stack<ExecutionStackFrame> stack;
    std::optional<Value> result;
public:
    Continuation(const OpTreeNode &o {
        stack.push(ExecutionStackFrame(o));
    }
    bool step() {
        if (stack.size()) {
            while (!stack.top().is_ready()) {
                stack.push(stack.top().next_op());
```

```
            }
            result = stack.top().execute();
            stack.pop();
            if (stack.size()) {
                stack.top().push_back(*result);
                return true;
            } else {
                return false;
            }
        } else {
            return false;
        }
    }
    std::optional<Value> get_result() { return result; }
};
```

This is where the two-way traversal happens. When `Continuation` is constructed, it sets `OpTreeNode` in the root of the stack with a new frame, which is the starting point for that continuation.

When a step is executed, first (if the stack is not already empty), it needs to traverse down `OpTree` and keep pushing to the stack until an operation that can be executed is found.

Once an operation is ready, I execute it and remove it from the stack, storing the result, but also pushing on the item lower in the stack (if it is not already empty). The `result` value of the last step always gets stored in `Continuation` for ease of introspection.

At this point, I can define the `Interpreter` object in terms of `Continuation`, and in terms of being constructed from `OpTree`, which is maintained in the `InterpretedProgram` class:

```
class Interpreter {
    std::shared_ptr<const OpTree> optree;
    Continuation continuation;
public:
    Interpreter(std::shared_ptr<const OpTree> o)
        : optree(o), continuation(o->root){};
    bool step() { return continuation.step(); }
    std::optional<Value> get_result() {
        return continuation.get_result(); }
};
```

Later, I will have to add support for concurrent continuations in the same interpreter, but for now, this is sufficient to exercise what I have built so far.

Finally, to conclude the overall global state of the interpreter, I can look at what `InterpretedProgram` looks like:

```
class InterpretedProgram {
    std::string source_file;
    std::shared_ptr<const OpTree> optree;
public:
    InterpretedProgram(std::string sf)
        : source_file(sf),
            optree(std::make_shared<const OpTree>(
                OpTree({operation::Int32Literal(0), {}}))) {}
    InterpretedProgram(std::shared_ptr<const OpTree> o)
        : source_file("-"), optree(o) {}
    Interpreter get_instance() {
        return Interpreter(optree);
    };
};
```

I currently have a placeholder for the parser by returning a single literal operation (`operation::Int32Literal`) if the name of the source file is provided. However, I also have an additional constructor that receives `OpTree` directly.

With this, I reach the rough shape of how the global interpreter state is going to be maintained. To exercise this, as well as the entire code up to this point, I can have a test case that steps through the execution of an operation tree that performs the equivalent of the `10 + 20` expression:

```
TEST(operations, literal) {
    using namespace networkprotocoldsl;
    operation::Int32Literal il1(10);
    operation::Int32Literal il2(20);
    operation::Add a1;
    auto optree = std::make_shared<OpTree>(
        OpTree({a1, {{il1, {}}, {il2, {}}}}));
    InterpretedProgram p(optree);
    Interpreter i1 = p.get_instance();
    Interpreter i2 = p.get_instance();
```

```
    ASSERT_FALSE(i1.get_result().has_value());
    ASSERT_FALSE(i2.get_result().has_value());
    ASSERT_TRUE(i1.step());
    ASSERT_TRUE(i2.step());
    ASSERT_EQ(Value(10), *(i1.get_result()));
    ASSERT_EQ(Value(10), *(i2.get_result()));
    ASSERT_TRUE(i1.step());
    ASSERT_TRUE(i2.step());
    ASSERT_EQ(Value(20), *(i1.get_result()));
    ASSERT_EQ(Value(20), *(i2.get_result()));
    ASSERT_FALSE(i1.step());
    ASSERT_FALSE(i2.step());
    ASSERT_EQ(Value(30), *(i1.get_result()));
    ASSERT_EQ(Value(30), *(i2.get_result()));
}
```

This test demonstrates that I can initialize a single `InterpretedProgram` instance from a manually created `OpTree`, then instantiate two different interpreters from that program and step through all the steps in the interpreter until I reach the end, when `step()` returns `false`, and that the result of the continuation has the expected value for each step.

The preceding changes can be inspected in pull request #3 (`https://github.com/PacktPublishing/Building-Programming-Language-Interpreters/pull/3/files`) in the GitHub repository.

In the next section, I will explore how to make an interpreter easy to embed into other systems.

Making it friendly to be embedded

If I were designing a language that would be responsible for executing the entire program itself, it would be much more reasonable not to think too hard about how the interpreter would be embedded into an existing process.

However, this programming language is specifically designed to be executed in the context of an existing program. Therefore, I need to make sure that the API is cooperative and defers scheduling decisions to the user of the language.

Given where I am in the implementation, the main thing to keep in mind is to make sure that the individual steps to be performed by the interpreter remain accessible to the user.

The other important aspect is defining how the interpreter will communicate with the native language, and how it will defer the execution of the interpreter until the native code signals that it is ready to continue.

As discussed in *Chapter 1, Defining the Scope*, this will involve making sure that I represent the switch between native and interpreted code as a top-level concept in the interpreter itself, allowing the execution of native callbacks to happen under the control of the user. This manifests by making sure that the native callbacks are not made inside of the regular operation.

In the previous section, I just had a boolean value representing whether the operation was ready to be executed or not, which is not going to be sufficient to differentiate the case where an operation will actually have to wait for the result of a native callback.

I will replace that boolean value with an `enum class` that will identify the additional state:

```
enum class ExecutionStackFrameState {
    MissingArguments,
    WaitingForCallback,
    WaitingCallbackData,
    Ready,
    Exited
};
```

You can see the change required for the introduction of this `enum class` in pull request #4 (`https://github.com/PacktPublishing/Building-Programming-Language-Interpreters/pull/4/files`).

However, this is still not sufficient, since `OperationConcept` doesn't specify a way for the interpreter to introspect whether some callback is needed, nor does it specify a way for the interpreter to receive the value from the callback.

There are some potential performance concerns regarding the fact that I am potentially checking every operation for the possibility of a callback, as well as storing whether I have made the callback and whether I received the callback results in every frame, but I will not try to perform an early optimization here. Instead, I will focus on getting the functionality in first.

The change to `OperationConcept` is, therefore, to introduce a boolean method to check whether a callback is needed, and then request a key to that callback so it can be dispatched later.

The principle here is that the interpreter will have a number of callback keys defined in the language. The integration with the native code will know about those callbacks and register them with the interpreter for the execution of the native code.

Using a key rather than the native function directly will allow external control over how callbacks gets dispatched. I will represent this as a method that returns an optional string by adding it to the concept definition:

```
{ op.callback_key() } -> std::convertible_to<std::optional<std::string>>;
```

Before going any further, I need to make sure that all existing operations conform to the new concept by making them return an uninitialized optional:

```
std::optional<std::string> callback_key() const {
    return std::nullopt;
}
```

With that being in place, I need to extend `ExecutionStackFrame` to store the required extra state:

```
std::optional<std::string> callback_key;
bool callback_called;
```

I must then check the operation for a callback key and handle the specific states:

```
template <OperationConcept O>
ExecutionStackFrameState is_specific_operation_ready(
    const O &o) {
        if (accumulator.size() <std::tuple_size<typename
O::Arguments>::value) {
            return ExecutionStackFrameState::MissingArguments;
        } else {
            callback_key = o.callback_key();
            if (callback_key.has_value()) {
                if (callback_called) {
                    return ExecutionStackFrameState::WaitingCallbackData;
                } else {
                    return ExecutionStackFrameState::WaitingForCallback;
                }
        } else {
            return ExecutionStackFrameState::Ready;
        }
```

```
    }
}
```

Finally, I need to offer a way to execute the callback itself with the dynamic arguments that were accumulated during the execution. I start by adding the introspection in `ExecutionStackFrame`:

```
std::optional<std::string> get_callback_key() {
    return callback_key;
}
void set_callback_called() {
    callback_called = true;
}
```

I then forward this visibility to `Continuation`, with the support for informing that the callback was executed, which will pop that operation out of the stack:

```
void set_callback_return(Value v) {
    assert(stack.size() > 0);
    assert(stack.top().get_callback_key().has_value();
    result = v;
    stack.pop();
    if (stack.size()) {
        stack.top().push_back(v);
    }
}
```

These methods are also present in the `Interpreter` class, which just forwards to the continuation. Now, I can introduce an operation that will receive a single value and be used to manage a callback:

```
class UnaryCallback {
    const std::string key;
public:
    UnaryCallback(std::string c) :key(c) {}
    using Arguments = std::tuple<Value>;
    Value operator()(Arguments a) const { return 0; }
    std::optional<std::string> callback_key() const {
        return key;
    }
};
```

With that infrastructure in place, I can now test the callback mechanism:

```
TEST(interpreter_global_state, callback) {
    using namespace networkprotocoldsl;
    operation::Int32Literal il1(10);
    operation::UnaryCallback uc1("multiply_by_2");
    auto optree = std::make_shared<OpTree>(OpTree({uc1, {{il1, {}}}}));
    InterpretedProgram p(optree);
    Interpreter i = p.get_instance();
    ASSERT_FALSE(i.get_result().has_value());
    ASSERT_EQ(ExecutionStackFrameState::WaitingForCallback, i.step());
    ASSERT_EQ(Value(10), *(i.get_result()));
    ASSERT_EQ(ExecutionStackFrameState::WaitingForCallback, i.step());
    ASSERT_EQ("multiply_by_2", *(i.get_callback_key()));
    i.set_callback_called();
    ASSERT_EQ(ExecutionStackFrameState::WaitingCallbackData, i.step());
    i.set_callback_return(
        std::get<int32_t>(*(i.get_result())) * 2);
    ASSERT_EQ(ExecutionStackFrameState::Exited, i.step());
    ASSERT_EQ(Value(20), *(i.get_result()));
}
```

This demonstrates that a user of the interpreter can check the state of the execution, dispatch its callbacks, report the result, and then continue the execution in the interpreter. The changes introduced here are in pull request #5 (`https://github.com/PacktPublishing/Building-Programming-Language-Interpreters/pull/5/files`) in the GitHub repository.

In the next section, I will approach how the interpreter can be extended to support multiple types of operations.

Refactoring for multiple types of operations

At this point, I already have a special case for the operations that require a callback to produce a value. Handling input and output from the event loop will require another set of special cases.

I also ended up adding the information about the callback key into the concept for the operation itself, which is not quite ideal, as it is likely that other types of operations will need their own data. This has the unfortunate side effect that everything in the operation tree will use the space needed by the superset of all specific requirements.

While I could most likely have foreseen this need when implementing the support for native callbacks, I also wanted to demonstrate how important it is to continuously evaluate the design decisions you make in your code. For that reason, I am explicitly going to navigate through the refactoring of the interpreter to allow abstracting away the different types of operations.

In my initial design, the execution of the operation could only return a value, and when the invocation happened, the expectation was that the complete preconditions were already met.

As I introduced the first type of operation that depended on external input, I realized that the interpreter needed to manage that additional interaction, so I added that to the general operation interface. As I'm now encountering the second type of operation, I am reminded of the saying that in computer science, there are only three valid integer answers for a software design question: zero, one, and infinite.

So, how can I abstract away the requirements of specific operations? The only outcome I can see is that I need to increase the surface of the concept of an operation. Let me reevaluate what the requirements of the two types of operations I identified so far are:

- A native callback needs to inform an identifier so the user can tell what needs to be invoked
- A native callback requires the user to submit the data to the operation before the execution can be unblocked
- I/O operations can be read or write
- There is a buffer of bytes to be sent to the network, or a buffer of bytes that have been read from the network
- An I/O operation requires the communication to have been finished

I also have to keep in mind the distinction between the data structure that represents the code itself in an immutable way and the requirement to keep track of mutable state for the specific type of operation.

The first step in this change is to delegate the decision on whether the external runtime information is already available or not to the operation itself. However, that means I need a way for the operation to describe what it needs in order to continue.

This is a point where I need to decide how generic I want the interface to be. This is a delicate balance because making it too generic will make it easier to support a wider variety of use cases, but it also introduces significant complexity, while making it too narrow means I will end up having to hardcode too many details.

There's no right answer to this question. It ends up being a complicated set of trade-off decisions, sometimes with calculations based a lot more on aesthetic than objective criteria.

In this particular case, I decided to consider the idea that I have different types of operations. Those operations have different data structures associated with them at runtime, and the user of the interpreter is going to be responsible for providing the right set of data for the right set of operations.

What becomes clear at this point is that the different types of operations will have different interfaces, and so I need different concepts for those different interfaces, starting with the refactoring of the operations that expect callbacks.

I'll start by simplifying `OperationConcept` so that it only describes the `Arguments` tuple:

```
template concept OperationConcept =
requires(OT op, typename OT::Arguments args) {
    { std::tuple_size::value } -> std::convertible_tostd::size_t;
};
```

Now, I can introduce `InterpretedOperationConcept`, which will be used for any operation where the execution is entirely handled internally by the interpreter, without the need for any runtime context beyond the execution stack itself:

```
template <typename OT>
concept InterpretedOperationConcept =
  requires(OT op,
           typename OT::Arguments args) {
    {OperationConcept<OT>};
    { op(args) } -> std::convertible_to<Value>;
};
```

You will notice that `operator()` only takes the `value` arguments from the execution stack. However, callback operations need additional runtime data, so I introduce `CallbackOperationContext`:

```
struct CallbackOperationContext {
    std::optional<Value> value;
    bool callback_called = false;
};
```

Finally, I define `CallbackOperationConcept`, which supports the interface for getting the callback key and reporting the callback status and value, and provides a different signature for `operator()`, allowing the operation's execution to manipulate the context:

```
template <typename OT>
concept CallbackOperationConcept =
  requires(OT op,
           typename OT::Arguments args,
           Value v,
           CallbackOperationContext ctx) {
    {OperationConcept<OT>};
    { op.callback_key(ctx) }
        -> std::convertible_to<std::string>;
    { op(ctx, args) }
        -> std::convertible_to<OperationResult>;
    {op.set_callback_called(ctx)};
    {op.set_callback_return(ctx, v)};
};
```

At this point, I have successfully rearchitected the mechanism for describing different types of operations. To prove that this approach actually works beyond what I have explored so far, I will start describing what I/O operations will look like.

Since one of the goals of the interpreter is to be decoupled from any particular library, I decided to go with a simple approach where the interpreter will hold a buffer where data is streamed in or out:

```
struct InputOutputOperationContext {
    std::string buffer;
};
```

`InputOutputOperationConcept` will describe any operation that interacts with that buffer, handling reads or writes. As with `CallbackOperationConcept`, the runtime value needs to be given to `operator()`:

```
template <typename OT>
concept InputOutputOperationConcept =
 requires(OT op,
          typename OT::Arguments args,
          InputOutputOperationContext ctx) {
    {OperationConcept<OT>};
```

```
    { op(ctx, args) }
        -> std::convertible_to<OperationResult>;
    { op.handle_read(ctx) }
        -> std::convertible_to<std::size_t>;
    { op.handle_write(ctx) }
        -> std::convertible_to<std::size_t>;
};
```

With that, I can replace the hardcoded properties in `ExecutionStackFrame` with a variant holding context information for the different concepts of operations. As part of this change, I also moved the logic of reporting a blocking operation to the operation itself, rather than the interpreter handling that.

The pattern here is that the dispatching of the operations will be implemented by matching the three different concepts of operations, while the variant is defined in terms of the specific operations. The individual operations are type-erased for the interpreter, and as long as they conform to one of the three operation concepts, the interpreter doesn't need specialized code for each operation.

I also took this opportunity to perform a general refactoring of the code to make it easier to understand, by better separating the implementations from the interfaces and pushing classes to their own specific translation units. The changes in this refactoring can be reviewed in pull request #6 (`https://github.com/PacktPublishing/Building-Programming-Language-Interpreters/pull/6/files`) in the GitHub repository.

In the next section, I will focus on the interface for I/O operations.

Designing the interface for I/O

As implied in *Chapter 1*, the goal is to make the interpreter independent of specific event loop frameworks, allowing the interpreter to be used in as many situations as possible.

Another consequence of that choice is that I only need to interact with the specific parts of the input and output operations that are relevant to how the protocols supported by this language are needed. In particular, that means I really only need to be able to handle the needs for the reads and writes.

I will go back to the sans I/O approach, where all that is needed is a mechanism to receive bytes, and to communicate which bytes have to be written.

I had a placeholder API for `InputOutputOperation` in the previous section; let me actually refine it now.

There is one subtlety that is relevant now, which is that the sequence of bytes received from the network does not necessarily match the number of bytes this specific operation needs. If there are fewer, the operation has to accumulate them and continue in the blocked state. If there are more, the operation has to be able to communicate that it did not consume all the bytes from the input.

Likewise, a `write` operation may not completely write everything the operation needs to output, at which point the operation should remain blocked, waiting for another opportunity for the write to continue.

I will consider that data will be read and given to the interpreter as `std::string_view`, and the operation will then return how many bytes from that input were consumed. If enough bytes are consumed, it will stop consuming more input, and the `step` function will return the value.

The `write` operation, however, will happen in two steps. The first one will provide access to the buffer that needs to be written, and the second one will allow notifying how many bytes from that buffer were written.

With that considered, here's the final interface for `InputOutputOperationConcept`:

```
template <typename OT>
concept InputOutputOperationConcept
 = requires(OT op,
            typename OT::Arguments args,
            InputOutputOperationContext ctx,
            size_t s) {
    {OperationConcept<OT>};
    { op(ctx, args) } -> std::convertible_to<OperationResult>;
    { op.handle_read(ctx, std::string_view) }
       -> std::convertible_to<std::size_t>;
    { op.get_write_buffer(ctx) }
      -> std::convertible_to<std::string_view>;
    {op.handle_write(ctx, s)};
};
```

Now, I should be able to introduce a test exercising a `ReadInt32Native` operation, which reads four bytes from the input data and returns an integer as a `Value`.

To make the test more interesting, I'll read two numbers from the input, use the `Add` operation to get the sum, and use a `WriteInt32Native` operation to produce the final integer.

The test will illustrate what the integration with the specific I/O operations will ultimately have to do, although I'll likely end up providing more helper functions to make it more ergonomic for the user.

I will not go over the entire test code, as you can see it in GitHub pull request #7 (`https://github.com/PacktPublishing/Building-Programming-Language-Interpreters/pull/7/files`) for the entire code, but I'll highlight some of the operations:

```
operation::ReadInt32Native r;
operation::Add add;
operation::WriteInt32Native w;
auto optree =
    std::make_shared<OpTree>(OpTree(
        {w, {{add, {{r, {}}, {r, {}}}}}}));
InterpretedProgram p(optree);
Interpreter i = p.get_instance();
```

The interpreter is initialized with `optree`, which will read two native integers, add them, and then write the result. Here's the segment that tries to execute one step, which ends up being blocked until input is submitted to the interpreter:

```
ASSERT_EQ(ContinuationState::Blocked, i.step());
ASSERT_EQ(ReasonForBlockedOperation::WaitingForRead,
    std::get<ReasonForBlockedOperation>(i.get_result()));
int input1 = 42;
int input2 = 900;
char buffer[8] = {};
std::memcpy(&(buffer[0]), &input1, 4);
std::memcpy(&(buffer[4]), &input2, 4);
size_t amount_read;
amount_read = i.handle_read({buffer, 2});
ASSERT_EQ(2, amount_read);
ASSERT_EQ(ContinuationState::Blocked, i.step());
ASSERT_EQ(ReasonForBlockedOperation::WaitingForRead,
    std::get<ReasonForBlockedOperation>(i.get_result()));
amount_read = i.handle_read({&(buffer[2]), 3});
```

```
ASSERT_EQ(2, amount_read);
ASSERT_EQ(ContinuationState::Ready, i.step());
ASSERT_EQ(Value(42), std::get<Value>(i.get_result()));
```

Finally, later on, after the Add operation returns, the next step will again be blocked until the data for writing is consumed from the interpreter:

```
ASSERT_EQ(ContinuationState::Blocked, i.step());
ASSERT_EQ(ReasonForBlockedOperation::WaitingForWrite,
    std::get<ReasonForBlockedOperation>(i.get_result()));
std::string_view write_buf = i.get_write_buffer();
ASSERT_EQ(4, write_buf.length());
ASSERT_EQ(4, i.handle_write(4));
int output;
memcpy(&output, write_buf.begin(), 4);
ASSERT_EQ(942, output);
ASSERT_EQ(ContinuationState::Exited, i.step());
ASSERT_EQ(Value(0), std::get<Value>(i.get_result()));
```

I understand that there's quite a lot going on here. So, I recommend checking out the code at the point of pull request #7 and familiarizing yourself further with everything that is happening. I will continue trying to focus on the specific points that communicate the design process for the runtime, as well as the techniques used to allow that implementation.

With this, the code is now at a point where it's fairly recognizable as an interpreter. There's an operation tree that is populated statically, as it would have been from the parser. The interpreter can then step through the execution, giving the caller feedback on whether it can proceed.

Summary

Structuring your C++ project in a way that facilitates test-driven development will allow you to very easily iterate on more and more complex features while mitigating the risk of breaking existing functionality. We learned this in this chapter. The history captured in the Git repository also plays an important role in understanding how the project evolves, as we saw in this chapter.

The building of a stack machine in C++ can greatly benefit from type erasure, whereby the code handling the stack does not need to constantly manipulate every single operation type. Instead, you should be able to categorize the operations in terms of what interfaces they need the interpreter to provide, which will allow you to reduce the amount of code that you need to write, without any loss in type safety. This was also covered.

At the same time, it's important to always continue reevaluating the overall structure of the code, and it is often a good idea to take a step back and reorganize the code to make it easier to extend it further, as mentioned in the chapter.

We also saw how decoupling the runtime context for the execution of the operation from the operation itself benefited the interpreter design. This decoupling allows the operation tree to be made entirely constant for the complete duration of the execution.

The interpreter now provides the user with the mechanism to continue stepping through the code, as long as there is nothing blocking the execution. Once something blocks it, be it because a callback needs to be made to native code or because an I/O operation is necessary, the user of the interpreter is then offered interfaces that allow moving the execution forward by providing the steps. This allows the interpreter to be easily embedded in many different scenarios, since the interpreter never blocks and never recurses.

In the next chapter, I will move one level of abstraction higher, from individual operations to functions with calls and returns, lexical pads, and other important features that will allow real programs to be executed.

11

Execution Frames, the Stack, and Continuations

In the previous chapter, I started the process of implementing the interpreter's stack machine. However, that implementation is not yet capable of handling control flow operations, such as conditionals or functions. In this chapter, I will add those capabilities, as well as discuss how the interpreter needs to manage the execution across multiple continuations.

More specifically, this chapter will work through the following:

- How an operation tree needs to be treated as a value in order to allow redirecting the execution
- The way in which the interpreter dynamically chooses what to invoke
- How a function is made by a sequence of operations, control flow, and variable scopes
- How the interpreter handles the calling of a function
- How to implement an end-to-end example of a function declaration and its invocation

By the end of this chapter, you will have a practical understanding of how an interpreter manages the stack machine across different sets of operations, including support for more complex control flow.

Code as a value

The implementation of the stack machine assumes that all inputs to an operation have to be resolved prior to the execution of the operation. This means the operation tree is traversed using a depth-first traversal until the interpreter finds an operation where all the inputs are resolved.

This is not sufficient, however, to represent more complicated control flow. Let's look at a conditional operation, using the Python language:

```
if a == 5:
    something()
else:
    something_else()
```

A naïve representation of the operation tree would look like the following:

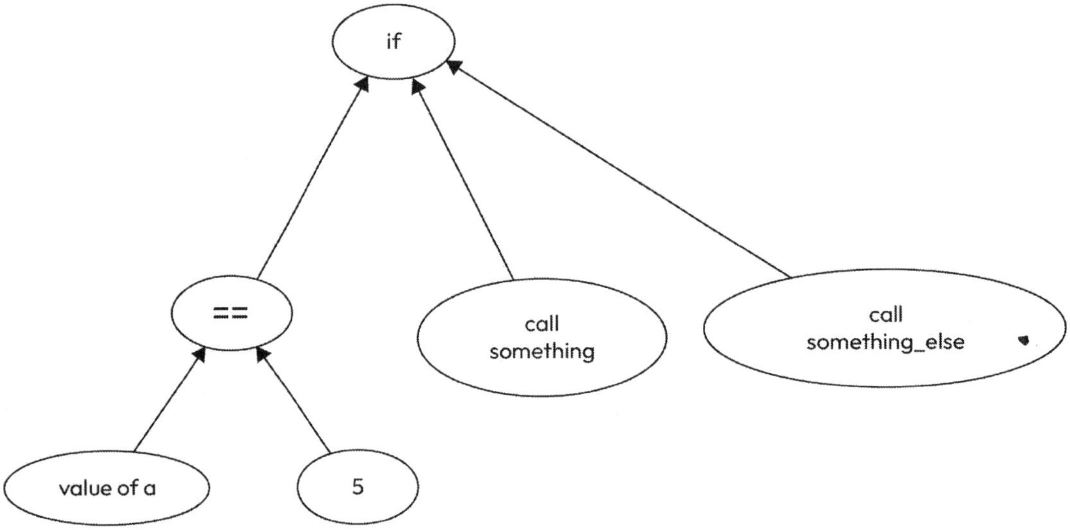

Figure 11.1: Naïve operation tree for a conditional

However, if we consider how the stack machine is currently implemented, this would result in both branches of the conditional being evaluated before the condition itself is evaluated. This is not what was intended.

To solve this problem, we need to start by being able to represent the code to be executed in each branch of the conditional as a value for the interpreter.

Since the stack machine will need to be able to hold the code to be executed as an argument to the conditional operator, we need to modify the `Value` type to include a representation for the executable code.

Because operations need values and values can now contain operation trees, our type system becomes mutually recursive: `Value` must include representations of `OpTree`, and `OpTree` nodes must refer to `Value`. Practically, that means forward declarations and careful ordering of headers are required. For clarity, I'll show only the minimal code necessary here; the full header arrangement can be found in the repository.

I start by introducing a new class to represent callable values (in the value namespace):

```
struct Callable {
    std::shared_ptr<const OpTree> tree;
};
```

The next step is to add it to the `Value` variant:

```
using Value = std::variant<int32_t, value::Callable>;
```

At this point, all the operations fail to compile, because they were only aware of what to do with a native integer, but since the value could be of a new type, this case needs to be handled too.

This means we also need a new value to represent the type error (also in the value namespace) if you try to, for instance, apply the `add` operator to a callable value:

```
enum class RuntimeError {
    TypeError
};
```

Then, the `RuntimeError` type also gets added to the `Value` variant:

```
using Value = std::variant<int32_t,
                           value::Callable,
                           value::RuntimeError>;
```

This tells the mechanism how we will propagate errors: the operators in the stack machine can simply return the error argument when they receive it. Here's what the implementation of the `add` operation looks like after the change:

```
static Value _add(int32_t lhs, int32_t rhs) {
    return rhs + lhs;
}
```

```
static Value _add(int32_t lhs, value::Callable rhs) {
    return value::RuntimeError::TypeError;
}
static Value _add(int32_t lhs, value::RuntimeError rhs) {
    return rhs;
}
static Value _add(int32_t lhs, Value rhs) {
    return std::visit([&lhs](auto rhs_v) -> Value {
                            return _add(lhs, rhs_v); },
                      rhs);
}
static Value _add(value::Callable lhs, Value rhs) {
    return value::RuntimeError::TypeError;
}
static Value _add(value::RuntimeError lhs, Value rhs) {
    return rhs;
}
Value Add::operator()(Arguments a) const {
    return std::visit([&a](auto lhs) {
                        return _add(lhs, std::get<1>(a)); },
                      std::get<0>(a));
}
```

This works by using the `_add` function when first visiting the left-hand-side argument to the operator, and then, when that has the right type, using `std::visit` again on the right-hand-side argument. The code changes for this section are in pull request #8 (`https://github.com/PacktPublishing/Building-Programming-Language-Interpreters/pull/8/files`) in the repository.

Now I can move toward implementing an operator that is able to start a different continuation based on callable values.

Invoking a callable value

The simplest use of a callable value is in a conditional operator, which needs to execute different branches and take them as arguments. Revisiting the operation tree in *Figure 11.1*, we get the following:

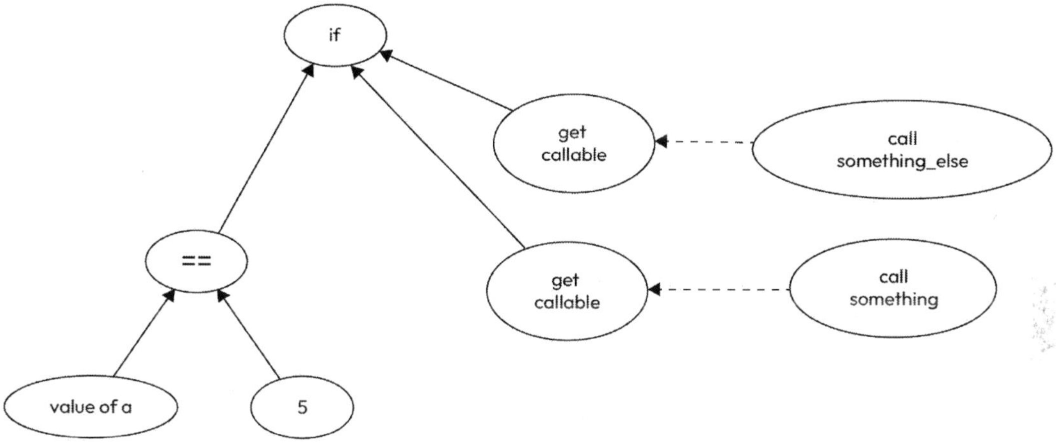

Figure 11.2: Operation tree with callable values

The dashed line in the diagram represents that the operation tree given to the operator that produces the callable is produced statically, just like it happens with the integral integers.

I will not list every code change here in the book, but before implementing the conditional, I also needed to introduce `bool` as a value type and introduce an equality operator. This change didn't require any different techniques from what I did before. You can see the changes in pull request #9 (`https://github.com/PacktPublishing/Building-Programming-Language-Interpreters/pull/9/files`).

Considering that the operation tree is constant for the execution of the code, I will need to create a mechanism by which the conditional operator will communicate to the interpreter that it needs to switch to a different continuation. We already have a similar thing happening with I/O or with the native callbacks.

The first step, therefore, is to create a new concept for operations that change control flow, along with an accompanying context object:

```
struct ControlFlowOperationContext {
    std::optional<Value> callable;
    std::optional<Value> value;
    bool callable_invoked = false;
};
template <typename OT>
concept ControlFlowOperationConcept =
 requires(OT op,
          typename OT::Arguments args,
          Value v,
         ControlFlowOperationContext ctx) {
    {OperationConcept<OT>};
    { op.get_callable(ctx) } -> std::convertible_to<Value>;
    { op(ctx, args) } -> std::convertible_to<OperationResult>;
    {op.set_callable_return(ctx, Value v)};
    {op.set_callable_invoked(ctx)};
};
```

The `ControlFlowOperationContext` type describes what data is needed for the execution of operations that match `ControlFlowOperationConcept`. The state stored in the context object gives the operation a way to keep track of its state, from not having decided which callable should be invoked, to having it invoked, and finally, getting the result of its evaluation.

The callable and value members start `null`, which indicates that the operation still needs to decide which callable to use. Once the callable is set, the operation knows that the callable can be given to the interpreter. When the interpreter invokes the callable, it notifies the operation, thus preventing repeated invocation of the callable. Finally, once the callable is evaluated, the resulting value is returned, which can be used as the result of the operation.

Additionally, I'll add new members to the `ReasonForBlockedOperation` enum to describe when the operation is waiting for a callable to be invoked, which will allow the interpreter to detect when a new continuation needs to be created.

Finally, at this point, I can implement the conditional operation. This implementation uses a similar technique to the previous operations, but it needs three arguments—one for the condition, then one for the callable when the condition is `true`, and another for when it's `false`:

```
class If {
public:
    using Arguments = std::tuple<Value, Value, Value>;
    OperationResult operator()(
        ControlFlowOperationContext &ctx,
        Arguments a) const;
    Value get_callable(ControlFlowOperationContext &ctx)
        const;
    void set_callable_invoked(
        ControlFlowOperationContext &ctx) const;
    void set_callable_return(ControlFlowOperationContext &ctx,
        Value v) const;
};
static_assert(ControlFlowOperationConcept<If>);
```

The implementation of this operation has some similarities with the other blocking operations, as it will only return a real value once the callable has been invoked, and it also offers a mechanism to keep track of whether that invocation has already happened or not.

That state also gets propagated through the continuation. I will not go into the details on adding that support to the continuation because it is not different from the code that is already there. I will also not go into the details of the operation that returns a callable for a static operation tree, as there's also nothing new there.

The important change is actually in the interpreter itself, as it now needs to react to when a continuation is blocked on a callable and invoke it. While this may not end up being the precise final design, for now, I will just create a stack of continuations, and when the continuation on the top of the stack has exited, we pop it and pass its return value back to the one below it.

The way this is implemented is by using `OperationResult` to identify that the operation is blocked and waiting for a callable to be invoked, and then the interpreter instantiates a new continuation and pushes it into the stack. At the same time, when a continuation exits, the interpreter checks whether there is another continuation to resume.

When a function call is encountered, the interpreter pushes a new continuation onto the stack. When that function returns, the continuation is popped, and its result is passed back to the caller. This avoids native recursion and prevents stack overflow:

```
ContinuationState step() {
    ContinuationState s = continuation_stack.top().step();

    if (s == ContinuationState::Blocked) {
        ReasonForBlockedOperation reason =
            std::get<ReasonForBlockedOperation>(continuation_stack.top().
get_result());

        if (reason == WaitingForCallableInvocation) {
            value::Callable callable =
                std::get<value::Callable>(continuation_stack.top().get_
callable());

            continuation_stack.top().set_callable_invoked();
            continuation_stack.push(Continuation(callable.tree));

            return continuation_stack.top().prepare();
        } else {
            return s;
        }
    }
    else if (s == ContinuationState::Exited) {
        Value r = std::get<Value>(continuation_stack.top().get_result());

        if (continuation_stack.size() > 1) {
            continuation_stack.pop();
            continuation_stack.top().set_callable_return(r);

            return continuation_stack.top().prepare();
        } else {
            return s;
        }
    }
    else {
```

```
        return s;
    }
}
```

The process begins by stepping the continuation at the top of the stack. This will give us the state after the step is done. If the continuation is blocked, the interpreter checks to see whether it's blocked for a callable, at which point it pushes a new continuation to the stack. Likewise, if the continuation has exited, it is popped from the stack, and the result is passed to the previous continuation that is now at the top. In all other cases, the interpreter just defers to its standard state-handling logic.

The changes for this section are in pull request #10 (`https://github.com/PacktPublishing/Building-Programming-Language-Interpreters/pull/10/files`), which includes all the code changes required for this implementation, where you can see, in detail, how the new operations don't look fundamentally different from the previous ones. The changes also include a test case that exercises this new functionality.

Next, I will start creating the definition of what a function context is, and how it is different from simply a callable value.

Making a function

The implementation currently just has the ability to transfer the control flow to a different operation tree. While it would be possible to represent a lot of different problems in this way, there are other capabilities that we normally associate with a function:

- Executing a sequence of statements
- Interrupting the control flow to leave the function immediately
- Using variables and defining how their names are scoped

So far, every operation only executes once, and the shape of the execution is known by the static type of the argument tuple for the operator. Let's look at the following example in Python:

```
print("Hello")
print("World!")
```

If we were to translate that into an operation tree, it would look something like this:

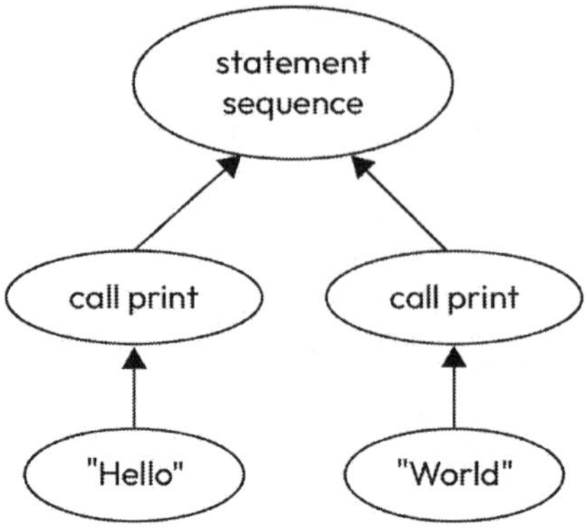

Figure 11.3: Operation tree for a sequence of statements

But if we tried to describe the "statement sequence" operator in the code as it is now, we would realize that we don't know the size of the argument tuple ahead of time. It is going to be determined by the shape of the interpreted code.

The other aspect that is worth exploring is how we deal with runtime errors. It wouldn't make a lot of sense to just ignore the error in the first statement and proceed to execute the second one. We probably want to interrupt the execution when a statement ends in an error.

> I should briefly discuss error handling. The approach that I am taking for this interpreter is inspired by functional programming languages, where errors get propagated through return values. That is, the return is either the expected value or an error value. There are a few other approaches that could be considered instead.
>
> The first would be what the C programming language does, which is to completely defer error handling to the user of the language, such that the runtime doesn't actually know about it. That's why, in C, it's common to have the return code as an integer, so that the user knows whether the operation succeeded or, otherwise, why it failed.
>
> The more common approach is to have an entirely separate infrastructure for raising errors through the call stack via exceptions, which is the case for C++ itself, but also most other programming languages, such as Python, Java, and JavaScript. I will leave researching how those mechanisms work as an exercise to you, as it would likely require an entire chapter in this book, at least, if I were to cover that.

I'll start by defining the statement sequence operator. Now, this is going to be special because it doesn't really look like any other operator, so it will not actually conform to `OperationConcept`. In fact, it is not really an operator; it just instructs the interpreter to do something different for the execution when it reaches the statement sequence node in the operation tree.

The definition for the `OpSequence` operator is simple:

```
class OpSequence {};
```

The fact that it doesn't conform to `OperationConcept` actually makes its implementation quite straightforward. I just need to offer overloads for a few functions in the logic behind the execution stack frame. Those overloads will be found when the variant for the operation is visited to implement the specific behavior.

> **Overload resolution**
>
> In this section, I'm making significant use of the overload resolution rules in the C++ language. The relationship between template argument deduction and argument-dependent lookup is what is being leveraged to allow the specific execution. If you are not very familiar with that, a good starting point is the *Overload Resolution* documentation in `cppreference.com` (`https://en.cppreference.com/w/cpp/language/overload_resolution.html`).

The first function to be overloaded is `initialize_context`, to just return a boolean, since this operation doesn't need any context:

```
static OperationContextVariant initialize_context(
                                const operation::OpSequence &o) {
    return false;
}
```

I want to emphasize how this works, since it may look a little bit like magic at this point. After all, the only thing we're doing is adding a new function overload definition; how is it that it results in a different behavior?

Looking at the place where `initialize_context` is called, you can see that it works by using `std::visit` on the operation, to dispatch different code depending on which alternative of the variant is actually active:

```
ctx = std::visit(
     [this](auto &o) { return initialize_context(o); },
     optreenode.operation);
```

This will, effectively, expand the lambda for each alternative of the variant. The `initialize_context` function then needs to accept the argument of the specific alternative.

So far, the implementation was using templates that required arguments conforming to specific concepts, meaning they would only be valid instantiations when the operation implemented that concept. Since the new operation does not meet those requirements, those templates would not be valid for it.

Considering that the behavior of the `OpSequence` operation is so special, we can just offer a direct overload for the function with the concrete type, which resolves the instantiation of the lambda for that alternative in the variant.

With that cleared, I can proceed to the next function that needs overloading:

```
static bool operation_has_arguments_ready(
    ExecutionStackFrame *frame,
    const operation::OpSequence &o)
{
    std::vector<Value> &acc = frame->get_accumulator();
    if (acc.size() < frame->get_children_count() &&
        !(acc.size() > 0 &&
          acc.back().holds_alternative<value::RuntimeError>()))
    {
        return false;
    }
    else
    {
        return true;
    }
}
```

This is where we actually make the interpreter navigate through the children of the `OpSequence` to execute them in order.

The original implementation of this function, which was a template requiring an argument to conform to `OperationConcept`, checked the size of the argument tuple against the size of the accumulator. In this overload, it instead checks the number of children operations in the tree, which is dynamic, based on its shape.

I want to highlight the second part of the condition:

```
!(acc.size() > 0 &&
  std::holds_alternative<value::RuntimeError>(acc.back())
```

This is actually all we need to do to make the execution stop when a runtime error happens in one of the operations. We want to stop execution if we already have a value accumulated and the last value is a runtime error.

At this point, I managed to convince the interpreter that the operation is not ready and that it should traverse to its children, as long as there are children operations to run, with the ability to bail out if a runtime error happens.

That leads to the last overload I need to specify:

```
static OperationResult execute_specific_operation(
    ExecutionStackFrame *frame,
    const operation::OpSequence &o
) {
    return frame->get_accumulator().back();
}
```

This is why the operation itself didn't need any members: the execution doesn't actually do anything, but rather just returns the result of the last operation evaluated.

The changes related to the operator sequence, including the tests, can be seen in pull request #11 (`https://github.com/PacktPublishing/Building-Programming-Language-Interpreters/pull/11/files`).

Now, I almost have something that looks like a function. The last thing missing is the ability to have named variables and have them be locally scoped to the function, and finally, the ability to call a function by name.

I discussed the concept of a lexical pad in *Chapter 8, Lexical Scopes*, and now it is time to code it. Different interpreters and compilers take different approaches to this, with different features and performance characteristics.

The lexical pad is an area where there is definitely a lot of room for optimization, such as eagerly resolving the names into a flat structure, or even going further and resolving all names from the pad at parse time.

The language design also informs the design of the lexical pad. In Python, the variables are only resolved at runtime, meaning it's valid to declare a function as follows:

```
def foo():
    print(a)
```

Even if statically we can't tell what the variable will point to, it will result in `NameError` (which I added as another member of the `RuntimeError` enum class) at runtime if nobody has defined the variable at the point the code is executed.

In C++, on the other hand, all variables need to be statically resolved, meaning there's no runtime overhead of identifying whether the variable is valid and where it is located.

The other significant design choice is whether it is possible to create a reference to the variable itself. For instance, in C++, you can write the following:

```
const char* something() {
    static const char* foo = "something";
    return foo;
}
```

That means the language runtime is not in control of all mechanisms by which a variable could have its value changed. That means you need to support a "reference" or a "pointer" to a variable as a first-class feature of the language.

In Python, on the other hand, it's not possible to get a "pointer" to a variable, and the interpreter can tell statically where the value may change.

The outcome of that choice is that you can have the lexical pad as a simpler dictionary, knowing that only the interpreter is allowed to override the value of a variable.

For the purpose of this exercise, I will take the simple approach of representing the lexical pad as a directed acyclic graph, where each pad optionally points to a parent scope where additional names can be resolved. References to variables won't be supported. With that, I can introduce the `LexicalPad` class:

```
class LexicalPad {
    std::unordered_map<std::string, Value> pad;
    std::optional<std::shared_ptr<LexicalPad>> parent;
public:
    LexicalPad(std::shared_ptr<LexicalPad> _parent)
      :parent(_parent) {}
    LexicalPad() {}
    Value get(const std::string &name);
    Value set(const std::string &name, Value v);
    void initialize(const std::string &name, Value v);
    void initialize_global(const std::string &name, Value v);
};
```

The important distinction I would like to make here is between the `set` and `initialize` methods. In this design, the `set` operation can only set the value for a variable that was already initialized, which means it is itself responsible for propagating the update to the parent pad. This means the interpreter doesn't need to, itself, identify what the correct pad is for updating the value of a variable. But it also means the language needs to identify the places where the variables are first initialized.

The implementations of those methods are fairly straightforward. The `get` operation is a simple lookup. If the name is not found, it tries its parent; otherwise, it returns `NameError`:

```
Value LexicalPad::get(const std::string &name) {
    auto it = pad.find(name);
    if (it == pad.end()) {
        if (parent.has_value()) {
            return parent.value()->get(name);
        } else {
            return value::RuntimeError::NameError;
        }
    } else {
        return it->second;
```

```
    }
}
```

The `set` operation is pretty much the same; it either returns the old value, if the variable was already initialized, or `NameError`:

```
Value LexicalPad::set(const std::string &name, Value v) {
    auto it = pad.find(name);
    if (it == pad.end()) {
        if (parent.has_value()) {
            return parent.value()->set(name, v);
        } else {
            return value::RuntimeError::NameError;
        }
    } else {
        Value old = it->second;
        it->second = v;
        return old;
    }
}
```

The `initialize` method is significantly more straightforward, as it just has to add the new name to the pad:

```
void LexicalPad::initialize(const std::string &name, Value v) {
    pad[name] = v;
}
```

And finally, `initialize_global` just searches for the root lexical pad before initializing a value:

```
void LexicalPad::initialize_global(
      const std::string &name, Value v) {
    if (parent.has_value()) {
        parent.value()->initialize_global(name, v);
    } else {
        pad[name] = v;
    }
}
```

Now that I have the definition for the lexical pad, I need to integrate it into the interpreter. For now, no operations need a lexical pad, and as I try to integrate it into the current code, it will become clear how deeply that needs to be coded in. Specifically, the lexical pad needs to be maintained alongside the overall state of the execution.

For now, I will have the interpreter instance hold the root lexical pad, which will contain any global values, and then use it to create a child pad when any continuations are created, and use the pad from the top of the continuation stack.

But this is not yet the right behavior, as we don't want a function to be able to access the variables from the function that called it. Instead, we need to have a way for a new continuation to be created with a lexical pad that has the root pad as a parent directly, rather than using the current continuation's pad.

As we already had a callable value, a simple solution is to add a simple boolean member, describing whether it should be run with a new lexical pad instead of inheriting from the caller:

```
bool inherits_lexical_pad = true;
```

To finalize, the code in the interpreter that instantiates a new continuation for a callable needs to correctly select the parent lexical pad for the new continuation in the `step` method:

```
std::shared_ptr<LexicalPad> parent_pad =
    callable.inherits_lexical_pad ?
    continuation_stack.top().get_pad() : rootpad;
continuation_stack.push(Continuation(
    callable.tree,
    std::make_shared<LexicalPad>(parent_pad)));
```

This will allow the lexical pad of a function being called to be disconnected from the lexical pad of the function that performed the call.

I am now very close to having all the features for a proper function to be defined. The only thing missing is the operations to manipulate the lexical pad—one for each of the methods we defined earlier.

As I did before, the first step is introducing a new operation concept for the operations that will require access to the lexical pad:

```
template <typename OT>
concept LexicalPadOperationConcept = requires(
      OT op,
```

```
        typename OT::Arguments args,
        std::shared_ptr<LexicalPad> pad) {
      {OperationConcept<OT>};
      { op(args, pad) } -> std::convertible_to<Value>;
  };
```

I will not go into the details of the implementation of the operations here, because there is nothing different from how other operations have been implemented. They are essentially just wrappers around the lexical pad class.

The other relevant change is in `ExecutionStackFrame` to support the additional context, but it follows the same approach I already used in the other operation concepts, so I will not cover it here.

The code introducing the support for lexical pads, the relevant operations to enable manipulating them, and the corresponding tests can be seen in pull request #12 (`https://github.com/PacktPublishing/Building-Programming-Language-Interpreters/pull/12/files`) in the repository.

Now that I can define a function, I need to be able to call it, which is what I'll cover in the next section.

Calling a function

The convention on how a function is called is a fundamental part of any runtime, interpreted or not. The function needs to be able to receive the arguments and produce the result. In the C++ language, for instance, that is specified as part of the **application binary interface** (**ABI**) of the specific platform.

In this interpreter, I will keep things simple. The arguments to the function will be represented as a single value that packs a dynamic list of values, which will then be bound to the parameters of the function.

The calling convention for the `FunctionCall` operation will be that `Callable` is given as the first argument and `DynamicList` as the second. The argument names are going to be described in `Callable`, and the `FunctionCall` operation will bind those arguments into `LexicalPad` according to their position.

So, the first step is adding a new type to the `Value` variant, which I am calling `DynamicList`. This will be simply a vector of values. I will not cover that in detail, since there's nothing new to it. You can see the changes to add the new type in pull request #13 (`https://github.com/PacktPublishing/Building-Programming-Language-Interpreters/pull/13/files`).

The next step is creating the operation that produces the list that will be used in the function call. Assembling the list looks a lot like the `OpSequence` operation, with the difference that it collects all the evaluated values, not just the last.

The similarity between `OpSequence` and `FunctionCall` justifies creating a new concept for operations that are simply processing other operations. This will allow reusing the code for both of them:

```
template <typename OT>
concept DynamicInputOperationConcept =
    requires(OT op, std::shared_ptr<std::vector<Value>> args) {
        { op(args) } -> std::convertible_to<Value>;
    };
```

With that, I can rework the overloads that were specific to `OpSequence` so that they are now defined in terms of this concept. The operation will then simply return the last entry in the arguments.

At the same time, I also did a small refactoring to make the accumulator in `ExecutionStackFrame` a `std::shared_ptr`, as that will allow avoiding the copy of the vector when turning it into a `Value`. Those changes can be seen in pull request #14 (`https://github.com/PacktPublishing/Building-Programming-Language-Interpreters/pull/14/files`). I will not discuss the details, as there's no new technique being applied there.

Now, I'm finally at the point where I can implement the function call itself. The `FunctionCall` operation needs to implement `ControlFlowOperationConcept`, just like the conditional operation does, which gives it access to communicate to the interpreter that a new continuation needs to be defined.

But I also need to find a way for the interpreter to bind the values from the dynamic list into the arguments for the callable. Given that the callable itself shouldn't be mutated, as it represents the code to be called, I decided to extend the concept to support returning the argument list, and extend the callable to have a list of argument names to be bound.

The `Callable` struct now looks like this:

```
struct Callable {
    std::shared_ptr<const OpTree> tree;
    std::vector<std::string> argument_names;
    bool inherits_lexical_pad;
    Callable(std::shared_ptr<const OpTree> t)
      : tree(t), argument_names({}),
```

```
        inherits_lexical_pad(true) {}
    Callable(std::shared_ptr<const OpTree> t,
        std::vector<std::string>& names, bool inherits)
      : tree(t), argument_names(names),
        inherits_lexical_pad(inherits) {}
};
```

I introduced the new member and new constructor, which will allow declaring a callable for a function.

`ControlFlowOperationConcept` now has a new required method:

```
{ op.get_argument_list(ctx) } →
  std::convertible_to<
    std::shared_ptr<std::vector<Value>>
  >;
```

And `ControlFlowOperationContext` has a new member:

```
std::shared_ptr<std::vector<Value>> arglist;
```

This arrangement will allow the operation to store the argument list in its context when it executes and to return the instruction to the interpreter that a new continuation has to be created.

Then, the interpreter should be able to bind the values from the argument list to the names in the callable before starting its execution. I just need to modify the code that was initializing the new continuation to perform the initializations in the pad based on the names and the argument list:

```
std::shared_ptr<LexicalPad> pad =
  std::make_shared<LexicalPad>(parent_pad);
std::shared_ptr<std::vector<Value>> arglist =
  continuation_stack.top().get_argument_list();
for (int i = 0; i < callable.argument_names.size(); i++) {
    if (i >= arglist->size()) break;
    pad->initialize(callable.argument_names.at(i),
                    arglist->at(i));
}
continuation_stack.push(Continuation(callable.tree, pad));
```

This implementation is rather simple. It doesn't check that arguments were actually given or whether there were extra ones. It also doesn't allow named arguments. But this is good enough for now, as any usage of an unbounded argument inside the function will result in `NameError`.

And the final piece is the implementation of the actual `FunctionCall` operation. It is very similar in its implementation to the conditional operator, so I will not cover it in too much detail. The main difference is that it will get the callable and the argument list from the input to the operation, store them in the context, and manage the state of the execution:

```
static OperationResult _function_call(ControlFlowOperationContext &ctx,
              value::Callable callable,
              value::DynamicList arglist) {
    ctx.callable = callable;
    ctx.arglist = arglist.values;
    return ReasonForBlockedOperation::WaitingForCallableInvocation;
}
```

This will be sufficient for the interpreter to dispatch the execution of the function with its own pad and argument bindings. The code changes introducing the new operation can be seen in pull request #15 (`https://github.com/PacktPublishing/Building-Programming-Language-Interpreters/pull/15/files`) in the repository.

In the next section, I will put everything together in a concrete example.

The end-to-end example

The design so far has a characteristic that perhaps is not completely clear from all the pieces that came together so far: function declarations themselves are part of the execution of the interpreter.

Let me explain. In a language that targets native code, it's usually the case that all the functions are known at compile time and there is a static mechanism by which those are resolved. In C++, for example, this is done by the linker, which will know the address that contains the instructions for a given function. In interpreter runtimes, however, it's very common that you will have a runtime lookup for a function.

The importance of this distinction is that it allows the interpreter to insert new entries for the resolution of functions after the interpreter starts. It leads to the point where the interpreter doesn't know what functions exist at first, and part of the startup of the program is turning the declarations in the interpreted code into entries in that resolution mechanism.

This is actually a very common approach. For example, when the Python code first starts, there's a first step where function declarations are done, and then the code in the top level gets executed. Just like I implemented here, declaring a function is an operation just like any other.

To make this easier to understand, I will present the operation tree showing the process of defining a factorial function and then calling that function, as you can see in *Figure 11.4*.

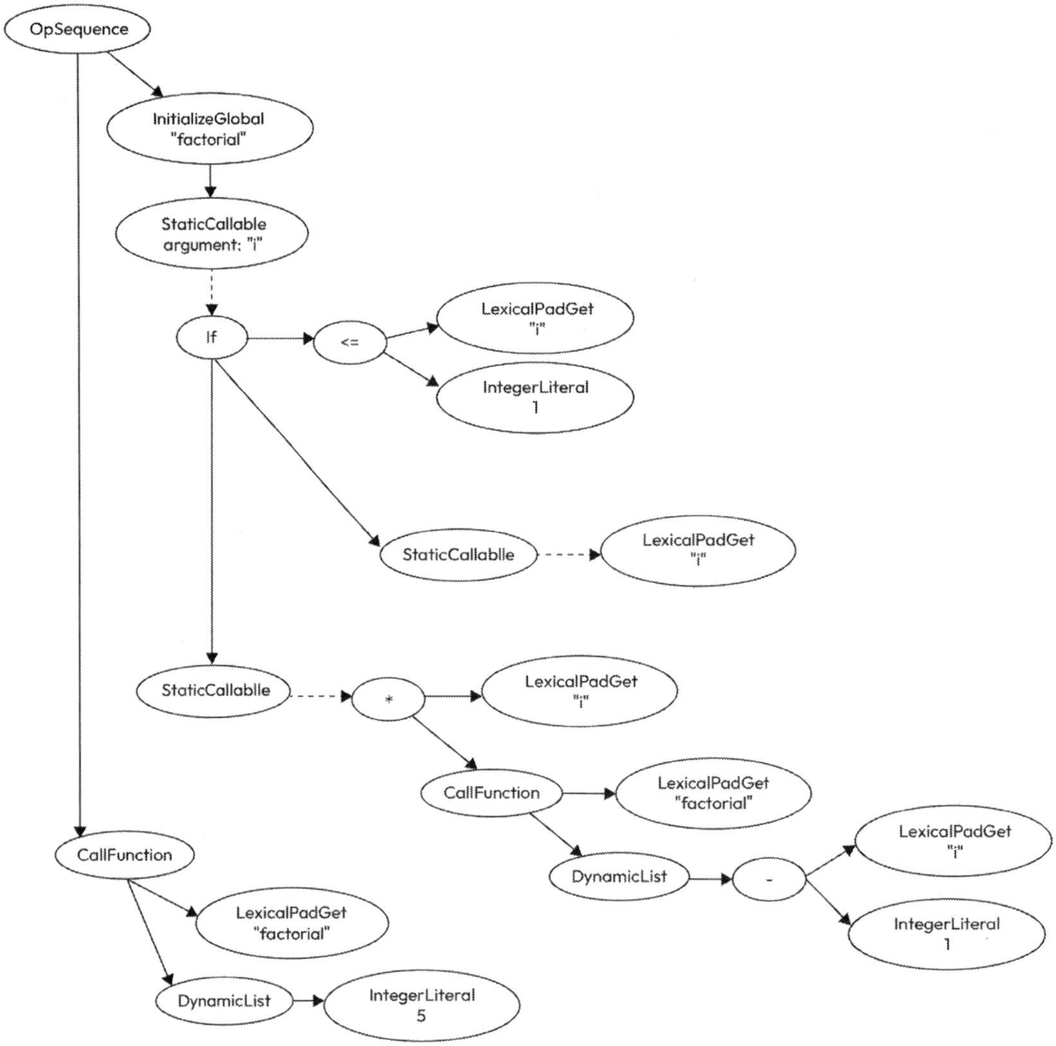

Figure 11.4: Complete operation tree for a program that declares a recursive factorial function and then calls it with 5 as an argument

The operations are the equivalent of the following code in Python:

```
def factorial(i):
    if i <= 1:
        return i
    else:
        return i * factorial(i - 1)
factorial(5)
```

The first thing that happens is the declaration of the function. This creates a callable value, stores it with the name `factorial`, and records that it takes an argument, `i`. Then, the function is invoked.

The dotted lines in the diagram represent the cases where the operations are only evaluated by something that expects a `Callable`, such as the `if` operator and the `CallFunction` operator.

I now have enough infrastructure in the interpreter to complete this entire operation tree. I just need to add a few missing operators, such as less-than-or-equal, multiplication, and subtraction. Then, I can have a final test case that contains that entire tree and exercises all the changes introduced in this section so far. All of that can be seen in pull request #16 (`https://github.com/PacktPublishing/Building-Programming-Language-Interpreters/pull/16/files`).

Summary

The stack machine that we had implemented so far was sufficient for trivial executions, but it could not handle more complex control flow operations.

To implement support for conditionals, I introduced the ability for the stack machine to reference the executable code as a value and for the interpreter to start executing that value. This is important because the branches in the operation tree should not be traversed until the operation selects which path to take.

The interpreter, for its part, needs to be able to recognize when it needs to switch from executing one particular stack to start executing a different one. The direction used here was to represent these different stacks as different continuations, with the state of the continuation allowing the interpreter to manage that transparently.

Beyond conditionals, it's also necessary to support a sequence of operations as well as the list of arguments to a function. That requires a new type of operation concept that doesn't depend on a static number of inputs, but rather on the shape of the operation tree itself.

In order to build functions, it is also important to support the lookup of symbolic names and their resolution to functions. For that, the lexical pad was introduced, and the relationship between the continuations and the lexical pad was established.

The calling convention for how a function is called was defined by taking the callable and a list of arguments as the inputs to the function call operation.

Finally, the end-to-end operation of the interpreter demonstrated how functions need to be defined at runtime in order to populate the dynamic lexical pads.

In the next chapter, I will focus on implementing the various operations that are necessary for the implementation of the network protocol language, focusing specifically on the support for the HTTP protocol, which is the design we have finalized so far.

12

Running and Testing Language Operators

In the past few chapters, I have explored different aspects of the runtime for the interpreter, from the execution model to how it interacts with I/O operations and native callbacks. There was a hint, particularly in the previous chapter, of the importance of designing the operators for the interpreter.

In this chapter, I will now focus on getting enough operations in place for the interpreter to be able to execute a more complete program. We will work through the following:

- Identifying the main flow of the program
- The operators we need and the data structures they manipulate
- Building the tests for the target use case
- Putting it all together into the real execution

By the end of this chapter, you will have a practical understanding of the way in which we translate the abstract concepts of executing a high-level programming language into the low-level primitives that the interpreter runtime can offer.

The execution flow

The last step of the design of the programming language in *Chapter 9, Putting It All Together and Creating a Coherent Vision,* ended with a state machine diagram (see *Figure 9.2*) that represented a high-level execution of the program for processing an HTTP request.

That, however, is something that still needs to be translated into lower-level operations that can actually be used by the interpreter that has been built up to this point. Currently, the interpreter operation tree is not able to represent the states and transitions we described there.

This is particularly relevant when you take into consideration that the programming language and its high-level state machine are meant to encompass both the client and the server side of that protocol, while the execution itself has to be radically different in those cases.

But before I can work on that translation, I need to define a target execution in this interpreter. This serves two purposes: it demonstrates that the interpreter is capable of implementing HTTP servers and clients, and it guides the later chapters, where I translate the high-level state machine into the operation trees that I produce here.

What I am doing is approaching the design from both ends at the same time: building confidence in the capabilities of the interpreter runtime while developing a refined sense of what the language will look like. This will guide the two ends to converge later, which will ground the implementation and avoid getting into dead ends.

The first step I want to consider is the overall flow of the execution. There is a higher-level state machine that talks about the state of the overall protocol, and a lower-level state machine that describes the rules for each specific message. In terms of processing input data, that means I will need to be able to inspect what is coming over, and then make a control flow decision based on what that inspection tells me.

This can potentially apply to both levels of the state machine, let's say, in the case where there may be more than one message acceptable at a given point. This is not the case for the simple HTTP description I gave before, but it does apply at the lower-level state machine, where it needs to make control flow decisions to know whether the next line is, for instance, yet another HTTP header or whether it is the end of the headers and the beginning of the contents.

As the parsing happens, the interpreter will also need to start accumulating all the data that has been parsed, such as the verb that was received and the HTTP version the client requested.

All of that also has to happen following the execution model of an operation tree, which, in the end, should produce the data for the message.

In previous chapters, I used a graphical representation for the operation tree, but that representation is not going to be practical for the amount of code that needs to be presented here, so I will use a text-based syntax instead:

```
(operation <static-parameters, ...> dynamic_parameters, …)
```

Here, the static parameters are the ones that are not evaluated at runtime, such as the argument for the name of the variable in the `LexicalPadGet` operator, and the dynamic operators are the ones evaluated as other operations, recursively.

Without further ado, here's the operation tree for handling the server-side processing of the HTTP request:

```
(OpSequence
  (LexicalPadInitialize <"verb">
   (ReadOctetsUntilTerminator <" ">) ),
  (LexicalPadInitialize <"request_target">
   (ReadOctetsUntilTerminator <" ">)),
  (ReadStaticOctets <"HTTP/">),
  (LexicalPadInitialize <"major_version">
   (ReadIntegerFromASCII)),
  (ReadStaticOctets <".">),
  (LexicalPadInitialize <"minor_version">
   (ReadIntegerFromASCII)),
  (ReadStaticOctets <"\r\n">),
  (LexicalPadInitialize <"headers">
   (GenerateList
    (StaticCallable
      <(OpSequence
        (TerminateListIfReadAhead <"\r\n">),
        (DynamicList
         (ReadOctetsUntilTerminator <":">),
         (ReadOctetsUntilTerminator <"\r\n">)))>))),
  (DynamicList
   (LexicalPadGet <"verb">),
   (LexicalPadGet <"request_target">),
```

```
    (LexicalPadGet <"major_version">),
    (LexicalPadGet <"minor_version">),
    (LexicalPadGet <"headers">)))
```

Let's work through what is happening step by step. The first thing to notice is that this is wrapped in an `OpSequence` operator. As discussed previously, the operator will execute one argument at a time, stop in case of error, and return the last value. Let me isolate just that, to make it clearer:

```
(OpSequence
  ...
  (DynamicList
   (LexicalPadGet <"verb">),
   (LexicalPadGet <"request_target">),
   (LexicalPadGet <"major_version">),
   (LexicalPadGet <"minor_version">),
   (LexicalPadGet <"headers">)))
```

The last operation in `OpSequence`, in this case, simply returns the values as they have been set in the lexical pad. As I was working through writing this operation tree, I realized that the only variables I initialized were the ones that would belong to the returning data structure. That turned out to be an interesting simplification I could make; I didn't start with that idea from the beginning.

The point that I'm trying to make is precisely that the process of designing the interpreter has to be an iterative process where you learn about the opportunities to make the interpreter simpler to write by building from the bottom up in the execution of real code.

Now, I can cover how the various values are added to that lexical pad, and a few of them look very similar:

```
  (LexicalPadInitialize <"verb">
   (ReadOctetsUntilTerminator <" ">) )
```

The `ReadOctetsUntilTerminator` operator was something I did anticipate when I first drew that state diagram, because this particular use case came up a lot. It consumes the octets until the expected terminator is read, and returns the value that was read. Then, that value is used as the argument to the `LexicalPadInitialize` operator, populating the lexical pad that will be returned in the end.

The headers, however, are a list of key-value tuples, so they require some special treatment. Let me isolate that:

```
(LexicalPadInitialize <"headers">
 (GenerateList
  (StaticCallable
    <(OpSequence
      (TerminateListIfReadAhead <"\r\n">),
      (DynamicList
       (ReadOctetsUntilTerminator <":">),
       (ReadOctetsUntilTerminator <"\r\n">))))>))),
```

The first thing to note here is the `GenerateList` and `TerminateListIfReadAhead` pair. Together, they decide when the list ends, and allow the calling of `StaticCallable` multiple times to produce each value of the list.

The other thing is the `DynamicList` operator, which consumes its arguments in order when those have the side effect of consuming the data from the stream until their respective terminators are reached.

The remainder of the HTTP request message is meant to be handled as a stream, so the interpreter is not really playing a big role there.

Now, it is time to look at the inverse case, where the client is the one sending the message instead. The first thing I need to understand is how the data is going to be sent to the interpreter. There would be multiple options here, of course, but I have a very simple one at hand, which is to use the lexical pad again.

I will just presume that when calling the code that writes the HTTP request, it will receive the arguments as parameters to its function. Let me start with the whole code first:

```
(StaticCallable
 <(OpSequence
   (WriteOctets (LexicalPadGet <"verb">)),
   (WriteStaticOctets <" ">),
   (WriteOctets (LexicalPadGet <"request_target">)),
   (WriteStaticOctets <" ">),
   (WriteStaticOctets <"HTTP/">),
   (WriteOctets
    (IntToAscii(LexicalPadGet <"major_version">))),
```

```
    (WriteStaticOctets <".">),
    (WriteOctets
     (IntToAscii(LexicalPadGet <"minor_version">))),
    (WriteStaticOctets <"\r\n">),
    (FunctionCallForEach
     (LexicalPadGet <"headers">),
     (StaticCallable
      <(OpSequence
        (WriteOctets (LexicalPadGet <"key">)),
        (WriteStaticOctets <":">),
        (WriteOctets (LexicalPadGet <"value">)),
        (WriteStaticOctets <"\r\n">))>,
        ("key", "value")>)),
    (WriteStaticOctets <"\r\n">)),
     ( "verb", "request_target", "major_version",
     "minor_version", "headers" )>)
```

Now, let me break it down into its parts, starting with the outermost layer:

```
(StaticCallable
 <(OpSequence
   ...)
  ( "verb", "request_target", "major_version",
    "minor_version", "headers" )>)
```

In the previous chapter, when covering function calls and the lexical pad, I defined that the arguments to a function would be passed as a list, and that the names of the arguments would be static arguments to the construction of the callable. That means the caller will just have to assemble a list of values to assign to each one of the members of the pad.

It's important to note that I used the same sequence of inputs for the writer as what I'm returning from the parser. This means we have a stable representation of what the HTTP message is.

Then, we can perform the sequential writes, which all look similar:

```
(WriteOctets (LexicalPadGet <"verb">)),
(WriteStaticOctets <" ">),
```

There's not a lot of mystery there. However, at some point, we need to iterate over the headers:

```
(FunctionCallForEach
  (LexicalPadGet <"headers">),
  ...),
```

Again, there could be many ways to implement this, but a very simple way is to recognize that since the headers are a list of lists, I can use the inner list as the argument list for a function call. So, this operation will simply iterate over the headers, using the list with the key and value as the argument to the function. This brings us to the following:

```
(StaticCallable
     <(OpSequence
       (WriteOctets (LexicalPadGet <"key">)),
       (WriteStaticOctets <":">),
       (WriteOctets (LexicalPadGet <"value">)),
       (WriteStaticOctets <"\r\n">))>,
       ("key", "value")>))
```

Like the external callable, the key and value are translated into entries in the lexical pad, which are then used in `OpSequence` to write the header.

The goal of this exercise is to prove that the execution model for the interpreter is actually capable of performing the program. At this point, it is still possible that we would have to go back to the earlier design and rethink some of the choices we made. But, more importantly, it's still early enough that making those changes would not be catastrophic to the project.

Next, I will focus on identifying, implementing, and testing all the operators and data structures we listed so far.

Identifying and implementing operators

It is possible to categorize the operators I just introduced into two categories: I/O operators, which either read from or write to the network socket, and list operators, which either consume a list or produce it.

I/O operators

The first pair of operators that I want to consider is `ReadStaticOctets` and `WriteStaticOctets`. These are static octet operators and are fairly simple, in the sense that the values they write or expect to read are defined statically, and therefore, they don't even need dynamic arguments.

I'll start by implementing the `WriteStaticOctets` operator. This is implemented using the same concept that was used before in *Chapter 10, Initialization and Entry Point*—`InputOutputOperationConcept`—which includes the context necessary for the execution.

The declaration of the operation is very similar to the declaration of the `ReadInt32Native` operation, so I will focus instead on the definition of key methods, starting with `operator()`, which performs the actual execution of the operation:

```
OperationResult WriteStaticOctets::operator()(
  InputOutputOperationContext &ctx,
  Arguments a) const {
  if (ctx.buffer.length() == 0) {
    ctx.buffer = contents;
    ctx.it = ctx.buffer.begin();
  }
  if (ctx.it != ctx.buffer.end()) {
    return ReasonForBlockedOperation::WaitingForWrite;
  } else {
    return 0;
  }
}
```

When the context is initialized, the buffer is empty, and therefore the operation knows that it needs to set the buffer to the value of the static contents and initialize the iterator for the operation. And as long as the iterator is not at the end of the buffer, it means the operation is blocked on the write.

To complement this, we need the implementations of `get_write_buffer` and `handle_write`:

```
std::string_view WriteStaticOctets::get_write_buffer(
  InputOutputOperationContext &ctx) const {
  return std::string_view(ctx.it, ctx.buffer.end());
}
```

This tells the interpreter what's next to be written. The expectation is that the runtime will push the contents of `string_view` to the socket, and then, however many bytes got written (since we want to support non-blocking I/O) are communicated via `handle_write`:

```
size_t WriteStaticOctets::handle_write(
  InputOutputOperationContext &ctx, size_t s) const {
  size_t consumed = 0;
  while (s > 0 && ctx.it != ctx.buffer.end()) {
    s--;
    consumed++;
    ctx.it++;
  }
  return consumed;
}
```

The `handle_write()` function is then responsible for advancing the iterator within the context, such that in the next round, when the interpreter asks for a write buffer, it points to whatever wasn't written yet. Once the iterator is moved to the end, it will cause the operation to conclude.

The `ReadStaticOctets` operation, however, does have something different about it, as it needs to be able to interrupt the execution in case the expected contents were not sent in the connection. And if the contents sent don't match the expected, the operation should fail with a runtime error:

```
OperationResult ReadStaticOctets::operator()(
  InputOutputOperationContext &ctx, Arguments a) const {
  if (ctx.buffer.length() < contents.length()) {
    return ReasonForBlockedOperation::WaitingForRead;
  } else {
    if (strncmp(ctx.buffer.c_str(), contents.c_str(),
        contents.length()) == 0) {
      return true;
    } else {
      return value::RuntimeError::ProtocolMismatchError;
    }
  }
}
```

The first thing the operation does is check whether the buffer has received enough octets to match the expected constant value. If not, the operation indicates that it is blocked, waiting for more data. If, however, there is enough data, the operation checks whether the received bytes match the constant value; if not, it raises a runtime error, indicating that the data didn't match the protocol.

To complement this, we need the `handle_read` method:

```
size_t ReadStaticOctets::handle_read(
  InputOutputOperationContext &ctx,
  std::string_view in) const {
  if (in.length() < contents.length()) {
    return 0;
  } else {
    ctx.buffer = std::string(in.begin(),
      contents.length());
    return contents.length();
  }
}
```

The important thing to consider in the `handle_read` method is that it receives an input buffer, and like the POSIX read method, it returns how many bytes were actually consumed by the operation. The assumption here is that the input data will be appended until the buffer gets to the right size, at which point the operation can consume and evaluate it.

The complete code for introducing the static octet operations (both for reading and writing) can be seen in pull request #17 (`https://github.com/PacktPublishing/Building-Programming-Language-Interpreters/pull/17/files`).

The dynamic operations handling octets need to be able to represent a range of octets as a value, since these operations will need to be able to read and write the octets dynamically from the result of other operations. For that, I introduce the `Octets` alternative to the `Value` variant, which is a shared pointer to a `const` string:

```
struct Octets {
  std::shared_ptr<const std::string> data;
};
```

This will allow the operations that have to deal with a dynamic string to be implemented. And at this point, we can see how the general approach of using `variant` and `visit` makes the code much easier to maintain, as adding alternatives to `Value` resulted in no impact on any of the other operations.

The `WriteOctets` operation is very similar to `WriteStaticOctets`; the only difference is that the value of the octets is received from the operation tree, instead of being statically defined in the constructor. Therefore, during the execution of the operation, the operation copies this value into the buffer that is the context for the I/O operation. As with the other operators, the process starts with visiting the value to dispatch the specific action:

```
OperationResult WriteOctets::operator()(
  InputOutputOperationContext &ctx, Arguments a) const {
  return std::visit([&ctx](auto arg) {
    return _execute_operation(ctx, arg);
  }, std::get<0>(a));
}
```

The next implementation returns an error if the value is of the wrong type:

```
static OperationResult _execute_operation(
  InputOutputOperationContext &ctx, auto unknown) {
  return value::RuntimeError::TypeError;
}
```

This is followed by the override that copies the data from the value into the buffer in the context:

```
static OperationResult _execute_operation(
  InputOutputOperationContext &ctx, value::Octets &oct) {
  if (oct.data->length() == 0) {
    return 0;
  } else if (ctx.buffer.length() == 0) {
    ctx.buffer = *(oct.data);
    ctx.it = ctx.buffer.begin();
  }
  if (ctx.it != ctx.buffer.end()) {
    return ReasonForBlockedOperation::WaitingForWrite;
  } else {
    return 0;
```

```
    }
  }
```

The handle_write method ends up being identical to the one in WriteStaticOctets, since all it needs to do is make sure the iterator is consumed.

Finally, since some of the values that need to be written are integers (such as major_version), I also need a mechanism to convert an int32_t value into an Octets value. For that, I introduced the IntToAscii operator, which does a simple conversion. I am not going to repeat the code that visits the value, since it's very similar to what I have already presented. The conversion logic looks like this:

```
static Value _inttoascii(int32_t v) {
  std::ostringstream os;
  os << v;
  return value::Octets{
    std::make_shared(std::string(os.str()))
  };
}
```

In pull request #18 (https://github.com/PacktPublishing/Building-Programming-Language-Interpreters/pull/18/files), you can see the complete code for the implementation of the IntToAscii and WriteOctets operations.

Consuming a dynamic value can happen both in the ReadOctetsUntilTerminator and ReadIntFromAscii operations. The only significant difference between those and ReadStaticOctets is that they have a slightly different condition on how to consume the input.

Because of the dynamic nature of reading, I had to introduce a new ready member to the context object, which then can be set by the handle_read method whenever the condition to end the read is met.

In the case of ReadOctetsUntilTerminator, the handle_read method looks like this:

```
size_t ReadOctetsUntilTerminator::handle_read(
  InputOutputOperationContext &ctx,
  std::string_view in) const {
  auto pos = in.find(terminator);
  if (pos == in.npos) {
    return 0;
  } else {
```

```
    ctx.buffer = std::string(in.begin(), pos);
    ctx.ready = true;
    return pos + 1;
  }
}
```

Here, processing occurs only once the terminator is found.

In the case of `ReadIntFromAscii`, it will only process the read once it has found a non-digit character:

```
size_t ReadIntFromAscii::handle_read(
  InputOutputOperationContext &ctx,
  std::string_view in) const {
  size_t consumed = 0;
  auto it = in.begin();
  for (; it != in.end() && *it >= '0' && *it < '9'; it++) {
    consumed++;
  }
  if (it != in.end()) {
    ctx.buffer = std::string(in.begin(), consumed);
    ctx.ready = true;
    return consumed;
  } else {
    return 0;
  }
}
```

In both cases, the buffer in the operation context gets updated with the data that was read, and the `ready` member is set to `true`, allowing the execution to proceed.

The operation execution for `ReadOctetsUntilTerminator` just converts the buffer into an `Octets` value and returns it.

In the case of `ReadIntFromAscii`, it also needs to perform the translation of the buffer from the ASCII representation to `int32_t`:

```
OperationResult ReadIntFromAscii::operator()(
  InputOutputOperationContext &ctx, Arguments a) const {
  if (ctx.ready) {
    if (ctx.buffer == "0") {
```

```
        return 0;
      } else {
        long conv = strtol(ctx.buffer.c_str(), NULL, 10);
        if (conv == 0) {
          return value::RuntimeError::ProtocolMismatchError;
        } else {
          if (errno == ERANGE ||
              converted > INT_MAX || converted < INT_MIN) {
           return value::RuntimeError::ProtocolMismatchError;
          } else {
           return (int32_t)converted;
          }
        }
      }
    } else {
      return ReasonForBlockedOperation::WaitingForRead;
    }
  }
```

This operation must handle the case where the number is invalid for the `int32_t` representation and return an error in that case. Pull request #19 (`https://github.com/PacktPublishing/Building-Programming-Language-Interpreters/pull/19/files`) contains the complete code for the `ReadOctetsUntilTerminator` and `ReadIntFromAscii` operations.

List operators

There are a few new operators to handle the fact that the protocol needs to be able to have a section of it that is meant to be repeated. From the side of the code writing the message, it needs to be able to iterate over the list of headers. And when reading the message, it needs to be able to generate a list of headers from the data that came in.

When writing the message, we can just iterate over the lists. The `FunctionCallForEach` operation is sufficient for that case. However, when reading the message, we need to react to a dynamic number of headers. For this, we need a pair of new operations.

The first one is GenerateList, which will invoke a callable until interrupted and accumulate all the values produced into a list. The second one is TerminateListIfReadAhead, which will peek into the next upcoming bytes and interrupt the GenerateList operation if the terminator is read.

This negotiation between the GenerateList and TerminateListIfReadAhead operations has a certain similarity with how we have been dealing with RuntimeError, where every operation knows that if it takes RuntimeError as input, it should just propagate it down without actually doing anything.

To support this, I am introducing this new value type—ControlFlowInstruction—which is an enum that contains, for now, the InterruptGenerator member:

```
enum class ControlFlowInstruction { InterruptGenerator };
```

Then, I need to add ControlFlowInstruction as an alternative to the Value variant, which will require me to change every operation to make it interrupt the execution and propagate the value. Basically, in every place where RuntimeError was handled specially, we have to handle ControlFlowInstruction as well.

I am not going to list every change, since they're all very similar, but I will show what overrides were added to the _add function in the Add operator:

```
static Value _add(
  int32_t lhs,
  value::ControlFlowInstruction rhs) {
  return rhs;
}
static Value _add(
  value::ControlFlowInstruction lhs,
  auto rhs) {
  return lhs;
}
```

This allows the control flow instruction to be propagated and to be handled by the operator that is expecting it. You can see the complete code introducing this in pull request #20 (https://github.com/PacktPublishing/Building-Programming-Language-Interpreters/pull/20/files).

With that, implementing the `TerminateListIfReadAhead` operation becomes significantly trivial. The `handle_read` method will peek and store the data in the buffer, but never actually consume anything:

```
size_t TerminateListIfReadAhead::handle_read(
  InputOutputOperationContext &ctx,
  std::string_view in) const {
  ctx.buffer = in;
  return 0;
}
```

But that gives the operation itself the context to decide whether the list should be interrupted or not:

```
OperationResult
TerminateListIfReadAhead::operator()(
  InputOutputOperationContext &ctx, Arguments a) const {
  if (ctx.buffer.length() == 0) {
    return ReasonForBlockedOperation::WaitingForRead;
  } else if (ctx.buffer.length() < terminator.length()) {
    if (ctx.buffer ==
        terminator.substr(0, ctx.buffer.length())) {
      return ReasonForBlockedOperation::WaitingForRead;
    } else {
      return false;
    }
  } else {
    if (ctx.buffer.substr(0, terminator.length()) ==
        terminator) {
      return
        value::ControlFlowInstruction::InterruptGenerator;
    } else {
      return false;
    }
  }
}
```

The only thing special about this operation is that it will peek at the input octets, but then never actually consume them, and if the terminator octets are in the input buffer, then return `ControlFlowInstruction`. You can see the complete code for this change in pull request #21 (`https://github.com/PacktPublishing/Building-Programming-Language-Interpreters/pull/21/files`).

The counterpart `GenerateList` operator will simply invoke a callable, accumulating values until it receives `ControlFlowInstruction`, and return the list of values it accumulated. I will start with the outermost logic of the function, and then explain each detail:

```
OperationResult GenerateList::operator()(
  ControlFlowOperationContext &ctx,
  Arguments a) const {
  if (ctx.callable.has_value()) {
    // will explain in the next block
  } else {
    return std::visit( [&ctx](auto &callable) {
     return _generate_list(ctx, callable);
    }, std::get<0>(a));
  }
}
```

When the operator is first executed, there's no context of the callable, because that is a dynamic value from the operation tree. Therefore, in the first case, we need to visit the value and set it in the context. I will not list that part of the code as it is similar to the example presented earlier in this chapter.

Once the callable is set, the operator repeatedly invokes it until the control flow signal instructs to interrupt the list. But first, the interpreter must ensure that the callable has been invoked and that a result is available. So, the next layer of the function is as follows:

```
if (ctx.callable_invoked) {
  if (ctx.value.has_value()) {
    // will explain in the next block
  } else {
    return
     ReasonForBlockedOperation::WaitingForCallableResult;
  }
} else {
```

```
    return
     ReasonForBlockedOperation::WaitingForCallableInvocation;
  }
```

This logic implements the mechanism for interacting with callables, as described in the previous chapter, where we use the `callable_invoked` and the `value` members of the context to drive the state machine with the interpreter. Finally, once we have a value produced by the callable, we can apply the logic with the control flow instruction:

```
if (std::holds_alternative<value::ControlFlowInstruction>(
      ctx.value.value())) {
  if (std::get<value::ControlFlowInstruction>(
         ctx.value.value()) ==
       value::ControlFlowInstruction::InterruptGenerator) {
    return value::DynamicList{ctx.accumulator};
  }
}
ctx.accumulator->push_back(ctx.value.value());
ctx.callable_invoked = false;
ctx.value.reset();
return
  ReasonForBlockedOperation::WaitingForCallableInvocation;
```

Any time the callable returns anything other than `InterruptGenerator`, that value is added to the accumulator of the context, and the state machine for the callable invocation is reset (by resetting the `callable_invoked` and `value` members). Once the control flow instruction is received, the operation will produce a dynamic list with the values produced. You can see the complete code for this operation in pull request #22 (`https://github.com/PacktPublishing/Building-Programming-Language-Interpreters/pull/22/files`).

Finally, we can also implement the `FunctionCallForEach` operation, which will just invoke the callable for each of its arguments. I am cheating a little bit for simplicity. Since this operator is being used for writing HTTP headers, I can rely on the fact that the headers are represented as a list where the first element is the key and the second is the value. Then, those get bound to the named arguments of the callable that prints them out.

In most cases, however, you would need to wrap the elements of input in order to be able to handle non-list and list arguments at the same time. But this simple form is enough for the problem at hand.

This is an interesting thing to keep in mind when designing the operators in an interpreter: sometimes you will need variations of the same operation to be used in different contexts.

This operator will take two dynamic arguments, the first being the callable to be invoked, and the second the list through which to iterate. There's an assumption here, as I mentioned previously, that the argument is a list of lists, where each inner list will contain the arguments to the callable invocation. Again, I will not list the code that collects the dynamic values provided to the operation, as it's very similar to what was already done. Instead, I will focus on the execution itself.

This implementation is actually very similar to the `GenerateList` operator, as it also needs to invoke the same callable multiple times. I will focus on the innermost block, since that's where the two operators differ:

```
ctx.accumulator->push_back(ctx.value.value());
if (ctx.accumulator->size() < ctx.arglist->size()) {
  ctx.value.reset();
  ctx.callable_invoked = false;
  return
   ReasonForBlockedOperation::WaitingForCallableInvocation;
} else {
  return value::DynamicList{ctx.accumulator};
}
```

Like `GenerateList`, `FunctionCallForeach` is also accumulating the results of the callable and producing the output. It's also resetting the `callable_invoked` and `value` members to trigger the state machine transition within the interpreter. The thing to note here is that it's comparing how many values it accumulated with the argument list that it received. This behavior is complemented by the implementation of the `get_argument_list` method:

```
std::shared_ptr<const std::vector> FunctionCallForEach::get_argument_list(
 ControlFlowOperationContext &ctx) const {
  return std::get<value::DynamicList>(
    ctx.arglist->at(ctx.accumulator->size())
  ).values;
}
```

This method will just return the element of the argument list in the context object that corresponds to the number of values accumulated so far. This will result in the invocation of the callable until all elements in the input list have been traversed. You can see the complete code in pull request #23 (`https://github.com/PacktPublishing/Building-Programming-Language-Interpreters/pull/23/files`).

With all operators needed for this example implemented, I can finally move on to creating the tests that demonstrate the execution of our HTTP parser and writer.

Testing the operators

For the purpose of this exercise, I am not creating as many unit tests as would probably be advised. (I haven't gone into the details of unit tests in the text, but you can check them out in the repository.) This is just a simplification of the fact that this interpreter is not meant for actual production use. A project building a real interpreter should definitely have significantly more unit tests than what I'm writing here.

That being said, in addition to unit tests, it's also important to create test cases that exercise the integration of those operations in a more complex environment. That's what I will focus on now.

The first step is to lay out the `OpTree` for the code I want to test. This is essentially the data structure that represents what the compiler for the interpreter will have to do. This will be done directly in C++.

I used this approach before when implementing the factorial example in the previous chapter to check the control flow operators. This case is just making use of a larger set of operators. The goal is to start with a string that represents an HTTP message, use that string on the parser, then get the output of the parser and send it to the writer, and compare the two, as the output should match the original input.

And since the data structure that the writer code needs is the same data structure that the parser produces, we can just build an `OpTree` where we call the writer with the output of the reader:

```
(FunctionCall ( CallableForWriter ),
  ( FunctionCall ( CallableForReader ) ) )
```

Here, `CallableForWriter` and `CallableForReader` will be substituted by the C++ code that creates the `OpTreeNode` objects representing the operations I described at the beginning of the chapter.

This test is important because it will demonstrate how a user of the interpreter will interact with the input and output. For the sake of testing, we are using just a fixed string as an input and appending the output to a string stream.

You can see the full code for the test in pull request #24 (`https://github.com/PacktPublishing/Building-Programming-Language-Interpreters/pull/24/files`), but I will break down what the actual test code does. I'll not go through the declaration of `main_optree` here, as that has nothing new from what we have been doing before.

The first step is to initialize `InterpretedProgram` and then get an instance of an interpreter, as we have been doing in all other tests:

```
InterpretedProgram p(main_optree);
Interpreter i = p.get_instance();
```

Then, we create a string that will represent the input for the parser, a cursor representing how far we have read, and a `stringstream` sink to capture the output produced by the writer:

```
std::string input = "GET /foo/bar/baz HTTP/1.1\r\n"
                    "Accept: application/json\r\n"
                    "Host: Test Value\r\n"
                    "\r\n";
auto input_cursor = input.cbegin();
std::stringstream
   output_message_stream(std::ios_base::out);
```

Now, we can get on the main interpreter loop. I will talk about the outermost part of the loop first, and then fill in the details:

```
  while (true) {
    ContinuationState s = i.step();
    if (s == ContinuationState::Blocked) {
      // will fill in later
    } else if (s == ContinuationState::Exited) {
      break;
    }
  }
  ASSERT_EQ(input, output_message_stream.str());
```

Essentially, we keep running the interpreter until it tells us that it has exited the program. Once that is complete, we can assert that the input that was sent to the reader matches the output that was produced by the writer.

Now to the interesting part, which is to integrate the input and output operations. The first step is to understand why the operation is blocked. Again, I'll focus on the outermost part first:

```
auto reason =
 std::get<ReasonForBlockedOperation>(i.get_result());
 if (reason ==
     ReasonForBlockedOperation::WaitingForWrite) {
   // code for handling writes
 } else if (reason ==
     ReasonForBlockedOperation::WaitingForRead) {
   // code for handling reads.
 }
```

Handling the writes is pretty straightforward in this case, since all we have to do is get the buffer that is waiting to be written, and since we'll never block, we can just write the whole thing at once:

```
auto buffer = i.get_write_buffer();
output_message_stream.write(buffer.cbegin(), buffer.size());
i.handle_write(buffer.size());
```

The last step is telling the interpreter that we managed to write the entire buffer, which should unblock the operation.

Handling the read is a bit more complicated, because we need to consider the fact that the interpreter will read only as many bytes as each operator needs, so we need to keep a cursor in the input buffer and advance it accordingly:

```
ASSERT_NE(input_cursor, input.cend());
```

The code starts by validating that we're not at the end of the input. In reality, the interpreter would also need to know how to handle end-of-file, but for now, I will ignore that fact and just assert that we never reach that case.

The second step is to tell the interpreter that it can read some things. I give it the entire buffer, but it will tell me how much it actually consumed:

```
size_t movement =
  i.handle_read(std::string_view{input_cursor,
                                 input.cend()});
```

Finally, we check that we have enough buffer left and advance the cursor by the amount that the operator actually read. The extra complexity arises because distance returns a signed integer, while the number of bytes read is unsigned. So, we need to assert that the distance is positive and then statically cast it to an unsigned integer (`size_t`):

```
int buffer_left = std::distance(input_cursor, input.cend());
ASSERT_GT(buffer_left, 0);
if (movement <= static_cast<size_t>(buffer_left)) {
   std::advance(input_cursor, movement);
} else {
   input_cursor = input.cend();
}
```

With this, I have managed to exercise all the operators that will be needed for implementing the first version of the language. With that said, I also noticed that we were missing a mechanism for handling socket closures in real scenarios.

Adding that capability was a simple matter of adding a new `eof` member to the `InputOutputOperationContext` class, as well as a `handle_eof` method to `InputOutputOperationConcept`. The handling logic was then added to the various operators. I will not list all the changes as they are all very similar, but for illustrative purposes, I will explain the changes made to the `TerminateListIfReadAhead` operator.

The first step was adding the `handle_eof` method itself, which simply propagates the **end of file (EOF)** condition to the context object:

```
void TerminateListIfReadAhead::handle_eof(
    InputOutputOperationContext &ctx) const {
  ctx.eof = true;
}
```

Then, in the place where the operator would say that it is blocked on a read, it will also check for EOF and return `ProtocolMismatchError` if the socket is closed:

```
if (ctx.eof) {
  return value::RuntimeError::ProtocolMismatchError;
} else {
  return ReasonForBlockedOperation::WaitingForRead;
}
```

You can see the complete set of changes to introduce the support for EOF in pull request #27 (`https://github.com/PacktPublishing/Building-Programming-Language-Interpreters/pull/27/files`).

Finally, I also needed to give a way for the user to send input arguments to the interpreter, which was a simple matter of adding an extra argument to the `get_instance` method in the `InterpretedProgram` class, in order to initialize the `argv` global variable:

```
  Interpreter get_instance(
    std::optional<Value> arglist = std::nullopt) {
    std::shared_ptr<LexicalPad> rootpad =
        std::make_shared<LexicalPad>(LexicalPad());
    if (arglist.has_value()) {
      rootpad->initialize_global("argv", arglist.value());
    }
    return Interpreter(optree, rootpad);
  };
```

This change can be seen in pull request #28 (`https://github.com/PacktPublishing/Building-Programming-Language-Interpreters/pull/28/files`).

With this complete, I can move to start creating a real usage of the interpreter, which is what I will do in the next section, putting together something that looks more like the actual API that users will use.

Finalizing the integration

So far, all the examples have been created with the goal of just exercising the code written until this point. Now, we're finally at the point where we can create a scenario that will actually reflect how the user of the interpreter will actually interact with it.

There are several things that every user of this interpreter will have to do; therefore, it makes sense to introduce some infrastructure to manage those operations. I will begin with some underlying support types that will be needed when dealing with multiple threads.

The first one is `MutexLockQueue`. It provides a thread-safe queue to be used in order to communicate between threads. This is important so we can send data in sequence, such as for reads and writes, between the thread handling the I/O and the one handling the interpreter.

The second is `NotificationSignal`, which wraps a condition variable, allowing different threads to block waiting for other threads, such as when all the interpreters are waiting for data to come through the network. Then the I/O thread is able to signal to the interpreter thread that it now has work to do.

Finally, the third one is `TransactionalContainer`, which implements a lock-free mechanism to make changes to an object and prevents data races when you need to perform changes to that data.

Those types are just wrappers around standard C++ facilities to make the remainder of the interpreter code easier to write. They are a bit off topic to the development of the interpreter itself, but their code can be seen in pull request #29 (`https://github.com/PacktPublishing/Building-Programming-Language-Interpreters/pull/29/files`).

Moving to the actual infrastructure the user of the interpreter will need to interface with, I'll start with the `InterpreterContext` struct:

```
struct InterpreterContext {
  Interpreter interpreter;
  support::MutexLockQueue<std::string> input_buffer;
  support::MutexLockQueue<std::string> output_buffer;
  support::MutexLockQueue<std::pair<
      std::string, const std::vector<Value>>>
      callback_request_queue;
  support::MutexLockQueue<Value> callback_response_queue;
  std::promise<Value> interpreter_result;
  void *additional_data;
  std::atomic<bool> eof = false;
  std::atomic<bool> exited = false;
  InterpreterContext(const Interpreter &interp)
    : interpreter(interp) {}
  InterpreterContext(Interpreter &&interp)
    : interpreter(std::move(interp)) {}
```

```
    InterpreterContext() = delete;
    InterpreterContext(const InterpreterContext &) = delete;
    InterpreterContext &operator=(const InterpreterContext &)
      = delete;
  };
```

The struct represents the information that you need in order to manage an `Interpreter` object. So, it starts with the interpreter itself, and then it has four queues: for input to be read, output to be written, callbacks that need to be made, and the response of those callbacks. Those queues are what will allow the interpreter to run in its own thread, separate from I/O threads and from code handling native calls.

The next member is `interpreter_result`, which is a `std::promise<Value>` object representing the value to be produced at the end of the execution of the interpreter. In other words, that's how the user of the interpreter will be able to inquire about the value returned by the interpreter. For instance, if you have an HTTP client, you will need to be able to receive the response from the interpreter.

The `additional_data` member is a plain void pointer that allows the user to store arbitrary data associated with an interpreter. This makes it possible to avoid global variables and keep the context of the interpreter self-contained.

The `eof` member is the mechanism that the I/O thread will use to indicate when you can't read or write anymore, and will instruct the operations on how to deal with that.

The `exited` member communicates to the other threads that this interpreter is no longer executing, and that it may be cleaned up from the system.

An interpreter like this, however, is probably very rarely used as a single instance in a system. If you have an HTTP server, for instance, you probably want to manage one instance for each connection in a centralized way. That's where the `InterpreterCollection` type comes in:

```
struct InterpreterSignals {
  support::NotificationSignal wake_up_interpreter;
  support::NotificationSignal wake_up_for_output;
  support::NotificationSignal wake_up_for_input;
  support::NotificationSignal wake_up_for_callback;
};
struct InterpreterCollection {
  const std::unordered_map<
```

```
    int, std::shared_ptr<InterpreterContext>> interpreters;
  const std::shared_ptr<InterpreterSignals> signals =
      std::make_shared<InterpreterSignals>();
};
```

This represents a set of interpreters running at a given moment, along with the necessary notification channels to be used by the threads managing them. The integer key in the interpreter's `unordered_map` represents the file descriptor that the interpreter is attached to.

Using the file descriptor this way is, of course, a design decision that only really makes sense in the context of this particular interpreter. All the decisions that we have been making up to this point have led to this particular format. When building your own interpreter, you will need to make a design that is appropriate for your particular scenario.

It's important to realize that `InterpreterCollection` has only `const` members; that's because that makes it safe to be shared across all threads to introspect what is running and communicate with the interpreters using the various members in `InterpreterContext`.

So, if the collection is constant, and the interpreter collection starts without any interpreter, how is the user supposed to start anything? That's where `InterpreterCollectionManager` comes in:

```
class InterpreterCollectionManager {
  support::TransactionalContainer<InterpreterCollection>
    _collection;
public:
  const std::shared_ptr<const InterpreterCollection>
    get_collection();

  std::future<Value>
  insert_interpreter(int fd, InterpretedProgram program,
                     std::optional<Value> arglist =
                      std::nullopt,
                     void *additional_data = NULL);
  void remove_interpreter(int fd);
};
```

This offers a thread-safe interface to insert new interpreters (attached to a given file descriptor) and to remove the interpreters when they're no longer needed.

The principle is that any thread can at any point get an immutable snapshot of the collection, use it, and then in the next moment, ask for it again and perhaps get an updated version.

It is implemented with `TransactionalContainer`, which I described earlier. The implementation has some interesting parts to talk about. I will only get into the details for one of the methods—`insert_interpreter`—since the implementations of the others are very similar:

```
std::future<Value> InterpreterCollectionManager::insert_interpreter(
    int fd, InterpretedProgram program,
    std::optional<Value> arglist,
    void *additional_data) {
  std::shared_ptr<InterpreterContext> ctx =
    std::make_shared<InterpreterContext>(
       program.get_instance(arglist));
  ctx->additional_data = additional_data;
  _collection.do_transaction(
      [&fd, &ctx](std::shared_ptr<
          const InterpreterCollection> current)
          -> std::shared_ptr<const InterpreterCollection> {
        auto new_interpreters = current->interpreters;
        new_interpreters.insert({fd, ctx});
        return std::make_shared<InterpreterCollection>(
            std::move(new_interpreters), current->signals);
      });
  _collection.current()->
     signals->wake_up_interpreter.notify();
  return ctx->interpreter_result.get_future();
}
```

This creates a new interpreter context, stores the additional data, and forwards the argument list. Then, it uses the `do_transaction` method to atomically replace the current collection with one with the extra interpreter.

Finally, it signals the interpreter thread to wake up, since it may have been without anything to do at that moment, and then returns the future for the promise associated with that interpreter.

And with that, we can now present the interface that actually drives the interpreter—`InterpreterRunner`:

```
struct InterpreterRunner {
  using callback_function =
    Value (*)(const std::vector<Value> &);
  std::unordered_map<std::string, callback_function>
    callbacks;
  std::atomic<bool> exit_when_done = false;
  void interpreter_loop(InterpreterCollectionManager &mgr);
  void callback_loop(InterpreterCollectionManager &mgr);
};
```

The `callbacks` member will hold function pointers for the native callbacks, registered by their associated keys. The `exit_when_done` member is what tells the runner that the loops should end when no more work is available.

The `interpreter_loop` and `callback_loop` methods will just keep running whatever is available to run until they are ready to leave. The idea is that there will be one thread running the interpreter loop, another thread running the callback loop, and other threads managing the I/O.

Both methods have a similar structure, where there is an infinite loop that gets broken once all interpreters have finished executing, and no new interpreters are expected. The `exit_when_done` boolean value provides a mechanism to handle the case where we run out of interpreters because there are no active connections, but where we're still accepting new connections. Once we are no longer expecting any new connections, we want to make sure any existing interpreter has a chance to finish running.

I'll dive into the loop. The first step is initializing some important variables for this iteration of the loop:

```
auto collection = mgr.get_collection();
```

This represents the collection at a particular point in time. Because the data structure has been built as `shared_ptr` to `const` values, it means we can safely hold onto this snapshot of the collection for the duration of this iteration.

Next, we initialize a counter to keep track of how many interpreters in the collection are currently active:

```
int active_interpreters = 0;
```

This counter is important because we want to be able to recognize that there's no work to do and wait until work becomes available.

Next is where the two functions start to diverge. In the case of `interpreter_loop`, we need to keep track of how many interpreters are still ready for execution after this step:

```
int ready_interpreters = 0;
```

While in the callback loop, we need to keep track of whether any callback was executed in this iteration, and if not, we want to wait for a notification:

```
int callbacks_count = 0;
```

Both methods will then iterate over all interpreters in the collection:

```
for (auto &[fd, context] : collection->interpreters) {...}
```

The implementation of both loops is where both methods become really different, so before going into that, I'll dive into how the iteration of the main loop finishes. In both cases, we start with the following:

```
if (mgr.get_collection() == collection) {...}
```

The loop is never interrupted when the collection changes, because it's likely that new work is available, but if there wasn't a change, then we can look into handling the end of the iteration:

```
if (active_interpreters == 0) {
  if (loaded_exit_when_done) {
    // notify threads that may be waiting
    break;
  } else {
    // wait for notification
  }
} else {
  // potentially wait for notification
}
```

This is where `exit_when_done` logic is handled. If there are no active interpreters, and we're ready to exit, that's when we break out of the main loop. But this is also where the notifications to the other threads need to be sent, or where threads wait for notifications from other threads.

Looking more specifically at the `interpreter_loop` method now, whenever there's no work to do, the thread will wait on the interpreter notification:

```
if (ready_interpreters == 0) {
  collection->signals->wake_up_interpreter.wait();
}
```

While in `callback_loop`, whenever we didn't fire any callback, the thread waits for the callback notification:

```
if (callbacks_count == 0) {
  collection->signals->wake_up_for_callback.wait();
}
```

This establishes the general shape of the loops. They will perform work for each interpreter, and whenever there's nothing else to do, either leave the loop if the entire system is being shut down or wait for a notification.

Now, if `interpreter_loop` and `callback_loop` are both waiting on notifications, something needs to wake them up, and that's the other part of the code in the loop. I'll focus on `callback_loop` first and explain how it wakes up `interpreter_loop`:

```
auto cbdata = context->callback_request_queue.pop();
if (cbdata.has_value()) {
  callbacks_count++;
  const auto &key = cbdata.value().first;
  const auto cb_it = callbacks.find(key);
  if (cb_it == callbacks.end()) {
    context->callback_response_queue.push_back(
      value::RuntimeError::NameError);
  } else {
    auto fp = cb_it->second;
    context->callback_response_queue.push_back(
      fp(cbdata.value().second));
  }
```

```
    collection->signals->wake_up_interpreter.notify();
  }
```

callback_loop doesn't interact with the interpreter directly, but rather interacts with callback_request_queue and callback_response_queue, which are associated with each interpreter. And whenever a callback request comes in, it gets resolved in the callback map, and the result of calling the function is submitted to callback_response_queue. Then, finally, the callback loop notifies the interpreter that it is now unblocked.

This is how the initial design goal of decoupling the callback invocations from the interpreter is achieved. It's also important to note that it would be reasonably easy to use a thread pool for the actual execution of the callbacks instead of a single thread. In fact, both implementations could easily exist side by side.

Callbacks are not the only way the interpreter may be blocked; the other operations we identified that can cause that are I/O operations. That being said, we explicitly don't want to commit to any specific implementation. It is the responsibility of the users, as they adapt the specific I/O library they're using, to use the queues for input and output, and to notify the interpreter accordingly.

With that said, I'll dive into how interpreter_loop iterates through the interpreters in the collection. The general shape of the iteration is as follows:

```
auto state = context->interpreter.step();
switch (state) { ... }
```

Each iteration takes a step in the interpreter and checks its state. For each of the states, I'm going to work through each of the cases:

```
case ContinuationState::MissingArguments:
case ContinuationState::Ready:
  ready_interpreters++;
  active_interpreters++;
  break;
```

Those are states related to regular interpreted operations. The interpreter yields after every operation in order to allow the execution of multiple interpreters in the same thread using what is called a trampoline function. In these cases, the interpreter does not wait for notifications; it simply reruns in the next iteration:

```
case ContinuationState::Exited:
  context->exited.store(true);
```

```
    collection->signals->wake_up_for_output.notify();
    OperationResult r = context->interpreter.get_result();
    if (std::holds_alternative<Value>(r)) {
      Value v = std::get(r);
     context->interpreter_result.set_value(v);
  } else {
     context->interpreter_result.set_exception(
       std::make_exception_ptr(
         InterpreterResultIsNotValue(r)));
  }
  break;
```

There are two important things happening in the preceding block. First, whenever an interpreter exits, `wake_up_for_output` gets notified. This allows the I/O layer to close a connection on behalf of the interpreted program (such as when a protocol mismatch happens). Second, the output of the exited interpreter is set to the promise of the interpreter. But if the interpreter ends in something that is not a value, then it results in an exception.

Finally, we can handle the cases where the interpreter is blocked:

```
case ContinuationState::Blocked:
 active_interpreters++;
 if (handle_blocked_interpreter(
      *context, *collection->signals)) {
   ready_interpreters++;
 }
 break;
```

I will now dive into the `handle_blocked_interpreter` function, but before that, I want to point out the fact that whenever we are able to do something about the blocked interpreter, we need to make sure it gets back to the next iteration again and not block it. The `ready_interpreters` variable is how that is ensured:

```
OperationResult r = context.interpreter.get_result();
if (std::holds_alternative<ReasonForBlockedOperation>(r)) {
   ReasonForBlockedOperation reason = std::get(r);
   switch (reason) { ... }
}
return true;
```

This code unpacks `OperationResult` and then evaluates the reasons why the interpreter could be blocked. If, for some reason, that evaluation falls through, it is assumed the interpreter loop should run another iteration.

Now, I'll go into the various states.

First, let's see the internal reasons why the interpreter may be blocked:

```
case ReasonForBlockedOperation::WaitingForCallableInvocation:
case ReasonForBlockedOperation::WaitingForCallableResult:
      return true;
```

These correspond to the interpreter working through callables, so we can just tell the interpreter to continue execution.

Next, we have the I/O operations:

```
case ReasonForBlockedOperation::WaitingForRead:
  return handle_read(context, signals);
case ReasonForBlockedOperation::WaitingForWrite:
  return handle_write(context, signals);
```

This is where the data is pushed and pulled from the I/O buffers in the interpreter context. This is where the interpreter notifies the I/O layer whenever it needs to perform input or output.

The `handle_read` function will consume the data from the input queue and pass it to the interpreter, but it needs to handle the fact that the operations may not consume an incomplete sequence, and so it needs to keep appending them. I will break it down, starting with the outermost part:

```
auto buffer = context.input_buffer.pop();
if (buffer.has_value()) {
  // will expand next
} else {
  if (context.eof.load()) {
    context.interpreter.handle_eof();
  } else {
    signals.wake_up_for_input.notify();
  }
}
return false;
```

If the interpreter is blocked, waiting for a read, but there's nothing in the queue, we need to check whether the socket was closed and pass that information to the interpreter. Otherwise, we wake up the I/O thread to check whether there's anything to read. Depending on the I/O library being used, that notification might not be used, but I wanted to keep the design compatible with libraries that do not try to read until asked for. The `return false` statement at the end indicates the interpreter is still blocked.

Now, let me step into the case where there is value in the buffer:

```
size_t consumed =
  context.interpreter.handle_read(buffer.value());
if (consumed == 0) {
  // will expand next
} else {
  if (consumed < buffer.value().size()) {
    context.input_buffer.push_front(
      buffer->substr(consumed));
  }
  return true;
}
```

As I discussed earlier in the chapter, the `handle_read` function will return how many octets were consumed. And if the interpreter consumes less than what was read, the remaining data must be pushed back to the front of the queue. But if, on the other hand, the operation doesn't consume anything, then we should see whether there's more data in the queue:

```
auto nextbuffer = context.input_buffer.pop();
if (nextbuffer.has_value()) {
  auto joined = buffer.value() + nextbuffer.value();
  consumed = context.interpreter.handle_read(joined);
  if (consumed < joined.size()) {
    context.input_buffer.push_front(
      joined.substr(consumed));
  }
  return true;
} else {
  context.input_buffer.push_front(buffer.value());
}
```

If there's something else in the queue, it is concatenated with what we had and given to the interpreter. If not all of it is consumed, it needs to be pushed back to the front of the queue again, so it can be given to the interpreter in the next iteration.

This is yet another good illustration of how the very specific design choices lead to specific runtime characteristics of the interpreter. In this case, because of how the operations were designed in a way to reduce how much state the interpreter holds, by just refusing to read data if it's incomplete, that complexity gets moved to a different part of the interpreter, where now we need to concatenate the input data.

The `handle_write` function, on the other hand, ends up being significantly simpler, since I'm not actually performing the I/O here, but rather just pushing the data to `output_queue`. Because the language doesn't offer the primitives for the specifics on how the system calls for writing on the socket are handled, I can significantly simplify this by just assuming that putting data in the output queue is equivalent to actually writing it:

```
if (context.eof.load()) {
  context.interpreter.handle_eof();
  return true;
} else {
  auto buffer = context.interpreter.get_write_buffer();
  std::string copy(buffer);
  context.output_buffer.push_back(copy);
  context.interpreter.handle_write(buffer.size());
  signals.wake_up_for_output.notify();
  return true;
}
```

As with `handle_read`, it also notifies that there's output in the queue, in case the I/O library is waiting.

Finally, we have the callback states:

```
case ReasonForBlockedOperation::WaitingForCallback:
 return handle_start_callback(context, signals);
case ReasonForBlockedOperation::WaitingCallbackData:
 return handle_finish_callback(context, signals);
```

This is where the callback requests are pushed, callback responses are pulled into the interpreter, and the interpreter notifies the callback thread whenever there's a callback that needs to be called.

I'll start with handle_start_callback:

```
context.callback_request_queue.push_back(
  std::make_pair(
    context.interpreter.get_callback_key(),
    context.interpreter.get_callback_arguments())); context.interpreter.
set_callback_called();
signals.wake_up_for_callback.notify();
return true;
```

This pushes the callback key and its arguments into the queue handled by the callback that was discussed before, and then notifies that thread so it can wake up to make the call.

Finally, handle_finish_callback takes the response from the queue and sends it to the interpreter:

```
auto v = context.callback_response_queue.pop();
if (v.has_value()) {
  context.interpreter.set_callback_return(v.value());
  return true;
} else {
  return false;
}
```

If nothing is in the queue, it means the interpreter is still blocked.

The key takeaway here is the relationship between the different threads running the different parts of the interpreter, the native code, and the user-managed I/O layer via the queues and condition variables. The data is communicated across threads via MutexLockQueues in each interpreter context, and whenever a thread does something that may unblock another, it signals via a notification.

This reinforces the design principle that I have been refining throughout of isolating the interpreter from the handling of I/O and the running of native code, by ensuring that data flows through thread-safe queues, which allow the user to decide how those are going to be scheduled. Had I made different choices up to here, I would probably have ended up with a very different picture. My objective here is for this to be a practical example of the process, not just a how-to. You can see the complete code in pull request #30 (https://github.com/PacktPublishing/Building-Programming-Language-Interpreters/pull/30/files).

And at this point, it is possible to assemble a real usage of the interpreter by writing an incomplete HTTP server, attaching it to a socket, accepting new connections, running the interpreter to read the request, calling a native function to handle it, and then using the return of the callback to write a response.

At this point, we have a functional interpreter runtime, even though we are not able to run the code written in the language we designed. This makes it a good moment to validate the design and implementation by emulating what a user of your interpreter would do.

So, I implemented a test case in the repository that uses a specific library as the I/O layer and integrates with the interpreter in the way that was described in this chapter. It still builds the `InterpretedProgram` objects by assembling hardcoded `OpTreeNode` objects, but it is a good enough proof that once we do assemble an operation tree, we'll be able to actually execute it in the real world.

I will leave it as an exercise for you to come up with a different implementation using different I/O libraries. It is not my goal here to go into the specifics of any of those libraries, but if you are curious about how a user would use this interpreter at this point, you can look at pull request #31 (`https://github.com/PacktPublishing/Building-Programming-Language-Interpreters/pull/31/files`).

Using tests to show how a real user of your interpreter will have to perform the integration is a good way to build confidence that you are building something that actually fits the use case that you started with.

Summary

When implementing the interpreter runtime, it's important to visualize a real example of the usage of the language to identify which operators need to be implemented. In this case, laying out the operations for writing and parsing an HTTP message helped identify various new operators and helped create test cases that demonstrated that they work as expected.

With those particular needs identified, I could focus on implementing each operator, finalizing with a test case that showed that the interpreter was able to parse a message to a data structure and then use that data structure to reproduce the same message.

With that, I could get to build what the API for the user of the library would look like, and build a test case that exercised the interpreter in a very real scenario, integrating with a specific I/O library to have a basic HTTP server and client communicate over real network sockets.

This closes the work on the runtime of the interpreter. In the next chapter, I will begin the process of translating the source code of the language into the operation tree that the interpreter already knows how to execute.

Part 4

Interpreting Source Code

In this part, the first version of the complete interpreter comes together. I will work through the four different layers needed to handle the source code—lexing, parsing, analyzing, and generating—up to the point where the source code actually runs. By the end, I will make a concrete use of the language, just as a user of that language would.

This part has the following chapters:

- *Chapter 13, Lexing: Turning Text into a Stream of Tokens*
- *Chapter 14, Parsing: Turning a Stream of Tokens into a Parse Tree*
- *Chapter 15, Analyzing: Turning a Parse Tree into an Abstract Syntax Tree*
- *Chapter 16, Generating: Turning an Abstract Syntax Tree into Instructions*
- *Chapter 17, Proving That It Works*

13

Lexing: Turning Text into a Stream of Tokens

Now that I have an interpreter runtime capable of executing the instructions that my programming language needs, it is time to start the process of transforming source code into those instructions.

The first step in this process transforms the sequence of characters into a sequence of typed tokens. This allows the subsequent steps to work at a higher level of abstraction than plain text, simplifying the process of specifying the language grammar.

In this chapter, I will do the following:

- Identify the different types of tokens in the language and the data each needs to store
- Specify the rules for how those tokens are matched
- Evaluate different libraries that can be used to implement a lexer and compare them with writing one from scratch
- Implement the actual process that transforms a sequence of characters into a sequence of tokens

By the end of this chapter, you will have practical experience on how to design and implement a lexer for your own programming language.

Identifying token types and their data structures

Back in *Chapter 9, Putting It All Together and Creating a Coherent Vision*, I finalized the format for the programming language that would specify how a network protocol would look. Let me take some snippets from there to start the discussion:

```
message "HTTP Request" {
    when: Open;
}
```

In the lexing phase, the goal is not to establish any hierarchy between the meaning of the text, but rather to identify which chunks of that text play which role in understanding it.

Looking at the preceding snippet, the output could be a list of tokens, as shown in *Table 13.1*:

Token type	**Additional data**
Keyword	`message`
String	`HTTP Request`
Open brace	
Identifier	`when`
Key-value separator	
Identifier	`Open`
Statement end	
Close brace	

Table 13.1: Token types and their associated data

This will allow the grammar later to be specified in terms of those tokens, such as "*when you find the message keyword, followed by a string and an open brace, it means that you are starting a block for a message that will end with the matching close brace.*"

But I'm not yet writing the grammar. I'm only working on the lexer, so the important question that I have to ask is: what are the types of tokens that I need in order to be able to write a grammar later, and what data will I store for them?

One common example of specialization in lexers is the differentiation between identifiers and keywords. In the preceding example, I decided to use a *keyword* for `message` but an *identifier* for `Open`.

There's not a well-defined rule on how you are supposed to make those choices, but a reasonable principle is that whenever you have something that is structural to the language, you probably want to have made it a keyword, and when you have something where the content changes but the structural meaning doesn't change, you want to make it an identifier.

Even the use of words such as *keyword* and *identifier* is already an arbitrary choice that I'm making right now, although it's a fairly common choice in language implementations. The way that you define those types will drive how your parsing will work later.

But you don't need to worry too much about it at this point. As programming languages evolve, the way the lexer is implemented also changes to cater to specific requirements. As you evolve your implementation, it's very likely that you iterate on the lexer and the parser at the same time, since they work in a very tight cooperation.

It's probably better to just jump in. I will go back to the full source code that I defined in *Chapter 9*, and make a first pass at defining types for the lexer for all the tokens used in that example.

It is common to represent a token by an enum and then have a token type that contains that enum, along with a slot for additional data for the token types that need it. However, I am taking a different approach: instead of enums, I will use `std::variant` to represent the token type.

One important side effect of this choice is that for all the tokens that do not need any additional data, the type can be an empty struct, as in this example:

```
namespace networkprotocoldsl::lexer::token::keyword {
    struct For {};
    struct In {};
    struct Message {};
    struct Parts {};
    struct Terminator {};
    struct Tokens {};
}
```

In other cases, such as for identifiers or literals, we need some additional data:

```
namespace networkprotocoldsl::lexer::token::literal {
    struct Integer { int value; };
    struct String { std::string value; };
}
```

In these cases, we simply store a member with the specific data.

The final `Token` type then looks like this:

```
namespace networkprotocoldsl::lexer {
    using Token = std::variant<
     token::Identifier,
     token::keyword::For,
     token::keyword::In,
     token::keyword::Message,
     token::keyword::Parts,
     token::keyword::Terminator,
     token::keyword::Tokens,
     token::literal::Integer,
     token::literal::String,
     token::punctuation::AngleBracketClose,
     token::punctuation::AngleBracketOpen,
     token::punctuation::Comma,
     token::punctuation::CurlyBraceClose,
     token::punctuation::CurlyBraceOpen,
     token::punctuation::Equal,
     token::punctuation::KeyValueSeparator,
     token::punctuation::StatementEnd
    >;
}
```

The reason for using a variant instead of an enum is that it will allow the code using the tokens to use `std::visit` instead of `switch` statements. This provides a type-safe way of handling the data associated with each token, while if the token were an enum, that safety would have to be deferred to runtime.

I introduce the initial types that I identified so far in pull request #32 (`https://github.com/PacktPublishing/Building-Programming-Language-Interpreters/pull/32/files`).

In the next section, I will start working on the definition of how the lexer should work.

Specifying the rules of the lexer

A lexer works by matching the input text against a set of rules and performing actions based on those rules. The action that we need is to append a token to the stream, or, in some cases, ignore it.

The rules are easily defined as a set of named regular expressions. The lexer is going to find the longest matches for each of these regular expressions in order to execute the corresponding action, using the order in which the rules are specified to resolve ambiguities.

Here is the list of regular expressions for each of the token types that have been identified so far:

Token name	Regular expression
KeywordFor	for
KeywordIn	in
KeywordMessage	message
KeywordParts	parts
KeywordTerminator	terminator
KeywordTokens	tokens
LiteralInteger	[0-9]+
LiteralString	\"(\\[\"\\ntr]|[^\"\\])*\"
PunctuationAngleBracketClose	>
PunctuationAngleBracketOpen	<
PunctuationComma	,
PunctuationCurlyBraceClose	\}
PunctuationCurlyBraceOpen	\{
PunctuationEqual	=
PunctuationKeyValueSeparator	:
PunctuationStatementEnd	;
WhiteSpace	[\t\n]+
Identifier	[a-zA-Z][a-zA-Z0-9]*

Table 13.2: Regular expressions defining each token type

Most lexing libraries simply accept a list of rules and their corresponding regular expressions. More complicated languages will, of course, have significantly more complicated lexing rules, but in the case of this language, so far, it's fairly straightforward.

Since it's so simple, it could be tempting to just implement the state machine for lexing by hand. But there is no reason to reinvent the wheel.

In the next section, I will evaluate a few different options for libraries that can be used for this task.

Evaluating different lexer libraries

The most traditional implementation of a lexer is, without a doubt, Flex (`https://github.com/westes/flex`). It is used by many programming languages, or at least it's the starting point for many of them. It works with a code generator, which interleaves the code required to match the regular expressions with the actions that need to be executed.

Its main advantage is its ubiquity: there's probably not an operating system in which you can't get Flex to work, and it has been extensively optimized and reviewed over the years. Its main disadvantage is the contrived rules of its code generator, where you're expected to write C code interleaved with the lexer rules that Flex parses, which then get converted into a final C file.

re2c (`https://re2c.org/`) and RE/flex (`https://github.com/Genivia/RE-flex`) are lexers that take a similar approach to Flex, in the sense that you have a separate programming language interleaved with your code, which then gets generated into the target programming language. They both convert the regular expressions into a deterministic finite automaton.

The advantage is that the generated code is going to be incredibly efficient, as it considers all rules at once in a single processing loop using plain jumps. As with Flex, the main disadvantage is the fact that you have the code generation step with a different syntax, which can make IDE integration and static analysis more awkward.

The last library I want to cover is `lexertl` (`http://www.benhanson.net/lexertl.html`). This library aims to provide the same capabilities as Flex, but fully integrated in C++. That means you don't need to learn a different language or deal with the complexity of adding code generation to your build process. A plain C++ API makes it easier for people learning how to create lexers, and for that reason, I am choosing it for this exercise. The knowledge you gain with this could easily be translated into a more efficient implementation if you need it later.

It's worth noting that, in practice, a lot of libraries and frameworks for lexing and parsing actually present a single integrated interface that performs both the lexing and parsing. I will cover those more specifically in the next chapter. In this chapter, I focused only on the libraries that work exclusively on lexing.

I am choosing to keep lexing and parsing separate in order to give me more flexibility on how I will implement the parser later. It is also simple enough to implement that if I end up joining them later, it won't be a significant waste of effort. I also wanted to make sure we went through the exercise of implementing both separately, in case you decide not to use a parser that has an integrated lexer as well.

In the next section, I will focus on the actual implementation of the lexer.

Getting a stream of tokens

The general shape of the implementation of a tokenizer is that you declare a set of rules, and you then iterate over the input. The lexer signals that it matched a specific rule, or that it failed to match any rule, meaning the input was not recognized.

In practice, that means that I need to execute specific code whenever a rule is matched. Since the goal is to produce a vector of tokens, I can declare a simple struct to declare a rule and the action I want to run:

```
struct TokenRule {
    std::string_view pattern;
    std::function<void(std::vector<Token> &,
                       const std::string_view &)> pusher;
};
```

This declaration allows me to have both the regular expression for a rule and the code that gets executed when the lexer matches that rule in a single place. The first argument is the vector that is going to be used as the token accumulator, while the second (`std::string_view`) contains the text that was matched.

Now, I can convert the rules I had created before into a vector of token rules:

```
const std::vector<TokenRule> token_rules = {
    {"for",
     [](std::vector<Token>& tokens, const std::string_view &)
       { tokens.push_back(token::keyword::For()); }},
       …
```

This is a good example of the token types that require no extra data. The only thing the action code does is push a token object of the corresponding type into the accumulator.

I will not include the code for all the tokens, because they all look very similar. The ones that need to do something with the text, such as the `Identifier` token, are a bit different:

```
    {"[a-zA-Z][a-zA-Z0-9]*",
     [](std::vector<Token>& tokens,
        const std::string_view & str)
       { tokens.push_back(
         token::Identifier{std::string(str)}); }}
```

Here, we can see that the `Identifier` token contains the name of the identifier, which is created and pushed into the vector.

Here is the case where we do nothing, which is the case when matching whitespace:

```
    {"[ \\t\\n]+",
     [](std::vector<Token> &, const std::string_view &)
     {}}, // No action for whitespace
```

Whitespace is not significant in the language; therefore, it shouldn't be represented in the token stream.

One last example I want to give is the `LiteralString` token, as it demonstrates the care required when escaping the regular expressions and removing the extra characters that were matched by the lexer but that are not part of the literal value itself:

```
{"\\\"(\\\\[\"\\\\ntr]|[^\"\\\\])*\\\"",
 []( std::vector<Token> &tokens,
     const std::string_view &str) {
   tokens.push_back(token::literal::String{
     unescape_string(
       std::string(str.substr(1, str.length() - 2)))});
 }},
```

The literal string also needs an extra step to interpret escaped characters, such as `\n`, by converting the two-character sequences from the original text into the corresponding escaped characters. I will not cover the function here as it's a simple loop that replaces the escape sequences with the real characters.

It's important to note that up to this point, we have nothing specific to the `lexertl` API; we simply have a list of rules and actions to be taken whenever the rules are matched. All of those are just constant definitions.

I can now start building the actual `tokenize` function. I'll start with the outermost layout, then go step by step:

```
std::optional<std::vector<Token>> tokenize(
    const std::string &input) {
    std::vector<Token> ret;
    // will expand next
    return ret;
}
```

The function returns an `optional` type because that's how we're going to communicate that the lexer failed when it finds something that doesn't match any of the rules. Then, we declare a local accumulator vector, which will be returned at the end of the function.

Now, we need to use the `lexertl` API. The first step is populating a `rules` object, which is the way the library represents the collection of rules:

```
lexertl::rules lexer_rules;
for (unsigned short i = 0; i < token_rules.size(); ++i) {
    lexer_rules.push(token_rules[i].pattern.data(), i + 1);
}
```

This adds all the rules, using their position in the array as their identifier, which is how `lexertl` communicates which rule was matched. Note that because `0` is reserved for the end of input in the `lexertl` API, we added `1` for the index.

Now, we can actually build the state machine for this particular lexer:

```
lexertl::state_machine sm;
lexertl::generator::build(lexer_rules, sm);
```

This builds a lexer state machine from the rules. If you have any invalid regular expressions, this is where the lexer will raise an exception.

Finally, we can iterate over the input, appending the tokens to our return vector:

```
lexertl::smatch results(input.begin(), input.end());
while (true) {
    lexertl::lookup(sm, results);
    if (results.id == 0) {
        break;
    } else if (results.id == results.npos()) {
```

```
            return std::nullopt;
        } else {
            // Adjust for zero-based index
            size_t rule_id = results.id - 1;
            if (rule_id < token_rules.size()) {
                token_rules[rule_id].pusher(ret, results.str());
            }
        }
    }
```

The `smatch` type tracks the iterator as it progresses through the state machine, going from `input.begin()` to `input.end()`. It will return `0` when the string has ended, `npos()` if it found an invalid match, and the matched rule ID in the case of a successful match. Since I populated the rules based on the constant `TokenRule` vector, I can index back into that constant to determine which action should be executed. As discussed before, these actions will push tokens into the `ret` vector being passed as an argument.

The `tokenize` function returns a vector of tokens wrapped in an `optional` type. It will return `std::nullopt` if the lexer fails; otherwise, it returns the vector of tokens.

Testing the tokenizer

With that, I can also write a test for the tokenizer where I confirm that it successfully returns the sequence of tokens that I expect for a given input:

```
std::string input(
    "message \"HTTP Request\" { when: Open; }");
auto output = lexer::tokenize(input);
```

The first step in the test is to set up a string with a snippet of the code in the language, and use the `tokenize` function I just wrote to produce a vector of tokens:

```
ASSERT_TRUE(output.has_value());
ASSERT_EQ(8, output->size());
```

I now validate, using Google Test's macros, that the function produced a value and that it has eight tokens, which I listed at the beginning of the chapter:

```
ASSERT_TRUE(
    std::holds_alternative<lexer::token::keyword::Message>(
        output->at(0)));
ASSERT_TRUE(
    std::holds_alternative<lexer::token::literal::String>(
         output->at(1)));
ASSERT_EQ("HTTP Request",
    std::get<lexer::token::literal::String>(
         output->at(1)).value);
```

Finally, the test validates that each element in the vector has the type and the contents that we expected, validating that we have exactly the list of tokens that we expected from the snippet. You can look at the complete code for the lexer and the test in pull request #33 (`https://github.com/PacktPublishing/Building-Programming-Language-Interpreters/pull/33/files`).

Summary

When creating a lexer, the first step is to identify what kinds of tokens you have and what data needs to be stored for each one of them. In this exercise, I decided to model the tokens as a variant with different types for each token.

Then, you need to define the regular expressions for how each token is matched, which will set the rules for what kind of input gets accepted in your language. I went ahead and noted the tokens that were needed for the sample code I had laid out before.

It is very unlikely that you will have a benefit in implementing a lexer by yourself; therefore, it's important to evaluate various options of existing libraries. I decided to use the `lexertl` library because of its plain C++ API, which makes it easier to teach.

Finally, I implemented the lexer by just using the `lexertl` API, translating the rules that I had identified before. I included a test to validate that I get the correct set of tokens when processing a specific input.

In the next chapter, I will go one level of abstraction higher by starting to implement the parser, which converts the sequence of tokens into a hierarchical data structure, known as a parse tree.

14

Parsing: Turning a Stream of Tokens into a Parse Tree

The sequence of tokens produced by the tokenizer is easier to work with than the raw text, but if you were to try and convert those tokens directly into operations, you'd find yourself struggling a lot. The reason for that is that most programming languages have a hierarchy of how the code is represented, and in order to understand the code, we need it to be represented at a higher level of abstraction.

In this chapter, I will focus on the process of converting a sequence of tokens into a parse tree, which is the name we give to the data structure representing how the code needs to be read. To do that, we will do the following:

- Identify what data structures we need to represent the code in a way that encapsulates its hierarchy
- Define a grammar that specifies how the tokens need to be matched in order to assemble those data structures
- Evaluate different options of libraries and frameworks that help implement parsers
- Implement a custom parser engine using modern C++ features
- Put everything together and add the complete parser implementation to the interpreter codebase

By the end of this chapter, you will have a practical understanding of how we raise the level of abstraction from tokens to the parse tree, as well as experience in implementing it.

Types of parse nodes and their data structures

As was the case with lexing, when you parse the code for your language, you want to be able to represent it in a data structure that represents what the code looks like. This is important because you will need to analyze that data structure in order to later produce a semantic understanding of what the code means and how it should be executed.

Unlike the lexer, however, the output of the parsing of the code is not represented as a sequence but rather as a tree, which represents the syntactical structure of the code. The parse tree, therefore, represents the syntax of the code in a hierarchical way, where you will be able to traverse the logical organization of the syntax, rather than a flat stream of tokens.

The strategy I am going to use to define the node types will follow the syntactical hierarchy from the inside out, since I know that the syntax of a message will include the attribute, but the attribute will not include a message.

We can start by looking at the top-level attributes of the message. A relevant section of the code in the language looks like the following:

```
    when: Open;
```

There are some attributes that exist in every message. For that reason, we don't need to worry about defining them right now. They will become part of the outer message type, so we'll focus on the attribute itself.

In this basic example, the only type of thing that can be on the value side is an identifier. So I will start by defining a node that represents a reference to an identifier:

```
struct IdentifierReference {
    std::string name;
};
```

This is a good example that shows how simple the start of this process is.

Now let's look inside the data section, where we have a line like the following:

```
        major_version: int<encoding=AsciiInt,
                           unsigned=True,
                           bits=8>;
```

In this case, things are significantly more complicated. We have an identifier, but we also have parameters for it. So, following the same inside-out approach, we can notice that we have a few different types of values in an attribute. Let's create types for each of those:

```
struct BooleanLiteral {
    bool value;
};
struct IntegerLiteral {
    int value;
};
```

Now, I need a way to specify that the value of a type parameter can be any of these:

```
using TypeParameterValue = std::variant<
    BooleanLiteral,
    IntegerLiteral,
    IdentifierReference
>;
```

With that, we can now create a map that represents all the attributes for the parameter type:

```
using TypeParameterMap = std::map<
    std::string,
    std::shared_ptr<const TypeParameterValue>
>;
```

At this point, we can finally create a node for the type itself:

```
struct Type {
    std::shared_ptr<const IdentifierReference> name;
    std::shared_ptr<const TypeParameterMap> parameters;
};
```

Now, if we look at the following snippet from the programming language, we'll notice that there is a problem:

```
element_type=tuple<
    key=str<encoding=Ascii7Bit,
            sizing=Dynamic,
            max_length=32768>,
    value=str<encoding=Ascii7Bit,
```

```
            sizing=Dynamic,
            max_length=32768>>,
```

The type parameter value may actually recursively reference other types with their own parameters. So, I need to adjust `TypeParameterValue` to allow a `Type` class as well:

```
class Type; // forward declaration
using TypeParameterValue = std::variant<
    BooleanLiteral,
    IntegerLiteral,
    IdentifierReference,
    Type
>;
```

I will not go into all the details on all the types that I am creating for the parse tree, since the process is pretty much the same for all syntax elements that I need to support.

The final type in this inside-out approach is the `ProtocolDescription` class, which allows traversing the entire syntax of the language:

```
using ProtocolDescription = std::map<
    std::string,
    std::shared_ptr<const Message>
>;
```

The code for the entire set of types can be seen in pull request #34 (`https://github.com/PacktPublishing/Building-Programming-Language-Interpreters/pull/34`). If you start from the `ProtocolDescription` type and traverse down, you will be able to explore the entire parse tree for the language.

In the next section, we will focus on specifying the grammar for the language and formalizing its final syntax.

Specifying the grammar for the parser

Before we get into the implementation, it's important to formalize the grammar that the language will use. This is important because it gives a complete picture of what the parser will need to do, and it will become the reference for the implementation.

As with defining the types for the parse tree, we will take an inside-out approach, gradually going all the way out toward the definition of the complete language. In fact, we will follow the same sequence that we followed when defining the types.

To represent the grammar for the language, at this point, we will use a syntax similar to **Extended Backus–Naur Form (EBNF)**, which is a standard language to describe grammars (I will explain its format as we work through its usage). We will reference the tokens that were defined in the previous chapter by prepending them with `token::`, so we don't have to specify them again here.

I will not go through every step, but I will traverse up to the `Type` definition:

```
IdentifierReference ::= token::Identifier
BooleanLiteral ::= token::literal::Boolean
IntegerLiteral ::= token::literal::Integer
TypeParameterValue ::=
   <BooleanLiteral> |
   <IntegerLiteral> |
   <IdentifierReference> |
   <Type>
TypeParameter ::=
   token::Identifier token::punctuation::Equals
   <TypeParameterValue>
TypeParameters ::= <TypeParameter>
   (token::punctuation::Comma <TypeParameter>)*
Type ::= token::Identifier
   [ token::punctuation::AngleBracketOpen
     <TypeParameters>
     token::punctuation::AngleBracketClose ]
```

If you're not familiar with the EBNF syntax, I will explain the elements that have been used here:

- The `A ::= …` statements define a new rule, which can be referenced later
- A term in angle brackets references another rule in the grammar, and the terms without brackets refer to tokens
- A sequence of terms means they appear in sequence in the grammar
- The use of square brackets means that the sequence is optional
- Parentheses create a grouping, which can be subject to modifiers, such as *, which implies zero or more occurrences

With that explanation, you should be able to read the grammar so far and see how it aligns with the types that were defined in the previous section and understand how we will likely be able to translate from the grammar directly to the parse tree.

But I want to call attention to the `TypeParameterValues` rule. In our parse tree type, I'm making it a map, rather than a list, even if syntactically, it appears as a sequence. That means that as part of the parsing, there's also some additional transformation that will be necessary.

This is a good example of how the parsing is also an opportunity to demonstrate that as we parse the programming language, we can also increase the level of abstraction of the semantics.

The remainder of the work of defining the grammar is essentially a matter of following the same process. I won't cover all of it, but you can see the final grammar in pull request #35 (`https://github.com/PacktPublishing/Building-Programming-Language-Interpreters/pull/35/files`).

In the next section, we will evaluate different library options to implement the parser.

Evaluating different parser libraries

As with lexers, there are various options of libraries that implement grammar engines. Those libraries offer different trade-offs, and it's important to consider which one is going to be most beneficial to your project.

The first library I want us to consider is **ANTLR**, because it is a very sophisticated framework for building lexers and parsers. If you think that your language will evolve into a lot more complexity, it may be beneficial to consider it. Its main drawback is the additional complexity involving code generators, which may also make debugging more challenging.

ANTLR will also implement its own lexer, and it will produce its own parse tree based on the grammar. If you want to increase the semantic meaning of the parse tree, such as transforming a list into a map, that will need to happen as a postprocessing step.

You also need to know about **Bison**, the counterpart to Flex. It is probably one of the most mature grammar engines. However, as it is based on preprocessing your code, you will need to mix C and C++. For this reason, integrating with more elaborate C++ types may rapidly lead to a very complex system.

That being said, it's easy to underestimate the importance of a mature engine. If you plan on your language supporting a much wider set of platforms, this may be an interesting choice.

Boost.Spirit, part of the Boost project, is also a mature library. It uses various overloads of C++ operators to make the syntax look like you are writing in a grammar syntax. It is a fairly flexible grammar engine. If you prefer keeping everything in C++, that is definitely a benefit, but it's definitely worth pointing out that its fairly uncommon use of operators can make it harder to read or maintain for developers unfamiliar with it.

Finally, I want to mention **PEGTL**, which is an implementation of a fairly new formalization of a type of grammar called **parsing expression grammar**, which restricts what kinds of grammars are considered valid by making certain ambiguities invalid. It also resolves some ambiguities by establishing that the order of the declaration of the rules can be used to define which path would be taken, even if they would otherwise be ambiguous.

This restriction allows the engine to be significantly simpler to use, but with the caveat that if your language has ambiguities in its grammar, it will not be able to produce a valid parser. For simple languages, the grammar will never need to support ambiguous rules; in fact, as a language designer, it is possible to accept that restriction and just never add any feature to the language that introduces any ambiguity.

There is ample documentation available online on each of these libraries, and most of the time, I would likely recommend using one of them. ANTLR in particular is very mature, and it's the de facto standard for new parsers. It is definitely worth the time to get familiar with these libraries.

That being said, I wanted to explore another option, which would be to build the parsing engine myself, particularly since I have been exploring the interesting things that we can do with the newer features of the C++ language, such as variant, lambdas, visit, and concepts.

I have also had the experience of building parsers in Haskell, and it always left me with the impression that the pattern matching used there was the most convenient way of describing a grammar.

While we don't have pattern matching in C++ (yet), we can definitely emulate it by using concepts, variants, and the visitor pattern. In the next section, we will build a grammar engine using these language features.

Building a grammar engine in C++

When you read about lexers and parsers, or read their implementations, it's often the case that the classification of tokens and parse tree objects is defined by enums or inheritance. However, in this project, I have built most of the composition using variants instead.

This generates a very important outcome, which is that the language itself has a type-safe way of traversing the different types of the variant, using `std::visit`. That means we don't need to implement `switch` statements to handle multiple types, nor do we need to use runtime type information to deduce what the actual type of a node in the parse tree is.

More importantly, it means that the compiler can generate the various type-safe code paths by itself, without the need for us to manipulate that ourselves.

Now, let's see how to go about implementing a parser.

The first step is to consider that the parser needs to traverse tokens. I will choose to represent this traversal using iterators, so I'll start by defining that the `begin` and `end` iterators will be the main input to the `parse` function.

The output of the `parse` function needs to be able to tell whether or not parsing succeeded, return the specific tree object, and show where the iterator was left.

Since I want to make this engine as generic as possible, I'll start by defining a `template` class that represents the traits of a given parser (inside the `support` sub-namespace):

```
template <typename TOKENITERATOR, typename NODEVARIANT>
struct ParseStateTraits {
    using TokenIterator = TOKENITERATOR;
    using ParseNode = NODEVARIANT;
    struct ParseStateReturn {
        std::optional<ParseNode> node;
        TokenIterator begin;
        TokenIterator end;
    };
};
```

The `TokenIterator` type will be able to de-reference the various types of tokens, which, in the case of this project, comes naturally out of the fact that the lexer returns a `std::vector<lexer::Token>` value, where `lexer::Token` is itself a variant. So, I can just create an alias for it:

```
using TokenIterator =
    std::vector<lexer::Token>::const_iterator;
```

The `ParseNode` declaration, on the other hand, will itself also be a variant of all the different types of tree objects that the parser can produce, which can simply be defined as follows:

```
using NodeVariant =
    std::variant<
      std::shared_ptr<const tree::BooleanLiteral>,
      std::shared_ptr<const tree::IdentifierReference>,
      std::shared_ptr<const tree::IntegerLiteral>,
      std::shared_ptr<const tree::StringLiteral>,
      std::shared_ptr<const tree::Type>,
      std::shared_ptr<const tree::TypeParameterPair>,
      std::shared_ptr<const tree::TypeParameterMap>,
      std::shared_ptr<const tree::TokenSequence>,
      std::shared_ptr<const tree::TokenPart>,
      std::shared_ptr<const tree::Terminator>,
      std::shared_ptr<const tree::ProtocolDescription>,
      std::shared_ptr<const tree::MessageSequence>,
      std::shared_ptr<const tree::MessagePart>,
      std::shared_ptr<const tree::MessageForLoop>,
      std::shared_ptr<const tree::MessageDataPair>,
      std::shared_ptr<const tree::MessageData>,
      std::shared_ptr<const tree::Message>>;
```

And with that, we can define the parameters that define how the generic parser needs to behave:

```
using ParseTraits =
  support::ParseStateTraits<TokenIterator, NodeVariant>;
```

With this, you may be starting to notice something interesting—the `NodeVariant` type defines all possible tree nodes, and those are also the types that are used to build the composite tree nodes, as follows:

```
struct IdentifierReference {
    std::string name;
    std::optional<
        std::shared_ptr<const IdentifierReference>> member;
};
```

This node represents a reference to an identifier, which may have a member access that is itself another identifier reference. The consistency of using shared pointers to constant structures means we'll be able to easily visit the nodes being parsed to construct the parse tree directly.

With that, we can start moving to the parsing engine itself. So far, I have identified what the entry point for it will be, something like the following:

```
ParseStateReturn r = MyGrammar::parse(begin, end);
```

Now, let's start to look into what needs to happen in the `parse` method. This is where everything comes together. The goal here is to allow defining a grammar in terms of matching the sequence of tokens by performing a visit on the token variant.

To make the explanation easier, I will start from the point where something is actually matched. Before implementing the grammar for `IdentifierReference`, let me start defining a grammar for `IntegerLiteral`, which is a simpler rule. I will start with just the conditions for a match:

```
class IntegerLiteral {
public:
    static ParseStateReturn match(
        TokenIterator begin, TokenIterator end,
        lexer::token::IntegerLiteral i) {
            return {
                std::make_shared<tree::IntegerLiteral>(i.value),
                  begin, end};
    }
```

Now, how would I go from the token iterator to passing the specific token type to a method named `match`? And how do we know whether the `match` method is there or not?

The trick here is to make the `parse` method a template with variadic template parameters, as follows:

```
template <typename... Args>
static ParseStateReturn parse(TokenIterator begin,
 TokenIterator end, Args... args) {
    if constexpr (is_match<ParseTraits,
                  ParserContext, Args...>::value) {
        return match(begin, end, args...);
    } else {
        auto next = *begin++;
        return std::visit(
        [&](auto t){
            return parse(begin, end, args..., next);
        }, next);
    }
}
```

Here, the `is_match` conditional is doing a lot of the heavy lifting by checking whether that particular method exists. This can be achieved using a combination of concepts and `constexpr` expressions:

```
template <typename ParseStateTraits,
          typename T, typename... Args>
concept has_match = requires(typename
          ParseStateTraits::TokenIterator begin,
          typename ParseStateTraits::TokenIterator end,
          Args... args) {
    {T::match(begin, end, args...)};
};
template <typename ParseStateTraits,
          typename T, typename... Args>
struct is_match {
    static constexpr bool value =
        has_match<ParseStateTraits, T, Args...>;
};
```

The concept takes the same variadic template parameters that we're using in the `parse` method, and then checks whether a `match` method taking those arguments exists for that type. Then, `is_match` just makes it easier to make a `constexpr` expression that we can use in the `if constexpr` condition.

So, at this point, the `parse` method will just expand recursively across all different types of the variant. However, that will quickly explode into a very large number of method calls. In fact, in this form, it will actually result in an infinite template expansion.

So, I need to introduce a way to limit the expansion. We call that a *partial match*. With that, the body of our `parse` function looks something like this:

```
    if constexpr (is_match<ParseTraits,
                  ParserContext, Args...>::value) {
        return match(begin, end, args...);
    } else if constexpr (is_partial_match<ParseTraits,
                 ParserContext, Args...>::value) {
         auto next = *begin++;
         return std::visit(
             [&](auto t){
         return parse(begin, end, args..., next);
         }, next);
    } else {
        return { std::nullopt, begin, end };
    }
```

Note that the `partial_match` function is never actually called. It is used only to indicate that the particular grammar rule needs more data. It tells the engine that it needs to advance the iterator and add the input token to the arguments in a new call to the `parse` function itself.

Now, the template recursion will immediately stop if there is no partial match, completely cutting off the exponential explosion that we would see before. With that, the `IntegerLiteral` class will look as follows:

```
class IntegerLiteral {
public:
    static void partial_match() {}
    static ParseStateReturn match(
      TokenIterator begin, TokenIterator end,
      lexer::token::IntegerLiteral i) {
```

```
        return {
            std::make_shared<tree::IntegerLiteral>(i.value),
              begin, end};
}
```

This already works quite well. The first invocation of `parse` will see a partial match for the empty set of arguments, then perform a visit on the first token. It will expand into a call to `match` when the token is of the right type, but will return `std::nullopt` for every other token type.

It is important to notice that the `is_partial_match` check in `RecursiveParser` is the place where the iterator is being advanced. Therefore, the `match` function is not expected to perform any advancing of the iterators. It simply returns the iterator at the point where it stopped when the match was concluded, meaning the machinery will continue from the next token already. In addition, the type of the parse node is intended to represent the parse tree object, even if the input is a token object. This is how I'll be able to transform tokens into a parse tree as the tokens are consumed.

Now, to finish this very first round, we need to make the `IntegerLiteral` grammar class actually support the `parse` method. For that, we will use the **Curiously Recurring Template Pattern (CRTP)** with a `RecursiveParser` template class:

```
template <class ParserContext, typename ParseStateTraits>
class RecursiveParser {
public:
    using ParseStateReturn =
        typename ParseStateTraits::ParseStateReturn;
    using TokenIterator =
        typename ParseStateTraits::TokenIterator;
    using ParseNode =
        typename ParseStateTraits::ParseNode;

    template <typename... Args>
    static ParseStateReturn parse(TokenIterator begin,
            TokenIterator end, Args... args) {
    // code from previous snippet
    }
};
```

Then, I can just add the inheritance into the `IntegerLiteral` class:

```
class IntegerLiteral
    : public support::RecursiveParser<IntegerLiteral,
                                      ParseTraits> {
    // code from before
}
```

With that, I should be able to parse an integer literal token into an integer literal parse tree node and write a little test for it:

```
TEST(LiteralsTest, IntegerLiteralMatch) {
    std::vector<lexer::Token> tokens =
      {lexer::token::literal::Integer(42)};
    auto result =
      parser::grammar::IntegerLiteral::parse(
         tokens.cbegin(),
         tokens.cend());
    ASSERT_TRUE(result.node.has_value());
    auto v = std::get<
                std::shared_ptr<
                  const parser::tree::IntegerLiteral>>(
                    result.node.value());
    ASSERT_EQ(v->value, 42);
}
```

This is great, but it's still not very useful. We need to be able to actually reference different rules from each other. For that, let's go back to `IdentifierReference`, whose grammar is a bit more complicated since it has member access as well.

Using what we have implemented so far, we can start matching the identifier token. However, we need to be able to recurse, and also handle the case where the identifier does not have member access (for example, `foo` versus `foo.bar`).

For that, we can introduce a new `constexpr` conditional:

```
} else if constexpr (is_recurse_maybe<ParseStateTraits,
                                      ParserContext,
                                      Args...>::value) {
    ParseStateReturn r =
        recurse_maybe<ParseStateTraits, ParserContext,
```

```
                    Args...>::type::parse(
            begin, end);
    if (!r.node.has_value()) {
        return ParserContext::parse(begin, end, args...,
                                    std::nullopt);
    } else {
        return std::visit(
          [=](auto t) {
             return ParserContext::parse(r.begin, end,
                                         args..., t);
          },
        r.node.value());
    }
```

The goal, in this case, is to attempt a different parser from where the iterator is. If it succeeds, we visit the parse node as the next element in the template parameter, and if it fails, we add a `std::nullopt` value in the template parameter.

It may not be obvious where I'm going with this, but what that allows me to do is the following:

```
class IdentifierReference
    : public support::RecursiveParser<IdentifierReference,
                                      ParseTraits> {
public:
    static void partial_match() {}
    static IdentifierMemberAccess*
        recurse_maybe(lexer::token::Identifier) {
        return nullptr;
    }
    static ParseStateReturn
        match(TokenIterator begin, TokenIterator end,
            lexer::token::Identifier i, std::nullopt_t) {
        return {std::make_shared<const
                tree::IdentifierReference>(i.name), begin,
                end};
    }
    static ParseStateReturn
    match(TokenIterator begin, TokenIterator end,
          lexer::token::Identifier i,
```

```
            std::shared_ptr<
                const tree::IdentifierReference> member) {
        return {std::make_shared<const
                tree::IdentifierReference>(i.name, member),
                begin, end};
    }
};
```

So, what that means is that after performing a partial match on the identifier token, the parser will recurse into a different class. If that class matches and returns a `tree::IdentifierReference`, we know this represents member access.

Of course, I still need to define `IdentifierMemberAccess`, which simply looks as follows:

```
class IdentifierMemberAccess : public
      support::RecursiveParser<IdentifierMemberAccess,
                               ParseTraits> {
public:
    static void partial_match() {}
    static IdentifierReference*
        recurse_one(lexer::token::punctuation::Dot) {
            return nullptr;
    }
    static ParseStateReturn
    match(TokenIterator begin, TokenIterator end,
          lexer::token::punctuation::Dot,
          std::shared_ptr<const tree::IdentifierReference> m) {
              return {m, begin, end};
    }
};
```

As you may have noticed, this requires a new `recurse_one` case as well, which will recurse back to `IdentifierReference` and return the `IdentifierReference` directly. This allows the parser to recursively capture member access expressions, such as `foo.bar.baz`, returning a tree structure of `foo` accessing the `bar` member, which in turn accesses the `baz` member.

The difference between `recurse_one` and `recurse_maybe` is whether they represent optional elements in the parse or not. In the case of `IdentifierReference`, it is possible that there isn't member access, but an `IdentifierMemberAccess` must match an `IdentifierReference` after the dot.

All of this gets expanded at compile time in a type-safe way, easily constructing the parse tree matching the structure of the language itself.

I will not get into all the details of the `RecursiveParser` implementation, since it is actually just variations on this same theme to support things such as alternatives and multiple matches.

You can see the entire implementation in pull request #38 (`https://github.com/PacktPublishing/Building-Programming-Language-Interpreters/pull/38`), which also includes the initial grammars that I used here, as well as additional ones.

In the next section, we will complete the entire grammar along with the tests required to show that the stream of tokens has been converted into a parse tree.

Getting the parse tree

Different parsing libraries will provide different approaches here. In some cases, you have more control, and in some cases less. With the grammar engine that I built for the project, however, it gives me complete control to assemble the parse tree in the way that makes the most sense to me.

In the previous section, I introduced a few initial parts of the grammar, building `IdentifierReference`. The code also included the literals and the data type declarations.

There is a reason why I started that way. You always want to build the grammar, as with the tree objects, from the inside out, since the outer syntactical elements need to reference the inner ones.

The process, from this point forward, is a simple matter of expanding the grammar and writing tests until the entire grammar is complete.

For that, I will start with the data section of the message, which needs first the pair defining the name of a variable and its type:

```
param: int;
```

So, we have an identifier, a colon, and another identifier, followed by a semicolon. Using the grammar engine, this results in the following declaration:

```
class MessageDataPair : public
    support::RecursiveParser<MessageDataPair, ParseTraits> {
public:
    static void partial_match() {}
    static void partial_match(lexer::token::Identifier) {}
    static Type *recurse_one(lexer::token::Identifier,
```

```
        lexer::token::punctuation::KeyValueSeparator) {
        return nullptr;
    }
    static void partial_match(lexer::token::Identifier,
        lexer::token::punctuation::KeyValueSeparator,
        std::shared_ptr<const tree::Type>) {}
    static ParseStateReturn match(
        TokenIterator begin, TokenIterator end,
        lexer::token::Identifier identifier,
        lexer::token::punctuation::KeyValueSeparator,
        std::shared_ptr<const tree::Type> type,
        lexer::token::punctuation::StatementEnd) {
        auto pair =
            std::make_shared<const tree::MessageDataPair>(
             identifier.name, type);
        return {pair, begin, end};
    }
};
```

The `MessageDataPair` class represents a rule in the grammar. It uses `partial_match` declarations to match the identifier token for the name of the data member. Then, it recurses into the `IdentifierReference` rule described earlier, which, if successful, will produce a `std::shared_ptr<const tree::Type>`. This is still a partial match until the final `match` declaration is reached, when `token::StatementEnd` is found.

The contents of the `match` function will then transform the sequence of tokens into the parse tree object, the `MessageDataPair`. So, whenever that rule is matched, it just returns the pair with the name and the type. Now, I just need to include the wrapping envelope:

```
data: { foo: int; }
```

I will not include the entire class, since it will start to become very repetitive, but the interesting part is the `match` method:

```
    static ParseStateReturn
    match(TokenIterator begin, TokenIterator end,
          lexer::token::Identifier identifier,
          lexer::token::punctuation::KeyValueSeparator,
          lexer::token::punctuation::CurlyBraceOpen,
```

```
        std::vector<std::shared_ptr<const
            tree::MessageDataPair>> fields,
            lexer::token::punctuation::CurlyBraceClose) {
      auto map = std::make_shared<tree::MessageData>();
      for (auto &pair : fields) {
          map->emplace(pair->first, pair->second);
      }
      return { map, begin, end };
  }
```

The part I want to highlight is the transformation that is already happening here, where the matching is already transforming the list of pairs into a map. This is going to be a lot more useful later, and it provides a better representation of the semantics of the syntax, even if the parsing needs the intermediate list of pairs.

We can conclude this with a test, to check that we're building the parse tree that we expect:

```
TEST(MessageDataTest, MessageDataMatch) {
    auto maybe_tokens = lexer::tokenize(
      "data: { param: int; other: foo<bar=42>; }");
    ASSERT_TRUE(maybe_tokens.has_value());
    std::vector<lexer::Token> &tokens = maybe_tokens.value();
    auto result =
        parser::grammar::MessageData::parse(tokens.cbegin(),
        tokens.cend());
    ASSERT_EQ(result.begin, tokens.cend());
    ASSERT_TRUE(result.node.has_value());
    auto map = std::get<std::shared_ptr<const
        parser::tree::MessageData>>(
        result.node.value());
    auto p1 = map->at("param");
    ASSERT_EQ("int", p1->name->name);
    auto p2 = map->at("other");
    ASSERT_EQ("foo", p2->name->name);
    auto p2map = p2->parameters;
    auto p2v1 = p2map->at("bar");
    ASSERT_EQ(42,
      std::get<std::shared_ptr<
```

```
        const parser::tree::IntegerLiteral>>(p2v1)->value);
}
```

The test starts by tokenizing a string. The resulting list of tokens is then given to the `parse` function of the `MessageData` class. The test then proceeds to validate that the data structure has the expected format with the expected values.

I am not covering the implementation of the parsing of the `tokens` section of the message, since it looks very similar to the code I introduced here. You can see the complete code for this section, including the tests, in pull request #39 (`https://github.com/PacktPublishing/Building-Programming-Language-Interpreters/pull/39`).

Before proceeding any further, I want to talk a little bit about the experience of implementing parsers. There will be points where you will inevitably get stuck and not really understand where things are wrong in your grammar.

This has certainly been the case for me, where a small mistake in the declaration can mean that something you think should match does not. When you have so much recursion in the execution, using an interactive debugger can be very frustrating.

Therefore, it's important to trace where the execution is in the token stream and what recursion path has been taken. In pull request #40 (`https://github.com/PacktPublishing/Building-Programming-Language-Interpreters/pull/40`), I introduced that feature in the grammar engine. The output looks something as follows:

```
(1) > partial_match MessageDataPair (0): fieldName : ...
 (2) > partial_match MessageDataPair (1): : FieldType ;
  (3) > recurse_one MessageDataPair (2): FieldType ;
   (4) > partial_match Type (0): FieldType ;
    (5) > recurse_maybe Type (1): ;
     (6) > partial_match TypeParameters (0): ;
      (7) > unknown TypeParameters (1):
     (6) < TypeParameters [FAIL]
    (5) < TypeParameters [FAIL]
   (4) < Type [FAIL] ;
    (5) > match Type (2): ;
   (4) < Type [SUCCESS] ;
  (3) < Type [SUCCESS] ;
   (4) > partial_match MessageDataPair (3): ;
    (5) > match MessageDataPair (4):
```

```
      (4) < MessageDataPair [SUCCESS]
     (3) < MessageDataPair [SUCCESS]
    (2) < MessageDataPair [SUCCESS] ;
   (1) < MessageDataPair [SUCCESS] FieldType ;
  (0) < MessageDataPair [SUCCESS] : FieldType ;
```

This trace gives you a clear view of how the execution works, including which areas of the grammar were explored, such as when the parser invokes `recurse_maybe`. The number in parentheses at the beginning of each line represents the level of recursion in the engine (how many recursive calls have been made to the `parse` function). When entering a rule, a greater-than sign shows which kind of match the parser looked for, the name of the rule, the number of tokens, and a visualization of the tokens. When leaving a rule, a lesser-than sign shows the name of the matched rule and the result in square brackets.

Most parsing libraries will offer some mechanism to trace the execution like this, and I definitely recommend learning how it works for whatever library you decide to use.

The work for finishing the grammar is an iterative process of adding more rules, and adding tests for those rules, until you get to the point where you can parse the entire source code.

I will not go into the details of every one of those. You can see the entire code for the completed grammar in pull request #41 (`https://github.com/PacktPublishing/Building-Programming-Language-Interpreters/pull/41`). The final test actually reads a file with the entire program I have been working with, and validates that the tree contains the data that is expected.

Summary

Creating a parser is an exercise in translating a sequence of tokens into a hierarchical data structure that represents the syntax of the language. This does not yet describe how the code will run, but it's an important step before that.

The first step is identifying what the data types are that you will need in your parse tree, and how the semantics of the language syntax are going to be represented in those objects.

That is going to be directly connected with the grammar for the language. It's important to explore the language definition in a way that is simple to get a complete picture. You may identify deficiencies at that point, and it's easier to make any changes before you actually implement the parser.

When writing a parser, it's important to evaluate all the different options that you have for existing libraries, their benefits, and their caveats. There are different kinds of grammars that require different levels of sophistication of the grammar engine. But as a language designer, it's also important to keep in mind that you also have the power to avoid language design choices that make the implementation harder.

That being said, with the features from C++20, such as concepts, there is a lot of power in the language itself. That means that it's not necessarily a bad idea to just implement the parser directly. In this case, I demonstrated that it's possible to implement an entire grammar engine capable of handling a domain-specific language in less than 400 lines of code.

Finally, once you have chosen or built a parsing library, comes the iterative process of going from the inner to the outer rules of the grammar, since they reference each other. As the parsing is done, you need to assemble the parse tree, using the types that you designed up front.

In the next chapter, I will focus on transforming the parse tree into an abstract syntax tree, bringing us closer to being able to actually execute the code.

15

Analyzing: Turning a Parse Tree into an Abstract Syntax Tree

The parse tree doesn't necessarily present itself in a way that makes it easy to process what the code is meant to do. Oftentimes, it contains redundant information or is organized in a way that is focused on allowing the grammar to be specified in a non-ambiguous way. Therefore, before we generate actual instructions, we need to transform the parse tree into a data structure that better represents the semantics of the language.

In this chapter, I will focus on the process of producing a representation of the code that represents the semantics of the execution of the code, even if it doesn't yet correspond to the actual interpreter operations. This will include the following:

- Exploring the differences between the parse tree and the abstract syntax tree and the different roles they play
- Modeling the types that we need to represent the semantics of the language
- Going through the code necessary to perform that transformation

By the end of this chapter, you will have practical experience in modeling the semantics of a programming language into an abstract syntax tree, as well as performing the actual transformation.

Difference between a parse tree and an abstract syntax tree

When implementing a parser, the primary concern is having a structure that correctly represents how the syntax of the language is laid out in text. When generating code, however, you need a representation that more precisely describes the semantics of the code.

The term we use for that second structure is **abstract syntax tree** (**AST**). It's referred to as *abstract* because it's not yet concrete execution code, nor is it a parse tree.

A parse tree must represent aspects that are specific to the rules of the grammar, even if those end up not being how the code itself is going to be executed. On the other hand, an AST abstracts away grammar-related details.

For instance, the parse tree for the language that I have been building is focused on the messages and the elements that form them. But what the language is actually describing is two different state machines—one for the server and one for the client—the possible transitions between those states, and which one of the agents is meant to be reading or writing them.

In fact, in *Chapter 9, Putting It All Together and Creating a Coherent Vision*, I specifically focused on that aspect when designing the language, and therefore it is a lot more useful if the AST actually represents those semantics.

The semantic analysis is the process that will transform the parse tree into the AST, which will bring our understanding of the code a lot closer to what will actually be executed.

In the next section, I will focus on modeling the data structures needed to represent the semantics of the programming language.

Modeling the node types and their data structures

Contrary to when we were designing the parse tree, in the case of the AST, it really makes sense to start from the top-level types rather than the details. This is not just a matter of preference—the modeling exercise here aims to describe the semantics of the language at a higher level than what we were working with when parsing.

Therefore, I will start with the definition of the `Protocol` class, which is the top-level node of the AST:

```
struct Protocol {
    std::shared_ptr<const Agent> client;
```

```
    std::shared_ptr<const Agent> server;
};
```

A protocol description has very different interpretations depending on which agent—client or server—you are thinking about. So, the approach I'm taking here is to create entirely independent parts of the tree representing the semantics of the client and the server.

In the parse tree, this was embedded into the syntax, but here, this is the main element. The semantics of the client and server agents go from simple identifiers in the syntax to being first-class citizens in the semantics of the language.

Next, I'll focus on the `Agent` class:

```
struct Agent {
    std::map<std::string,
             std::shared_ptr<const State>> states;
};
```

This design flips the parse tree inside out: instead of representing messages, it represents the states for each agent. The parse tree was indexed by the name of the messages, with the states being attributes in each one of them, while the AST will be indexed by the states, with the messages being the transitions that are valid in each state.

That's important because these states define the actual semantics that are being described by the language, even if the syntax is focused on the messages.

Now, let's move to the `State` class:

```
struct State {
    std::map<std::string,
        std::pair<Transition, std::string>> transitions;
};
```

Now we finally have the name of the message showing up in the tree. For instance, when the client is in the `"Open"` state, there are two transitions possible: the client may either close the connection or send a request.

Beyond knowing what the transition looks like, we also need to know what state the agent will be left with after the transition is executed.

Before getting into the transition, I want to exemplify, using pseudo-code, what the AST for the code of the HTTP protocol would look like so far:

```
Protocol(
  client=Agent(
    states={
      "Open": State(
        transitions={
          "HTTP Request": <Transition(…), "AwaitResponse">,
          "Client Closes Connection":
            <Transition(…), "Closed">
        }
      ),
      "AwaitResponse": State(
        transitions={
          "HTTP Response": <Transition(…), "Open">
        }
      ),
      "Closed": State(transitions={})
    }
  )
  server=Agent(
    states={
      "Open": State(
        transitions={
          "HTTP Request": <Transition(…), "AwaitResponse",
          "Client Closes Connection":
            <Transition(…), "Closed"
        }
      ),
      "AwaitResponse": State(
        transitions={
          "HTTP Response": <Transition(…), "Open"
        }
      ),
      "Closed": State(transitions={})
    }
  )
```

You've probably noticed that the client and server sections actually look the same so far, and that's perfectly expected, since the high-level state machine is the same for both agents. However, it's when we get to the transitions that things get very different. To explain, let me start with the definition of `Transition` itself:

```
struct AbstractTransition {
    std::shared_ptr<const parser::tree::MessageData> data;
    std::vector<Action> actions;
    AbstractTransition(
    const std::shared_ptr<const parser::tree::MessageData>
     &d,
    const std::vector<Action> &a)
    : data(d), actions(a) {}
};
struct ReadTransition : public AbstractTransition {
    using AbstractTransition::AbstractTransition;
};
struct WriteTransition : public AbstractTransition {
    using AbstractTransition::AbstractTransition;
};
using Transition = std::variant<std::shared_ptr<const ReadTransition>,
              std::shared_ptr<const WriteTransition>>;
```

This was not necessary, but it's important for the high-level state machine to understand what the role of the agent for that particular transition is. It would have been possible to encode whether a transition is a read or write via an enum, but using the type system of the C++ language to encode those semantics allows the compiler to catch incorrect usage, making some illegal states harder to represent.

Essentially, when the server is in the `"Open"` state, both transitions are `ReadTransition` objects, meaning the server's execution is passive. On the other hand, when the client has two `WriteTransition` objects in the `"Open"` state, it means the client has an active role at that point.

I also decided not to transform `MessageData` from the parse tree, because it already contains the necessary semantic fields (names, types, and terminator) in a normalized shape. If the parse tree had a lot of additional unnecessary structure, it would make sense to extract a cleaned semantic version of the data. The rule of thumb here is to remove unnecessary data when building the AST, but there's no need to create new data types when the representation is already good enough.

Now comes the point where the AST will look drastically different between the client and the server. We have to represent what the agent will actually have to do to perform that transition:

```
using Action = std::variant<
    std::shared_ptr<const action::ReadStaticOctets>,
    std::shared_ptr<const action::ReadOctetsUntilTerminator>,
    std::shared_ptr<const action::WriteFromIdentifier>,
    std::shared_ptr<const action::WriteStaticOctets>,
    std::shared_ptr<const action::Loop>>;
```

And surprisingly, those are the only actions that I needed to define when analyzing the code for the HTTP protocol. Let's go over each of them, starting with the two write actions:

```
struct WriteFromIdentifier {
    std::shared_ptr<const parser::tree::IdentifierReference>
        identifier;
};
struct WriteStaticOctets {
    std::string octets;
};
```

They are mostly self-explanatory. The first one writes data from a variable identified by `identifier`. The data section of the transition has the type information and any other details necessary to execute it. In the case of writing static octets, we can just store them directly in the AST node.

Let's go over the two read actions now:

```
struct ReadStaticOctets {
    std::string octets;
};
struct ReadOctetsUntilTerminator {
    std::string terminator;
    std::shared_ptr<const parser::tree::IdentifierReference>
         identifier;
};
```

They mostly mirror the two write actions, but in the case of reading dynamic content, we also need to know what the terminator is, beyond knowing to which variable it needs to write.

Finally, the last action we need to talk about is the loop action:

```
struct Loop {
    std::shared_ptr<const parser::tree::IdentifierReference>
        variable;
    std::shared_ptr<const parser::tree::IdentifierReference>
        collection;
    std::string terminator;
    std::vector<Action> actions;
    // constructors omitted for brevity
};
```

This represents which variable contains the collection and which one will be used in the loop. It also includes a recursive definition of actions needed to be executed in that loop.

I will not go into every single transition, because it would be very repetitive; I'll just represent the writing and reading of the HTTP request message, using the same pseudo-code syntax I used before.

First are the actions for the client writing the message:

```
WriteTransition(
    data=…,
    actions=[
        WriteFromIdentifier("verb"),
        WriteStaticOctets(" "),
        WriteFromIdentifier("request_target"),
        WriteStaticOctets(" "),
        WriteStaticOctets("HTTP/"),
        WriteFromIdentifier("major_version"),
        WriteStaticOctets("."),
        WriteFromIdentifier("minor_version"),
        WriteStaticOctets("\r\n"),
        Loop(
            collection="headers",
            variable="header",
            terminator="\r\n",
            actions=[
                WriteFromIdentifier("header.key"),
                WriteStaticOctets(":")
```

```
                WriteFromIdentifier("header.value")
                WriteStaticOctets("\r\n")
            ]
        )
    ]
)
```

You can see that, at this point, there's very little resemblance to the parse tree, and we are very specifically representing the execution semantics. To contrast, let's go over the actions for the server receiving the request message:

```
ReadTransition(
    data=…,
    actions=[
        ReadOctetsUntilTerminator(
            identifier="verb", terminator=" "),
        ReadOctetsUntilTerminator(
            identifier="request_target", terminator=" "),
        ReadStaticOctets("HTTP/")
        ReadOctetsUntilTerminator(
            identifier="major_version", terminator="."),
        ReadOctetsUntilTerminator(
            identifier="minor_version", terminator="\r\n"),
        Loop(
            collection="headers",
            variable="header",
            terminator="\r\n",
            actions=[
                ReadOctetsUntilTerminator(
                identifier="header.key", terminator=":"),
                ReadOctetsUntilTerminator(
                identifier="header.value", terminator="\r\n")
            ]
        )
    ]
)
```

At this point, I am very confident that we can correctly represent the semantics of the execution, and more importantly, we're getting closer to being able to generate the interpreter operations directly from this.

Whenever you are designing your own AST, that is the main goal that you should aim for. Try to remove any information that is only relevant for the parsing phase, and bring the semantics of the data closer to what is necessary to actually generate executable code.

Also, as in this case, feel free to completely introduce new concepts that were not present at all in the parse tree.

In the next section, I will focus on the code necessary to transform the parse tree into the AST.

Transforming one tree into another

There are various approaches that you can take to make that transformation. In some cases, it makes sense to do a manual navigation of the parse tree, and in other cases, it will make sense to use more advanced techniques to match the structures and generate the new one.

In the case of this particular AST, I ended up with a mix of the two. When assembling the high-level state machine, I used a manual traversal, but when generating the actions, I had to switch to something closer to a visitor pattern.

Regardless of the technique used, this is still a function that takes one tree and returns another:

```
std::optional<std::shared_ptr<const ast::Protocol>>
analyze(std::shared_ptr<
    const parser::tree::ProtocolDescription> &protocol);
```

There are different approaches to handling failures at this step. If failure is expected to be common and part of control flow—for example, during incremental parsing in the IDE—it's usually better to return a `std::optional` object or an error object to avoid exceptions. If failures are exceptional and indicate a programmer error or an unrecoverable parse state, throwing exceptions with rich diagnostics (such as source position or message) may be appropriate. My example uses `std::optional` because it fits a pipeline where the caller decides how to report/aggregate errors.

For transforming the tree, as for designing the types, I prefer to start explaining from the outside and then get into the details as the code evolves.

So, let's look at the main `analyze` function:

```
    auto maybe_client = analyze_agent(protocol, "Client");
    auto maybe_server = analyze_agent(protocol, "Server");
    if (maybe_client.has_value() &&
        maybe_server.has_value()) {
            return std::make_shared<ast::Protocol>(
                    maybe_client.value(),
                    maybe_server.value());
    }
    return std::nullopt;
```

This is fairly self-explanatory. As discussed in the previous section, the AST is divided in the very beginning between the client-side and server-side interpretations of the protocol.

Since we identify them by the `"Client"` and `"Server"` strings, we just need to tell the `analyze` function which side it needs to look at. As we move to the `analyze_agent` function, things start to get more interesting.

In this first part of the process, I will implement a manual traversal technique, because the shape of the parse tree is pretty static and, therefore, there's not much that needs to be discovered.

The transformation is, of course, profoundly dependent on what the data types of both the parse tree and the AST are, so the implementation will vary based on the specific context.

In my case, I need to identify the transitions triggered by the messages and the states for the agents. Let me start with just the signature for extracting the transitions:

```
static std::optional<std::map<std::string, ast::Transition>>
analyze_transitions(
        std::shared_ptr<
            const parser::tree::ProtocolDescription> &protocol,
        const std::string &agent_name);
```

This function returns a map, where the string key is the name of the message and the value is the transition itself. `ProtocolDescription` was introduced in the previous chapter, and it is a map where the key is the name of the message and the value is the `Message` node of the parse tree. With that, I should be able to assemble the states:

```
// get the transition generated by each message
auto maybe_transitions = analyze_transitions(protocol,
      agent_name);
if (!maybe_transitions.has_value()) {
    return std::nullopt;
}
auto &transitions = maybe_transitions.value();
// assemble the states and transitions together
std::map<std::string, std::shared_ptr<ast::State>> states;
for (const auto &message : *protocol) {
    auto when_state = message.second->when->name;
    auto then_state = message.second->then->name;
    // make sure the states are created
    for (const auto &state_name:{when_state, then_state}) {
        if (states.find(state_name) == states.end()) {
            states[state_name] =
            std::make_shared<ast::State>();
        }
    }
// we need to add the transition of this message from
// the when_state to the then_state
states[when_state]->transitions[message.first] =
    std::make_pair(transitions[message.first],
                   then_state);
}
```

This is, again, reasonably self-explanatory. I am just flipping the data structure around, from one based on the transitions, which more closely resembles the parse tree, to one based on the states, which is more useful for the semantics of the language, which is probably something you will also be doing in your own language.

The next step is to generate the transitions in the `analyze_transitions` function:

```
    auto transitions = std::map<std::string,
                                ast::Transition>();
    for (const auto &message : *protocol) {
        auto maybe_transition =
            message.second->agent->name == agent_name
            ? analyze_write_message(message.second)
            : analyze_read_message(message.second);
        if (!maybe_transition.has_value()) {
            return std::nullopt;
        }
        transitions[message.first] = maybe_transition.value();
    }
    return transitions;
```

This is where the semantics of the agent's behavior in the context of each message are encoded. For example, when handling the HTTP request message, I will call `analyze_write_message` for the client while calling `analyze_read_message` for the server.

This is a good example of how the semantics are being taken to a significantly higher level of abstraction, because we're taking various pieces of information from various parts of the parse tree and assembling them into a coherent description of what the program actually does.

For the last step of this manual traversal, I define the transitions themselves:

```
static std::optional<ast::Transition>
analyze_write_message(const std::shared_ptr<
    const parser::tree::Message> &message) {
    auto maybe_actions =
        parts_to_write_actions(message->parts);
    if (!maybe_actions.has_value()) {
        return std::nullopt;
    }
    return std::make_shared<const ast::WriteTransition>(
          message->data, maybe_actions.value());
}
static std::optional<ast::Transition>
analyze_read_message(const std::shared_ptr<
    const parser::tree::Message> &message) {
```

```
    auto maybe_actions =
        parts_to_read_actions(message->parts);
    if (!maybe_actions.has_value()) {
        return std::nullopt;
    }
    return std::make_shared<const ast::ReadTransition>(
            message->data, maybe_actions.value());
}
```

This implements the two different types for `ReadTransition` and `WriteTransition`, which defines, in our AST, the behavior of the agent on that particular transition.

Processing the actions for the message is where things get a bit more interesting, because it doesn't really have a fixed structure, and instead, I need to produce various AST nodes based on the list of `MessageParts`.

It gets even more interesting when you think about syntactic elements such as the `for` loop, since you essentially have recursive types, where you may have nested loops, so doing a full manual traversal will become very tedious very fast.

At this point, I realized that the engine that was used to transform the list of tokens into a parse tree could be used to process a list of message parts into the AST.

This may or may not be applicable to your own situation, but the important message here is to consider the possibility of exploring different programming techniques, taking some influence from more functional styles in order to make your code easier to write and maintain.

I will not cover both the read and write action analysis, because they look very similar in structure, but I think it is worth going through the read case in full.

If you think carefully about it, the process of transforming a tree is not that dissimilar to the process of parsing a sequence of tokens, but it does have a few differences, which I hope will become clear as I go.

Since I am using the same engine as I used for the parser, I need to start by defining the traits:

```
using ParseStateTraits =
    parser::support::ParseStateTraits<
        std::vector<
            parser::grammar::ParseTraits::ParseNode
        >::const_iterator,
```

```
        std::variant<
            std::vector<ast::Action>,
            ast::Action
        >
    >;
```

As a refresher, the first argument to ParseStateTraits defines the type of iterator that the parser will navigate through. Since I am working with the parse tree, I can use the original variant used when producing the parse tree as input. The second argument defines the output, which will be either a single action or a list of actions.

With that, I should be able to define the parts_to_read_actions function:

```
std::optional<std::vector<ast::Action>> parts_to_read_actions(const
std::shared_ptr<
        const parser::tree::MessageSequence> &parts) {
    auto full_sequence = unroll_variant(*parts);
    auto r = PartSequenceToReadActions::parse(
        full_sequence.cbegin(),
        full_sequence.cend());
    if (r.node.has_value()) {
        return flatten_actions(r.node.value());
    } else {
        return std::nullopt;
    }
}
```

There are a couple of things here that are potentially not obvious. The first is that the parse tree has a more specific type for the message parts, so I need to convert it into the type that matches the expected input:

```
template <typename V>
inline std::vector<ParseStateTraits::TokenIterator::value_type>
unroll_variant(const V &v) {
    auto r = std::vector<
        ParseStateTraits::TokenIterator::value_type>();
    for (const auto &part : v) {
        std::visit([&](auto &&arg) { r.push_back(arg); },
            *part);
    }
```

```
    return r;
}
```

The `unroll_variant` function will be used on various occasions, as we process different lists of nodes from the parse tree that have more specific types. This is a bit of a pessimization, because it causes the copying of the vectors, and it could be optimized away, but that would make the remaining code significantly more complicated.

The second non-obvious thing is the flattening of actions into a single vector. As we process the parse tree, we may end up with various vectors of actions, so we need to make sure we end up with just a flat list of actions:

```
inline void append_actions(
        std::vector<ast::Action> &actions,
        const std::vector<ast::Action> &new_actions) {
    actions.insert(
        actions.end(),
        new_actions.cbegin(), new_actions.cend());
}
inline void append_actions(
        std::vector<ast::Action> &actions,
        ast::Action new_action) {
    actions.push_back(new_action);
}
inline std::vector<ast::Action>
flatten_actions(ParseStateTraits::ParseNode node) {
    std::vector<ast::Action> actions;
    std::visit([&](auto &&t) {
        append_actions(actions, t);
    }, node);
    return actions;
}
inline std::vector<ast::Action>
flatten_actions(
    std::vector<ParseStateTraits::ParseNode> nodes) {
    std::vector<ast::Action> actions;
    for (const auto &node : nodes) {
        auto flattened = flatten_actions(node);
        actions.insert(actions.end(),
```

```
            flattened.cbegin(), flattened.cend());
    }
    return actions;
}
```

Basically, you can call `flatten_actions` with various different inputs, and you will always get back a single, normalized vector of actions. This will become more useful later.

With this set up, now I can start declaring the classes that will implement the parsing of message parts. Let's start from the outermost one:

```
class PartSequenceToReadActions
    : public parser::support::RecursiveParser<
        PartSequenceToReadActions, ParseStateTraits> {
public:
    static PartSequenceFragmentToReadActions
        *recurse_many() { return nullptr; };
    static void partial_match(std::vector<ast::Action>){};
    static void
        partial_match(std::vector<std::vector<ast::Action>>){};
    static void partial_match(std::vector<ParseNode>){};
    static ParseStateReturn match(
        TokenIterator begin, TokenIterator end,
        std::vector<ast::Action> actions, EndOfInput) {
        return {actions, begin, end};
    }
    static ParseStateReturn match(
        TokenIterator begin, TokenIterator end,
        std::vector<std::vector<ast::Action>> actions,
        EndOfInput) {
        std::vector<ast::Action> result;
        for (const auto &a : actions) {
            result.insert(result.end(), a.cbegin(), a.cend());
        }
        return {result, begin, end};
    }
    static ParseStateReturn match(
        TokenIterator begin, TokenIterator end,
```

```
        std::vector<ParseNode> others, EndOfInput) {
        return {flatten_actions(others), begin, end};
    }
};
```

As with the parser grammars, the key to understanding this code is following the number of arguments, so when the `PartSequenceToReadActions` parser starts, it calls `recurse_many` on `PartSequenceFragmentToReadActions`, which I'll define later. Then it performs a `partial_match` function on the result (which may be represented in a few different ways), but it only does a match with the `EndOfInput` argument, to make sure we parse the sequence completely.

In other words, in this first phase, the parser will match multiple fragments and ensure that no part of the sequence is left unmatched. If that's the case, the parse will fail and the analysis will stop.

The first part of this process is to define a rule for the parser engine in the form of a class that inherits from `RecursiveParser`. I will dive into the specific methods in the class one at a time:

```
class PartSequenceFragmentToReadActions
  : public parser::support::RecursiveParser<
    PartSequenceFragmentToReadActions, ParseStateTraits> {
public:
    // will cover later
}
```

The first step is to specify the partial matches for the empty sequence and for the token sequence from the parse tree. Essentially, I'm traversing all the parts of a message, and want to make sure they are consumed before attempting the specific matches, whether it's a token sequence or a `for` loop:

```
    static void partial_match(){};
    static void partial_match(
        std::shared_ptr<const parser::tree::TokenSequence>){};
    static void partial_match(
        std::shared_ptr<const parser::tree::MessageForLoop>){};
```

Now we can look at specific situations where we have a token sequence followed by a terminator. At this point, we can assemble a single action, related to the token sequence followed by the terminator. The following example illustrates this case:

```
tokens { a b c }
terminator { " " }
```

You can notice that this will explicitly recurse into the `parse` function for `TokenSequence`, in order to translate the tokens into the AST nodes:

```
static ParseStateReturn
match(TokenIterator begin, TokenIterator end,
    std::shared_ptr<const parser::tree::TokenSequence>
     token_sequence,
    std::shared_ptr<const parser::tree::Terminator>
     terminator) {
// Parse the token sequence, but add the terminator to
// the end
auto full_sequence =
    unroll_variant(token_sequence->tokens);
full_sequence.push_back(terminator->value);
auto r = TokenSequence::parse(
    full_sequence.cbegin(), full_sequence.cend());
return {r.node, begin, end};
}
```

When a token sequence is at the end of the message, it doesn't necessarily need a terminator. Since the previous `match` requires a terminator, the sequence at the end wouldn't match. The code would look like the following as the last sequence in the parts of the message:

```
tokens { " " }
```

To address this, we specifically use `EndOfInput` in the signature for the `match` function:

```
static ParseStateReturn
match(TokenIterator begin, TokenIterator end,
    std::shared_ptr<const parser::tree::TokenSequence>
        token_sequence, EndOfInput) {
    // Parse the token sequence
    auto full_sequence =
        unroll_variant(token_sequence->tokens);
    auto r = TokenSequence::parse(
        full_sequence.cbegin(), full_sequence.cend());
    return {r.node, begin, end};
}
```

Finally, now we can handle the case of the `for` loop with a terminator. The code for the `for` loop looks like the following:

```
for var in collection { … }
terminator { " " }
```

The code to handle the `for` loop is different than that for the token sequence case, because it essentially needs to recurse back to the `PartSequenceToReadActions` rule, since the body of the `for` loop follows the same rule as the outer message body:

```
    static ParseStateReturn
    match(TokenIterator begin, TokenIterator end,
          std::shared_ptr<const parser::tree::MessageForLoop>
            loop,
          std::shared_ptr<const parser::tree::Terminator>
            terminator) {
    auto l = std::make_shared<ast::action::Loop>(
        loop->variable, loop->collection,
        terminator->value->value);
    auto full_sequence = unroll_variant(*(loop->block));
    auto r = PartSequenceToReadActions::parse(
      full_sequence.cbegin(),
      full_sequence.cend());
    if (r.node.has_value()) {
      std::visit([&](auto &&t) {
         append_actions(l->actions, t); },
                 r.node.value());
      return {l, begin, end};
    } else {
      return {std::nullopt, begin, end};
    }
  }
};
```

The parser first performs the `partial_match` function on an empty sequence, then a partial match on `TokenSequence`, with a match on either `Terminator` or `EndOfInput`. It can also allow `MessageForLoop` followed by `Terminator`.

In the case of the `for` loop, it recurses into `PartSequenceToReadActions`, which will perform the same logic again, producing a list of actions, but it wraps it in the loop action (so it's not flattened).

In the case of `TokenSequence` followed by `Terminator`, the parser unrolls the variant and adds `Terminator` to the list. When followed by an `EndOfInput` type, it just processes the tokens.

The processing of `TokenSequence` is a bit different, because it needs to start a new context for processing. It recurses into an entirely new `parse` function, operating on a new sequence of inputs—in this case, what goes inside the `tokens` block.

Next, I'll go over `TokenSequence` itself:

```
class TokenSequence : public parser::support::RecursiveParser<
                  TokenSequence, ParseStateTraits> {
public:
    static IndividualTokenAction *recurse_many() {
        return nullptr; };
    static void partial_match(std::vector<ast::Action>){};
    static ParseStateReturn match(
          TokenIterator begin, TokenIterator end,
          std::vector<ast::Action> actions, EndOfInput) {
        return {actions, begin, end};
    }
};
```

Like the outside of the message parts, this parser just recurses over many token actions, just making sure that it goes to the end of the input. With that, we get to the final piece:

```
class IndividualTokenAction
    : public parser::support::RecursiveParser<
          IndividualTokenAction, ParseStateTraits> {
public:
    static void partial_match(){};
    static ParseStateReturn
    match(TokenIterator begin, TokenIterator end,
          std::shared_ptr<const parser::tree::StringLiteral>
          lit) {
        return {std::make_shared<
          const ast::action::ReadStaticOctets>(lit->value),
          begin, end};
```

```
    }
    static void partial_match(std::shared_ptr<
        const parser::tree::IdentifierReference>){};
    static ParseStateReturn
    match(TokenIterator begin, TokenIterator end,
            std::shared_ptr<const parser::tree::IdentifierReference>
            id, std::shared_ptr<const parser::tree::StringLiteral>
            lit) {
        return {std::make_shared<
            const ast::action::ReadOctetsUntilTerminator>(
            lit->value, id),
            begin, end};
    }
};
```

At this stage, the parser expects either a string literal, which means a straightforward `ReadStaticOctets` action, or an identifier, which needs to be followed by a string literal to tell what the terminator is.

That is essentially all the code needed to transform the parse tree into the AST. Of course, your language will have very different requirements, most likely, but I am hoping that this exercise has given you a practical understanding of the kinds of techniques that may be needed to transform a parse tree into an AST.

You can look at the code for the transformation on the write transitions as well as the final test code that inspects the entire AST for the HTTP protocol description in pull request #42 (`https://github.com/PacktPublishing/Building-Programming-Language-Interpreters/pull/42/files`).

Summary

An AST is a representation of the code that has a lot of higher-level semantics about how the code will actually be interpreted, while a parse tree is very focused on what's required by the grammar engine.

There are many things that will be present in the parse tree but can be eliminated from the AST; at the same time, there are entirely new data structures. This is important because it gets us closer to what will be needed to actually generate code.

Designing the types for the AST of your language will require a lot of thought, while keeping in mind the relationship with the interpreter itself, as you want to start representing the semantics of how the code will run.

In the case of the language being designed in this book, that involved transforming the messages described by the parse tree into the state machines of the different agents, as well as identifying what all the actions those agents will need to take are.

Once you define the types for your AST, you then need to engage various programming techniques to be able to transform one tree into the other. At some points, you will have to use a manual traversal, and in other cases, you may need more functional styles. In the example used here, I actually used the same engine that was used for the parsing.

In the next chapter, I will get to the final step of this process, which is to actually generate the executable code in terms of the interpreter operations.

16

Generating: Turning an Abstract Syntax Tree into Instructions

While the **abstract syntax tree (AST)** is now much closer to the semantics of the execution of the code from the programming language, it still does not represent actual executable instructions. The interpreter only knows how to process an operation tree, and we have now finally gotten to the point where we will complete the loop, all the way from source code to the executable instructions.

In this chapter, I will focus on the challenges and the practical approach involved in the transformation of the AST into the operations the interpreter can run. The following topics will be covered:

- Traversing AST nodes and transforming them into an operation tree, including identifying and creating any missing operations
- Producing the final operation tree for the entire program
- Integrating the final interface of the interpreter, from source code to execution
- Running the interpreter in a testing environment

By the end of this chapter, you will have practical experience in how to identify the right operations from the AST, how to translate them into the operation tree, and how to produce the final interpreter.

Matching AST nodes to interpreter operations

So far, I have been exercising the interpreter execution in a limited context. In *Chapter 9, Putting It All Together and Creating a Coherent Vision*, I presented two levels of state machines for the execution of the code. At a higher level, there is a state machine that defines when different messages can be expected and what state transition they represent. At a lower level, it defines how each message needs to be produced or consumed.

In *Chapter 12, Running and Testing Language Operators*, I implemented the operations required for processing the state of a single message in the context of both reading and writing it.

Now, as I see the AST that was produced in *Chapter 15, Analyzing: Turning a Parse Tree into an Abstract Syntax Tree*, it is clear that I am missing the operations for handling the higher-level state machine.

This is a good way to illustrate what this process will look like for your own interpreter, because I am starting from the first node in the AST—the high-level state machine—and then I am trying to visualize how its execution happens.

Looking back at the example source code that describes HTTP in *Chapter 9*, I can see that the server will need to be able to decide which one of the two transitions from the `"Open"` state will be taken, and that needs to happen before the interpreter actively consumes the data, since the message itself determines what happens.

When you go through this process on your own interpreter, you will likely need to create new operations, and this is mostly an exercise in imagination, as you have to create the mechanisms for the execution to happen.

Let's start by introducing one such operation—`TransitionLookAhead`.

Introducing the TransitionLookAhead operation

So far, when reading a message, there are only three possibilities:

- We expect a static string, such as when the server starts the response with `HTTP`
- We expect a string followed by a terminator, such as when the client sends `GET` followed by a space in the request
- We expect the closing of the connection, such as when the client doesn't want to send any more requests

Looking back at the AST, we know that the transitions have actions, so the intention is that this operation can be initialized based on the first action of each transition for a given state.

With that, I can define the following types:

```
struct EOFCondition {};
struct MatchUntilTerminator {
  std::string terminator;
};
using TransitionCondition =
    std::variant<EOFCondition,
                 MatchUntilTerminator,
                 std::string>;
```

This allows me to express a condition for a transition to be matched based on the three possibilities identified so far.

With that, I can define the operation itself. It will implement the `InputOutputOperationConcept` and will have the following member:

```
std::vector<std::pair<TransitionCondition, std::string>>
    conditions; // pair of condition and target state
```

This operation won't need any runtime parameters, and it can be implemented by simply checking what data the interpreter has received and returning `value::Octets` with the name of the matching transition.

As with the `TerminateListIfReadAhead` operation introduced in *Chapter 12*, this operation will never actually consume any input, but it will be looking at the buffer the interpreter has been accumulating while leaving the data to be processed by the operations in the actual message. The `handle_read` method simply stores the buffer in the operation context and returns `0` to indicate it is not going to consume anything:

```
std::size_t TransitionLookahead::handle_read(
    InputOutputOperationContext &ctx,
    std::string_view sv) const {
  ctx.buffer = sv;
  return 0;
}
```

When performing the lookahead, there are two possible outcomes. The first is that the condition for a transition hasn't yet been matched because the input is still too short, and the second is that it is already a mismatch, and the operation doesn't need to look further to know that.

I'll represent this with a function called `match_condition`, which will be used in `std::visit` of the `TransitionCondition` variant. Let's look at `EOFCondition` first:

```
std::pair<bool, bool>
TransitionLookahead::match_condition(
   InputOutputOperationContext &ctx,
   const EOFCondition &) {
  if (ctx.buffer.empty()) {
    if (ctx.eof) {
      return {true, true};
    } else {
      return {false, false};
    }
  } else {
    return {false, true};
  }
}
```

The first boolean in the pair represents whether the condition has already been matched, and the second represents that it already definitively doesn't match. Therefore, if the condition for the transition is the connection being closed, and the connection has been closed, it has already matched the condition, which is what the first `return` statement covers.

However, if the connection hasn't been closed, it may still be possible that it will be closed before any additional data is sent. Therefore, we only consider the condition completely resolved if any content has already been read.

When waiting for a terminator, the code is a bit simpler:

```
std::pair<bool, bool>
TransitionLookahead::match_condition(
    InputOutputOperationContext &ctx,
    const MatchUntilTerminator &c) {
  auto it = ctx.buffer.find(c.terminator);
  if (it != std::string::npos) {
    return {true, false};
  } else {
    return {false, ctx.eof};
  }
}
```

If the terminator is found, it means the condition is met. Otherwise, the condition is only definitively not met if the connection has already been closed.

Finally, we can get to the condition where a static string is expected:

```
std::pair<bool, bool>
TransitionLookahead::match_condition(
    InputOutputOperationContext &ctx,
    const std::string &c) {
  if (ctx.buffer.size() <= c.size()) {
    if (ctx.buffer.compare(0, ctx.buffer.size(),
                  c.substr(0, ctx.buffer.size())) != 0) {
      return {false, true};
    } else {
      return {false, ctx.eof};
    }
  } else {
    if (ctx.buffer.compare(0, c.size(), c) == 0) {
      return {true, false};
    } else {
      return {false, true};
  }
}
```

When comparing to a static string, we know how far we need to read before we have a definitive answer, but even with an incomplete string, we know that it already doesn't have a match.

Now I can finally get to the execution of the operation itself. I will start with the outermost part of the method and then dive into the details:

```
OperationResult TransitionLookahead::operator()(
  InputOutputOperationContext &ctx,
  const Arguments &) const {
  bool all_permanently_invalid = true;
  for (const auto &condition : conditions) {
    // more on that later
  }
  if (all_permanently_invalid) {
    return value::RuntimeError::ProtocolMismatchError;
  }
```

```
    return ReasonForBlockedOperation::WaitingForRead;
  }
```

The `TransitionLookAhead` operation will iterate through all the conditions. If they're all already invalid, it returns a `ProtocolMismatchError`, but if they're not yet a match and at least one of them could still be valid, it just returns that it's waiting for more data.

Now I can get into the body of the loop:

```
  const auto &cond = condition.first;
  const auto &target_state = condition.second;

  auto [is_valid, is_permanently_invalid] = std::visit(
      [&](const auto &c) {
        return match_condition(ctx, c);
      }, cond);
  if (is_valid) {
    return value::Octets{std::make_shared<std::string>(
      target_state)};
  }
  if (!is_permanently_invalid) {
    all_permanently_invalid = false;
  }
```

The code starts by calling `std::visit` on the `TransitionCondition` variant, using argument-dependent lookup to call one of the appropriate overloads listed earlier. If the condition matches positively, the operation will return an octet with the name of the target state, but if it does not match, it will check whether the condition could still be valid.

What I want to communicate here is the process of creating the mechanisms for the AST to become executable. One of the main benefits of creating your own interpreter is that you can create the operations that best suit the execution of your code. So don't be concerned about creating an overly specific operation if that would make your interpreter better.

This provides the logic that will be needed for `StateMachineOperation`, which is the subject of the next section. You can see the complete code for the `TransitionLookAhead` operation in pull request #44 (`https://github.com/PacktPublishing/Building-Programming-Language-Interpreters/pull/44`).

Introducing StateMachineOperation

Now that I have a mechanism for the interpreter to decide between different read transitions in a state, I need to implement the management of the high-level state machine as well.

I'm highlighting this operation because it is a good illustration of how much you can customize the interpreter by introducing fine-tailored operations for the specific use cases of your programming language. This is an operation that will do a lot of heavy lifting for the interpreter. It will not have any runtime parameters—all of its behavior will be defined in the operation tree itself.

At this point I also had to decide the general execution model for the state machine, so I decided to go with the following:

- When entering a state, the operation executes one `OpTree`
- The return of that execution should be a `value::DynamicList` with two elements
- The first element should contain a `value::Octets` with the name of the transition that is being taken
- The second element should contain a `value::Dictionary` that will be used in the transition
- When a transition starts, the values in the dictionary are translated as argument names for the transition's operation tree
- The transition's operation tree always returns a `value::DynamicList` with a single element of a `value::Dictionary`
- A transition has a static target state, and the `value::Dictionary` becomes the argument for the state's operation tree execution
- The `"Open"` and `"Closed"` states are special: the operation will automatically transition to the `"Open"` state, and automatically finish the execution when arriving at the `"Closed"` state

I think it's fair to say that this is a fairly complicated operation, but that complexity allows the entire state machine management to be centralized in this one operation. To be honest, it took me a lot of trial and error to arrive at this particular execution model, but that is the important lesson here.

Be open to thinking about the execution of your interpreter in the way that best fits the particular use case that you have. In this example, it was an exercise in making the integration simpler with a stable set of rules.

The way that I pictured the process is as follows:

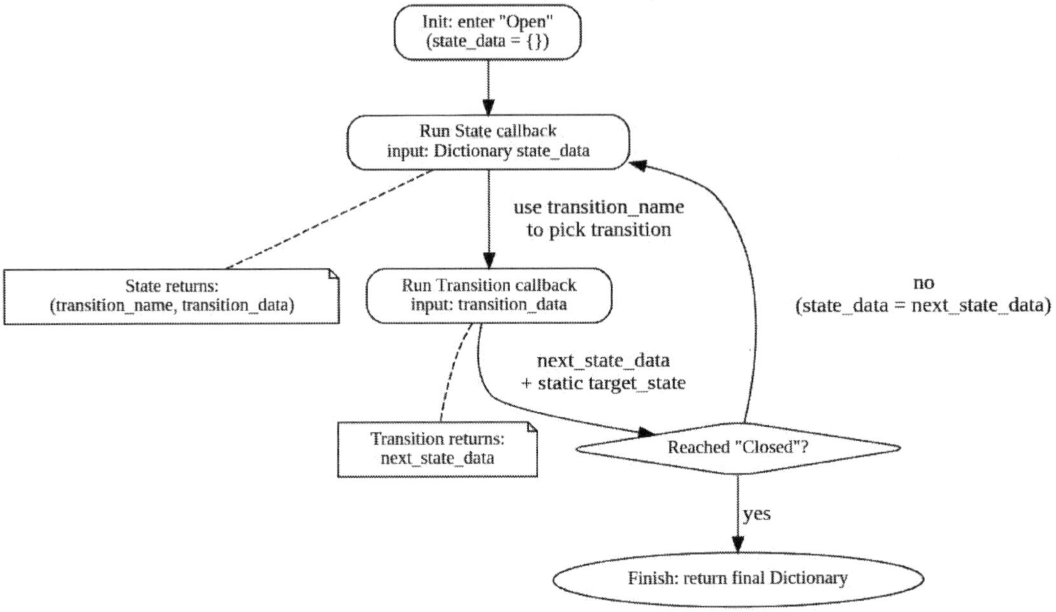

Figure 16.1: High-level description of StateMachineOperation

- The operation tree that knows how to read or write a message runs within a transition, either taking or returning the data from the message
- States where all transitions are write transitions will function as a native callback to the user of the interpreter, where the user will specify what transition to take and the parameters for it
- States where all transitions are read transitions will function by using the `TransitionLookAhead` operation to determine what the transition is

To encode that information, I defined the following data structures:

```
struct TransitionInfo {
  std::shared_ptr<const OpTree> callback_optree;
  std::vector<std::string> argument_names;
  std::string target_state;
};
using StateTransitionMap =
  std::unordered_map<std::string, TransitionInfo>;
struct StateInfo {
```

```
    std::shared_ptr<const OpTree> callback_optree;
    StateTransitionMap transitions;
};
using StateMap = std::unordered_map<std::string, StateInfo>;
```

And then the operation itself has a single data member:

```
StateMap states;
```

This structure encodes the entire behavior of the state machine.

`StateMachineOperation` implements `ControlFlowOperationConcept`, which allows it to submit callbacks and process their returned values. In order to allow the state to be tracked, the first step is to add a new member to the `ControlFlowOperationContext` object:

```
std::any additional_info;
```

This additional info member is necessary because the state machine needs to keep track of whether it is processing a transition or if it is processing the callbacks for a state. It would have been possible to use `std::variant` instead of `std::any` in this case, but this would have required exposing the implementation details of the operation.

To represent these modes, we define the following `enum class`:

```
enum class ProcessingMode {
  Transition,
  State,
};
```

To associate each state or transition with its name, we define the following pair types:

```
using StatePair = std::pair<
    std::string, StateMachineOperation::StateInfo>;
using TransitionPair = std::pair<
    std::string, StateMachineOperation::TransitionInfo>;
```

Finally, we put everything together, including whether we're coming from a given state (which may not exist when processing the transition to the `"Open"` state), as well as which transition we're executing and the target state:

```
struct ProcessingInfo {
  ProcessingMode processing_mode;
  std::optional<StatePair> from_state;
```

```
    std::optional<TransitionPair> transition;
    StatePair to_state;
};
```

This struct is completely encapsulated within the implementation of the operation, which prevents the leaking of those implementation details. This is where the usage of `std::any` instead of `std::variant` gives us that control. With that, I can start implementing the execution of the operation, from the outermost code, and then dive deeper:

```
OperationResult
StateMachineOperation::operator()(
  ControlFlowOperationContext &ctx,
  Arguments a) const {
  if (ctx.callable.has_value()) {
    // will cover next
  } else {
    auto it = states.find("Open");
    if (it == states.end()) {
      return value::RuntimeError::NameError;
    }
    ctx.accumulator = std::make_shared<std::vector>(
      std::vector{value::Dictionary()});
    ctx.additional_info = ProcessingInfo{
      ProcessingMode::Transition,
      std::nullopt,
      std::nullopt,
      *it
    };
    return _start_state_callback(ctx, states);
  }
}
```

The assumption is that there's always going to be a callable associated with the operation after it's initialized. Therefore, if there isn't a callable, the state machine transitions to the `"Open"` state, initializes an empty dictionary as the data for the `"Open"` state, since `"Open"` can't have any parameters, and populates the `additional_info` context member with the information that it's transitioning to the `"Open"` state.

The `_start_state_callback` function, in turn, initializes the state callback and allows the interpreter to execute it:

```
static OperationResult _start_state_callback(
  ControlFlowOperationContext &ctx,
  const StateMachineOperation::StateMap &states) {
  ProcessingInfo &info = std::any_cast<ProcessingInfo &>(
    ctx.additional_info);
  auto &s = info.to_state.second;
  ctx.callable = value::Callable{
    s.callback_optree, {"dictionary"}, true};
  ctx.value = std::nullopt;
  info.processing_mode = ProcessingMode::State;
  return
   ReasonForBlockedOperation::WaitingForCallableInvocation;
}
```

This describes that the state callback will have a single argument, which is a dictionary with the entire message that has led to this state. In the case of the `"Open"` state, it will be empty. It then tells the interpreter that the callback needs to be invoked.

This may seem a bit redundant now, since the code for the `"Open"` state could just have done it directly. However, the code to start the callback for any state is the same, and doing it with this function allows us to reduce duplication once we get to the other cases.

Now I can get back to the operation execution, in the case where a callback has been set, looking at the block that I skipped earlier:

```
if (ctx.callable_invoked) {
  if (ctx.value.has_value()) {
    // more on that later
  } else {
    return
      ReasonForBlockedOperation::WaitingForCallableResult;
  }
} else {
  return
   ReasonForBlockedOperation::WaitingForCallableInvocation;
}
```

This performs the usual interaction with the interpreter: having the callback called and the results submitted. After that, we can finally get into the processing of the callbacks themselves:

```
ProcessingInfo &info = std::any_cast<ProcessingInfo &>(
  ctx.additional_info);
if (info.processing_mode == ProcessingMode::Transition) {
  if (!info.transition.has_value()) {
    return value::RuntimeError::NameError;
  }
  return _process_transition_return(ctx, states);
} else {
  return _process_state_return(ctx, states);
}
```

The two functions being called—`_process_transition_return` and `_process_state_return`—unwrap the value returned by the callable, returning errors if the value doesn't have the expected type. Once the arguments are correctly identified, they actually perform the action. In the case of a state, the state callback returns two arguments: the name of the transition that is being taken and the dictionary with the data for that transition:

```
static OperationResult _process_state_return_with_args(
  ControlFlowOperationContext &ctx,
  const StateMachineOperation::StateMap &states,
  const value::Octets t,
  const value::Dictionary d) {
  ProcessingInfo &info =
   std::any_cast<ProcessingInfo &>(ctx.additional_info);
  if (info.to_state.first == "Closed") { return d; }
```

In addition, this is where the `"Closed"` state is treated specially, causing the operation to return the dictionary of the data from the last message that has led to this point.

Next, the previous `to_state` becomes the new `from_state`:

```
  info.from_state = info.to_state;
```

We then try to find the transition that was given to us in the value of `t`, returning a `NameError` if the transition name is not listed in the state:

```
  auto &s = info.to_state.second;
  auto it = s.transitions.find(*t.data);
```

```
    if (it == s.transitions.end()) {
      return value::RuntimeError::NameError;
    }
```

Since the callback told us which transition is being taken, we also know what the target state is, and we need to validate that it's a valid state:

```
    auto target_state_name = it->second.target_state;
    auto it2 = states.find(target_state_name);
    if (it2 == states.end()) {
      return value::RuntimeError::NameError;
    }
```

Finally, we can extract the named arguments from the dictionary for the execution of the transition, and trigger the start of the transition callback:

```
    auto maybe_args = _extract_arguments(
      it->second.argument_names, d);
    if (!maybe_args.has_value()) {
      return value::RuntimeError::TypeError;
    }
    ctx.accumulator = maybe_args.value();
    info.transition = *it;
    info.to_state = *it2;
    return _start_transition_callback(ctx, states);
```

The `_extract_arguments` function just goes over the argument names for the transition and transforms the dictionary into a list, as required by the `StaticCallable` arguments for the transition:

```
static std::optional<std::shared_ptr<std::vector<Value>>>
_extract_arguments(
    const std::vectorstd::string &names,
    const value::Dictionary &d) {
    auto args = std::make_shared<std::vector<Value>>();
    for (const auto &arg_name : names) {
      auto it = d.members->find(arg_name);
      if (it == d.members->end()) {
        return std::nullopt;
      } else {
        args->push_back(it->second);
```

```
      }
    }
    return args;
  }
```

This validates that the dictionary has all the expected values while traversing that list. And with this we assembled the data for the transition that will either read or write the message.

We can now look at what happens in the case of the transition:

```
  static OperationResult
  process_transition_return_with_args(
     ControlFlowOperationContext &ctx,
     const StateMachineOperation::StateMap &states,
     const value::Dictionary &d) {
    ctx.accumulator =
      std::make_shared<std::vector>(std::vector{d});
    return _start_state_callback(ctx, states);
  }
```

The `process_transition_return_with_args` function simply assembles the dictionary that was returned by the transition callback so the state callback can be called.

With this we have a complete picture of the state machine. At the start it will trigger a transition to the `"Open"` state, create a static callable for the execution, and start it. The `"Open"` state callback then returns which transition is going to be taken and the data needed for its processing, and then it iterates through states and transitions until it gets to the `"Closed"` state, which will cause the operation to conclude.

If, at any point, an invalid transition or invalid arguments are returned by either state or transition callbacks, the execution is interrupted by returning a runtime error. You can look at the complete code for the operation in pull request #45 (`https://github.com/PacktPublishing/Building-Programming-Language-Interpreters/pull/45`).

Now I can start the actual transformation.

Generating the code for StateMachineOperation

As the language I'm specifying has two different agents, it makes sense that I introduce two separate generators:

```
std::optional<std::shared_ptr<const OpTree>>
client(const std::shared_ptr<const sema::ast::Protocol>
       &protocol);
std::optional<std::shared_ptr<const OpTree>>
server(const std::shared_ptr<const sema::ast::Protocol>
       &protocol);
```

The functions take the protocol, which is the top level of our AST, and return, optionally, an `OpTree`. The optional is used in case we have anything in the AST that doesn't quite make sense; in those cases, the generator will just refuse to produce code.

The two functions are very similar. I'll work through the code section by section.

First check that the protocol is well formed with the relevant section specified:

```
if (!protocol || !protocol->server) {
  return std::nullopt;
}
```

Then the state map can be produced for the given section of the AST, and this is where the two functions have a significant difference, with each one getting the state of the corresponding agent:

```
auto state_map_opt =
  construct_state_map(protocol->server->states);
if (!state_map_opt) {
  return std::nullopt;
}
```

With that we can finally create the operation:

```
auto state_machine_operation =
   StateMachineOperation(*state_map_opt);
```

And then we can return the final `OpTree`:

```
auto optree =
  std::make_shared<OpTree>(
     OpTree{OpTreeNode{state_machine_operation, {}}});
return optree;
```

Now, `construct_state_map` is where things get interesting. In particular, an important limitation of the interpreter becomes evident.

If a state has a mix of read transitions and write transitions, we can't quite make it work, so we need to start by checking that all the transitions are of the same type. For that, first I define an enum that we can use to track the transition type:

```
enum class TransitionType { Read, Write };
```

And this is where it becomes important that the transition itself is represented as a variant between read and write transitions. This allows me to create a `visit_transition` function that will be used both to generate the `StateMachineOperation::TransitionInfo` for the given transition, which I'll cover later, and to gather related information. Let's first look at how it works for `WriteTransition`:

```
static std::optional<
  std::pair<TransitionType,
            StateMachineOperation::TransitionInfo>>
visit_transition(
    const std::shared_ptr<const sema::ast::WriteTransition>
    &transition, const std::string &target_state) {
  auto maybe_info = generate_transition_info(
     transition, target_state);
  if (!maybe_info)
    return std::nullopt;
  return {{TransitionType::Write, *maybe_info}};
}
```

And then we look at `ReadTransition`, which is almost identical but returns a different enum value:

```
static std::optional<
  std::pair<TransitionType,
            StateMachineOperation::TransitionInfo>>
visit_transition(
```

```
    const std::shared_ptr<const sema::ast::ReadTransition>
    &transition, const std::string &target_state) {
  auto maybe_info = generate_transition_info(
     transition, target_state);
  if (!maybe_info)
    return std::nullopt;
  return {{TransitionType::Read, *maybe_info}};
}
```

In order to explain what the function is doing, I will first talk about the general structure around traversing the states, where essentially we construct the state map that will be returned one state at a time:

```
StateMachineOperation::StateMap state_map;
for (const auto &state_pair : states) {
  StateMachineOperation::StateInfo state_info;
  // ... I will cover this later
  state_map[state_pair.first] = state_info;
}
return state_map.empty()
  ? std::nullopt
  : std::optional<
     StateMachineOperation::StateMap>{state_map};
```

Now I can dive into how each state is processed, starting by creating a variable to keep track of which types of transitions we've seen. This is important because the language doesn't support a protocol where a state fails to define which agent is doing the writing next. Later, the code will check if we have both a read and a write transition out of the same state, and treat that as a semantic analysis failure:

```
std::optional<TransitionType> state_transitions_type =
   std::nullopt;
```

Then we can iterate over all the transitions in that state, calling `visit_transition` for each of the transitions and storing the resulting transition information in the `state_info`. At the end, we check that we don't have mixed transition types:

```
for (const auto &transition_pair :
     state_pair.second->transitions) {
  const auto &transition = transition_pair.second.first;
```

```
    const auto &target_state = transition_pair.second.second;
    auto maybe_transition =
      std::visit([&](auto &t) {
          return visit_transition(t, target_state); },
      transition);
    if (!maybe_transition)
      return std::nullopt;
    auto [transition_type, transition_info] =
      *maybe_transition;
    state_info.transitions[transition_pair.first] =
      transition_info;
    if (state_transitions_type.has_value()) {
      if (state_transitions_type != transition_type) {
        return std::nullopt;
      }
    } else {
      state_transitions_type = transition_type;
    }
  }
```

I will cover the generation of the transition information in the next section. For now I will finish the logic for creating the state information.

First, I need to treat the `"Closed"` state differently, as I described before:

```
  if (state_pair.first == "Closed") {
    state_info.callback_optree = std::make_shared<OpTree>(
        OpTree(OpTreeNode{UnaryCallback(state_pair.first),
               {{LexicalPadGet{"dictionary"}, {}}}}));
  }
```

When the state is closed, it will just invoke the callback for the `"Closed"` state and let that be the return, which will end the execution of the state machine operation.

Now I can focus on the other cases. First, I need to handle the special case where there's no transition in a state, and presume it is a read state:

```
  if (!state_transitions_type)
    state_transitions_type = TransitionType::Read;
```

Then I can decide the different logic, starting with the write transition, which is the simplest, since the decision has to be made by the user of the interpreter, and so we completely delegate it to a callback:

```
switch (state_transitions_type.value()) {
case TransitionType::Write:
  state_info.callback_optree = std::make_shared<OpTree>(
    OpTree(OpTreeNode{UnaryCallback(state_pair.first),
              {{LexicalPadGet{"dictionary"}, {}}}}));
break;
```

The read transition, however, needs to generate the use of the `TransitionLookAhead` operation, so I'll break it down into a separate function, with the error handling via the optional:

```
case TransitionType::Read: {
  auto maybe_optree =
     generate_read_state_callback(state_pair.second);
  if (!maybe_optree)
    return std::nullopt;
  state_info.callback_optree = *maybe_optree;
}
break;
```

The implementation of the `generate_read_state_callback` function starts by iterating over the transitions in that state in order to accumulate the different conditions for the lookahead:

```
std::vector<std::pair<
       operation::TransitionLookahead::TransitionCondition,
       std::string>>
    conditions;
for (const auto &transition_pair : state->transitions) {
  const auto &transition = transition_pair.second.first;
  const auto &target_state = transition_pair.second.second;
  // more on that later
}
if (conditions.empty())
  return std::nullopt;
```

```
return std::make_shared<OpTree>(
  OpTreeNode{operation::DynamicList{},
    {{operation::TransitionLookahead{conditions}, {}},
     {operation::DictionaryInitialize{}, {}}}});
```

Now I can get into the body of the loop, starting again with the special case for transitions that will end in the "Closed" state, which depends on the end of the connection:

```
if (target_state == "Closed") {
   conditions.emplace_back(
     operation::TransitionLookahead::EOFCondition{},
     transition_pair.first);
```

And then I can handle the remaining cases by visiting the transitions to convert them into the right conditions:

```
auto maybe_condition = std::visit(
    [](auto &t) {
       return get_transition_condition(t); }, transition);
if (maybe_condition) {
   conditions.emplace_back(*maybe_condition,
                           transition_pair.first);
} else {
  return std::nullopt;
}
```

The get_transition_condition function is a series of overloads depending on the type of condition. I will not go through all of them, because they're fairly similar, but I will include one just for illustration purposes:

```
static
std::optional<
   operation::TransitionLookahead::TransitionCondition>
get_transition_condition(
   const std::shared_ptr<const sema::ast::ReadTransition>
   &read_transition) {
  if (!read_transition->actions.empty()) {
    return
     get_transition_condition(
       read_transition->actions.front());
```

```
    }
    return std::nullopt;
}
```

The `get_transition_condition` function will look at the first action of the read transition, which will then visit the action:

```
static
std::optional<
  operation::TransitionLookahead::TransitionCondition>
get_transition_condition(const sema::ast::Action &action) {
  return std::visit([](const auto &a) {
    return get_transition_condition(a);
    }, action);
}
```

It finally resolves to the specific action type and translates it into a condition:

```
static
std::optional<
    operation::TransitionLookahead::TransitionCondition>
get_transition_condition(
    const std::shared_ptr<
    const sema::ast::action::ReadOctetsUntilTerminator>
    &read_action) {
  return
    operation::TransitionLookahead::MatchUntilTerminator{
      read_action->terminator};
}
```

With that, I have the entire state machine operation built. The only thing remaining is actually producing the code for either reading or writing a message.

I wanted to go through this code, even if it's not necessarily going to match how you would write your own code generation, because this is an example of a simple imperative style of traversal of the AST for the main structure of the program. In this case, it handles the higher-level state machine of the programming language.

When you are writing your own generator, it is possible that your language will have those high-level structures as well (such as packages in Java), and it may be useful to treat them separately from the part that has to deal with finer control flow. It is also important to consider whether creating specialized operators, like I did here, is something you should do for that.

In the next section, I will get to the generation of the low-level control flow of the programming language—the reading and writing of messages.

Generating the entire program

In the previous section, I skipped over the `visit_transition` function, which will deal with the lower-level control flow of the program. This distinction is important, because here the user has a lot more flexibility in what the program can do, and therefore it's going to become important to use more flexible paradigms.

Let me start with an example of how this becomes more complex. In the programming language, each message has a data section, which describes the types of the data that are used in the message, and a parts section, which describes how they're used:

```
message "HTTP Response" {
    when: AwaitResponse;
    then: Open;
    agent: Server;
    data: {
        major_version: int<encoding=AsciiInt,
                           unsigned=True,
                           bits=8>;
        … other data
    }
    parts {
        tokens {
            "HTTP/" major_version "." minor_version
        }
        … other parts
```

So far we haven't really connected the two. The AST simply mentions that for a reading agent, it needs to read the `major_version` data until encountering `"."` as a terminator, while for a writing agent, it needs to write the `major_version` data and then a `"."`. But we want that data to actually have the type that was described in the language; therefore, we need to map the name to a specific type.

It gets more complicated because we also have `for` loops:

```
for header in headers {
   tokens { header.key }
   terminator { ":" }
   … other parts
}
terminator { "\r\n" }
```

This means that to resolve the variable name, the translation also needs to know that the `for` loop introduces a new variable and that it needs to navigate the type based on how the element of headers was defined.

For that, I will use a higher-order function that knows how to discover the type for a name in a specific context, but that can defer to the outer context if that name is not present in that context. To do that, we define the type for that function:

```
using ExtractTypeClosure =
    std::function<
     std::optional<
     std::shared_ptr<const parser::tree::Type>>(
           const std::string &)>;
```

This function will be passed along as an argument while we traverse the AST, and any time a new context is needed, we just wrap it in another function.

In the outermost functions—the ones that start the traversal of the transition—the resolution of the type from the name is simply defined as follows:

```
  auto get_type = [&](const std::string &name) {
    return extract_type(transition->data, name);
  };
```

It is important to notice that the `transition` and `name` variables are closed over into the `get_type` function, which means they can be referenced even when `get_type` is called deeper in the stack.

The outermost get_type can just look up the member at the top of the data section by name, since that's the context at that point. But in the case of a loop, the function needs to be a bit smarter, since it must recognize the name of the loop variable and extract it from the properties of the collection:

```
static std::optional<ExtractTypeClosure>
create_get_type_wrapper(const ExtractTypeClosure &get_type,
                        const std::string &variable,
                        const std::string &collection) {
  auto maybe_type = get_type(collection);
  if (!maybe_type)
    return std::nullopt;
  auto params = maybe_type.value()->parameters;
  auto it = params->find("element_type");
  if (it == params->end())
    return std::nullopt;
  auto element_type = it->second;
  return [=](const std::string &name)
      -> std::optional<std::shared_ptr<
          const parser::tree::Type>> {
    if (name == variable) {
      if (std::holds_alternative<
          std::shared_ptr<const parser::tree::Type>>(
              element_type)) {
        return std::get<
          std::shared_ptr<const parser::tree::Type>>(
              element_type);
      } else {
        return std::nullopt;
      }
    }
    return get_type(name);
  };
}
```

With this, the code traversing the for loop can define a new get_type that wraps the previous one, allowing it to correctly identify the type of the loop variable.

My goal with going through this example is to show that using functional patterns makes it significantly easier to deal with the flexibility we need to provide the user. This simple mechanism will work regardless of how many nested loops are created by the user.

Now that we have a mechanism to identify the members of the data for a transition, we can finally get to the `visit_transition` function, which then splits the code generation between the write and read transitions.

I will focus on the write transition for this explanation, but the logic for the read transition is quite similar. Let's start with the implementation of the `generate_transition_info` function:

```
auto optree = generate_transition_optree(transition);
if (!optree)
  return std::nullopt;
auto argument_names =
  extract_argument_names(transition->data);
if (!argument_names)
  return std::nullopt;
return StateMachineOperation::TransitionInfo{
         *optree, *argument_names, target_state};
```

This is where the integration with the state operation gets finalized, as the names from the data section will be used as argument names in the dictionary produced by the user. These argument names are simply the names of the top-level members of the data section.

Next we can look at the `generate_transition_optree` function for the write transition:

```
auto get_type = [&](const std::string &name) {
  return extract_type(transition->data, name);
};
auto maybe_ops =
  actions_to_optreenodes(transition,
                         transition->actions,
                         get_type);
if (!maybe_ops)
  return std::nullopt;
return std::make_shared<OpTree>(
  OpTree(OpTreeNode{OpSequence{},
         {{OpSequence{}, *maybe_ops},
          {DynamicList{}, {{LexicalPadAsDict{}, {}}}}}}));
```

As discussed before, this is where the outermost context for the names of variables is defined, and that gets sent to the `actions_to_optreenodes` function.

Before diving in, I want to note that this is already starting to build a proper operation tree. In this case, the operation tree being built is composed of an `OpSequence`, where the nodes produced from the actions run first, followed by returning whatever was in the lexical pad as a dictionary, which was part of the design of the state machine operator.

OK, now I'll focus on the conversion of the actions to operation trees, starting with the outermost part of that definition:

```
std::vector<OpTreeNode> operations;
for (const auto &action : actions) {
  auto maybe_op = std::visit(
    [&](const auto &a) {
          return visit_action(transition, get_type, a);
      }, action);
  if (!maybe_op)
    return std::nullopt;
  operations.push_back(maybe_op.value());
}
return operations;
```

Here, we use the final visitor pattern for the actions, where we can transform each action into its own `OpTreeNode`. If an action needs more than one node, it can always wrap them in an `OpSequence`.

I will not focus on all the actions as they are quite similar and you will be able to see them in the final code, but I do want to show at least one to complete the picture. For that, I will look at the code for the `WriteFromIdentifier` action. I start by getting the identifier and the type:

```
auto &identifier = action->identifier;
auto maybe_type = get_type(identifier->name);
if (!maybe_type)
  return std::nullopt;
```

Now, if the identifier doesn't have a member access, we can just write the octets based on the type of the identifier:

```
auto member = identifier->member;
if (!member.has_value())
  return write_octets_from_value(maybe_type.value(),
                                 variable_access);
```

However, if there is a member access, things get more interesting. We need to traverse the variable access through all the members. The outermost name of the identifier has to be something in the lexical pad. Therefore, we start with this:

```
OpTreeNode variable_access =
    OpTreeNode{LexicalPadGet(identifier->name), {}};
```

And now we can generate the `OpTree` that will recursively consume as many members as necessary, wrapping the outermost variable access:

```
auto maybe_access = recursive_variable_access(
    maybe_type.value(), member.value(), variable_access,
    std::nullopt);
if (!maybe_access)
  return std::nullopt;
auto [last_access, last_type] = *maybe_access;
return write_octets_from_value(last_type, last_access);
```

And this is where we check the types of the variables and can implement the member access. The outer type needs to have a parameter matching the name of the member, and we should be able to identify its type:

```
auto it = type->parameters->find(identifier->name);
if (it == type->parameters->end()) {
  return std::nullopt;
}
auto member_type =
  std::get<std::shared_ptr<const parser::tree::Type>>(
    it->second);
if (!member_type) {
  return std::nullopt;
}
```

Now, we need to check if it is the last member access, and if so, just return a `DictionaryGet` `OpTreeNode`, with the identifier name as the static value and the current access as the child node:

```
if (!identifier->member.has_value()) {
  auto last_access =
     OpTreeNode{DictionaryGet(identifier->name),
                                 {current_access}};
  return std::make_tuple(last_access, member_type);
```

If there is more to traverse, we need to recurse until the end, but only if the type of the member is a tuple:

```
} else if (member_type->name->name == "tuple") {
  auto outer_access =
     OpTreeNode{DictionaryGet(identifier->name),
                                 {current_access}};
  return recursive_variable_access(
         member_type, identifier->member.value(),
         outer_access, std::nullopt);
} else {
  return std::nullopt;
}
```

I skipped over some complexity in the code, but I hope that I can show how the operation tree gets built recursively while traversing the AST.

I do want to show one particular bit that I skipped, which was the `write_octets_from_value`:

```
if (type->name->name == "int") {
  return OpTreeNode{WriteOctets{},
                    {{IntToAscii{}, {value}}}};
} else if (type->name->name == "str") {
  return OpTreeNode{WriteOctets{}, {value}};
}
return std::nullopt;
```

This is where the loop is finally closed. It handles the type of the actual value, which is statically typed, and generates the correct operation tree for the writing to be done.

I know this chapter has been quite long already, but I do want to give you a practical sense of what writing this sort of generation looks like and how C++ features can be used in this context to write this code effectively.

In the end, the entire code generation step for this minimal implementation of the interpreter remains reasonably easy to follow. The complete code up to this point can be seen in pull request #46 (`https://github.com/PacktPublishing/Building-Programming-Language-Interpreters/pull/46`). I would recommend going through it, because there are many details that will be interesting but don't quite need a textual explanation here.

In the next section, I will work on finalizing the interface for how the user will instantiate the interpreter.

Integrating into the interpreter

So far we have been working on one step of the translation at a time. Now it's time to present to the user a final interface, where the user can give a path to a file and receive something that can be executed.

From the beginning, there was a plan for a constructor in the `InterpretedProgram` class that took a file path:

```
InterpretedProgram(std::string sf)
  : source_file(sf),
    optree(std::make_shared<const OpTree>(
        OpTree({operation::Int32Literal(0), {}}))) {}
```

But with what we know now, we know this is not a good interface. First, because we need to be able to have two different constructors—one for the client and one for the server—and second, because we need to be able to handle errors. Therefore, instead of a constructor, I will move this logic to have two static methods:

```
static std::optional<InterpretedProgram>
generate_client(const std::string& sf);
static std::optional<InterpretedProgram>
generate_server(const std::string& sf);
```

We start with the part that is common to both the client and the server: lexing, parsing, and analyzing the code:

```
std::optional<std::shared_ptr<const sema::ast::Protocol>> parse_
protocol(const std::string& sf) {
  auto maybe_tokens = lexer::tokenize(sf);
  if (!maybe_tokens.has_value())
    return std::nullopt;
  std::vector<lexer::Token> &tokens = maybe_tokens.value();
  auto maybe_ast = parser::parse(tokens);
  if (!maybe_ast.has_value())
    return std::nullopt;
  return sema::analyze(maybe_ast.value());
}
```

Finally, I can then generate either the client or the server interpreted program:

```
std::optional<InterpretedProgram> InterpretedProgram::generate_
client(const std::string& sf) {
  auto maybe_protocol = parse_protocol(sf);
  if (!maybe_protocol.has_value())
    return std::nullopt;
  auto maybe_client =
    generate::client(maybe_protocol.value());
  if (!maybe_client.has_value())
    return std::nullopt;
  return InterpretedProgram(maybe_client.value());
}
std::optional<InterpretedProgram> InterpretedProgram::generate_
server(const std::string& sf) {
  auto maybe_protocol = parse_protocol(sf);
  if (!maybe_protocol.has_value())
    return std::nullopt;
  auto maybe_server =
    generate::server(maybe_protocol.value());
  if (!maybe_server.has_value())
    return std::nullopt;
  return InterpretedProgram(maybe_server.value());
}
```

And with that I can change the test to use the new functions. You can see the use of the new interface in pull request #47 (`https://github.com/PacktPublishing/Building-Programming-Language-Interpreters/pull/47`). This brings the entire interface to a simple-to-use point.

And thinking about that entry point for the interpreter, particularly when the programming language is meant to be used as a library, is going to make a lot of difference for the users. Of course, the interface of this entry point is also important if it's meant to be a stand-alone executable, and you should research the various interfaces provided by interpreters before settling on yours.

In the next section, I will go over the actual execution of the interpreter, which shows how the users of this language can use the interpreter.

Executing code in our programming language for the first time

When I explained the state machine operator in the first section, I explained how the interaction with the user code would look, and now it's finally time to see that realized.

The main mechanism that the interpreter offers to the user for interacting is the definition of a set of callbacks for the various states the client or the server may be in. This goes back to the `InterpreterRunner` that was described in *Chapter 12*, and now it makes a lot more sense in the context of the programming language. Let me show the code for the server, leaving the actual code in the callbacks for later:

```
InterpreterRunner server_runner{
  .callbacks =
    {
     {"AwaitResponse",
      [](const std::vector<Value> &args) -> Value {
         // ...
      }},
     {"Closed",
      [](const std::vector<Value> &args) -> Value {
         // ...
       }},
    },
  .exit_when_done = true};
```

The preceding code essentially defines which part of the execution is going to interact with the user code. This is a direct outcome of the design of the state machine operation. It determines where the callback is made and how the return value is used.

To make this more concrete, let me go over the code for the `AwaitResponse` callback. I'll break it down into steps to make it easier. The first step is retrieving the dictionary that was the result of the transition leading to this state, which would be the transition reading the request from the client:

```
value::Dictionary dict =
   std::get<value::Dictionary>(args[0]);
std::cerr << "Member count: " << dict.members->size()
          << std::endl;
std::cerr << "Server received request: "
          << std::get<value::Octets>(
               dict.members->at("request_target"))
               .data->c_str()
          << std::endl;
```

This code prints out some information to illustrate that the members of the dictionary are the data members described in the protocol.

Now, the return value of the state is important because it must indicate not only which transition is going to be taken, but also what the arguments for that transition are, which, again, should match the data defined in the protocol:

```
return value::DynamicList{
 {_o("HTTP Response"),
  value::Dictionary{
  {{"response_code", 200},
   {"reason_phrase", _o("Looks good")},
   {"major_version", 1},
   {"minor_version", 1},
   {"headers",
    value::DynamicList{
     {value::Dictionary{
      {{"key", _o("Some-Response")},
       {"value", _o("some value")}}},
      value::Dictionary{
      {{"key", _o("TestHeader")},
       {"value", _o("Value")}}}}}}}}}}};
```

To make this code simpler, I wrapped the creation of `value::Octets` in the small `_o` function. The important thing here is that I'm returning data that the interpreter knows how to handle, but it's still expressed in plain C++ syntax, which can be conveniently created using brace syntax.

Finally, here is the code for the `"Closed"` callback, which simply acknowledges the closure. The data in its dictionary will end up being the final value returned by the interpreter:

```
std::cerr << "Server Close" << std::endl;
return value::DynamicList{{_o("N/A"), args.at(0)}};
```

The code in the file `tests/027-translate-ast-to-optree.cpp` has this complete interaction, including actually spawning multiple threads and later asserting that the data exchanged across the I/O layer actually matches the expected results.

I will not go into details on that because it's quite similar to the test introduced in *Chapter 12*. However, contrasting the code from this chapter with the code from that chapter will be useful for you to understand how we went from just the interpreter runtime to a complete end-to-end interpreter.

As with that chapter, I also included code implementing the integration with an existing I/O library, and as before I will leave it as an exercise to you to consider how other libraries could be integrated.

Summary

It is important to always be open to re-evaluating whether your interpreter will need new operations. This becomes particularly relevant if you have situations where it's significantly easier to implement the behavior in native code rather than using other primitives from the interpreter.

Additionally, you may find yourself having to alternate between imperative and functional paradigms when actually converting the AST into the interpreter operations. Sometimes the higher-level constructs are not as flexible, making direct assembly more practical. But when traversing the areas of the language where the user has a lot more flexibility, functional patterns can provide a much more straightforward solution.

With all that done, you will be in a position to figure out the final way in which the user will get the entire translation, from source code to execution, in a simple interface.

Finally, we can have code that looks like what a user would create and can run through the interpreter to manage the protocol. This is where we can see the real usage scenario and get the confidence that the interpreter actually works from end to end.

In the next chapter, I will reflect on this entire trajectory and whether the objectives set in the beginning were actually achieved, hopefully giving you a better sense of what you are getting into if you decide to embark on building your own interpreter.

17

Proving That It Works

I am now reaching the conclusion of this journey. In *Chapter 1, Defining the Scope,* I set out to guide you through the journey of designing a programming language and an interpreter using a real-world use case of interacting with network protocols.

Now, it is time to look back on that journey:

- Revisit what the goals were that were set in the beginning, and start evaluating whether I have met all of them, and if not, whether it is still a useful result
- Check back on what the acceptance criteria were that were defined, and whether they have been met
- Work through a significant usage of the new programming language and interpreter
- Reflect on the whole trajectory

By the end of this chapter, you should be able to establish your own framework on how you will evaluate the success of your own effort to solve a problem with a new programming language and interpreter.

Revisiting our goals

As this has been quite a long journey, it's important to take time to reflect on what goals were set in the beginning and how far we've come. Let me go through them one by one.

Domain-specific language (DSL) for specifying network protocols

This was the primary motivation for building the programming language and interpreter. The idea was that manually writing the code to handle the state machine of a network protocol is very error-prone, and, in fact, errors in that code are likely an important source of vulnerabilities in networking code.

This is an area where I can say with confidence that the interpreter does serve as a useful proof of concept, showing that the DSL proposed here effectively abstracts away the state machine of the protocol from the user. Later, in the *Working through an example* section, I will walk through a significantly more complicated example usage of the language, which will illustrate just how much of the state machine handling is taken by the interpreter.

Synchronous request–response protocols

This is at the same time a statement of a goal and a statement of a non-goal. Essentially, I made the problem statement limited to a specific subset of network protocols—particularly the ones that have straightforward requests and responses.

In the previous chapter, I demonstrated that the interpreter is capable of handling a simplified HTTP protocol, with the correct handling of the request–response behavior. To prove the design further, I will use the programming language to model **Simple Mail Transfer Protocol** (**SMTP**), which is going to be a good testing exercise for the language.

Transfer of control at multiple points

Initially, I aimed to be able to reject an HTTP request as soon as the query path was submitted, without ever processing the entire request. This is a good example of something that ended up being shaved from the first version of the programming language. The language does provide points where control is transferred, but at this moment, that happens at the end of a message, not at arbitrary points.

The decision to simplify this process came from realizing that while this is a good feature for the language in general, it became clear as I was working through it that it was not strictly necessary for the **minimum viable product** (**MVP**). More importantly, it would still be possible to split the HTTP request, allowing for processing the verb separately. So, while the aforementioned feature is not directly supported by the language, you can still achieve the goal.

Transferring values to the native language

An interpreter that knows how to read an HTTP request but that doesn't tell you what it is would not have been a particularly useful interpreter. We do have a working solution for this, where at the end of a message, a dictionary is sent to the native language.

One feature that was removed from the first release was the ability to be able to represent these data structures in other formats, beyond the one that is native to the interpreter. The decision to remove this feature from the MVP came naturally from the recognition that it was possible to implement a client and server using this language while operating directly on the interpreter values.

This is clearly an area where future development would be beneficial, but I think it's fair to say that using the interpreter's native type system doesn't make it unusable. But that's something that only working through an example will answer.

Using captured values within the protocol

The example I had when listing this goal was that I would be able to use the value of the `Content-Length` header in HTTP in order to parse the body of the request. This was also trimmed from the first version of the language, leaving the format of the protocol entirely static. The support for streams ended up being removed from the MVP, as many protocols do not require it, although this is a clear high priority for future versions of the interpreter.

This journey of scoping down the first version of a project to truly the size of an MVP is an important aspect of software development. Working through those decisions and the journey of getting to that MVP is also an important part of that process, and one I wanted to share with you as part of the narrative.

In the next section, I will reflect on the acceptance criteria that I set in *Chapter 1*.

Checking our acceptance criteria

While reducing the scope of goals is a natural outcome of achieving the first release of any software product, the acceptance criteria set a much more precise bar for success.

As with the goals, let me walk you through each one of them.

Initialize the interpreter once

For an interpreter that handles network protocols, I set as a principle that the interpreter should only be initialized once, especially in the case of a network server, as it will have to handle the same protocol multiple times. This was something that I carefully kept in mind throughout the design and implementation of the interpreter. From the very beginning, I started with the `InterpretedProgram` type, which contains a read-only execution model for the program.

This has driven not only how the interpreter itself was designed, but also how the translation of source code into the executable instructions in the form of the read-only `OpTree` objects allows the reuse of those across all the instances of the execution, creating a clear separation between the executable instructions and the runtime data used in the execution stack.

This design represented a choice that limited what the interpreter can do, as it doesn't have access, as other interpreters do, to rewrite its own code. While this may significantly reduce the interpreter's flexibility, for an interpreter that is meant to handle network protocols, it is actually a desirable restriction.

Make the interpreter drive the interaction with the network

This was perhaps the main criterion, since the principle was to reduce the number of programming errors in the handling of the state machine of any given protocol. The final interpreter that was built actually completely hides the network communication from the user, as the user only sees the messages in the form of the structured data described in the protocol itself.

I think it is fair to say that this particular acceptance criterion was satisfied from the ground up of the design of the programming language and the interpreter.

Transfer control at specific points

The final requirement was that the transitions between the interpreter and the native code would happen at specific points of the execution. This concept got represented through native callbacks, which are executed when the protocol gets into a state, while transitions are implemented by the interpreter itself.

That means that we not only reduced the chances of errors in handling the immediate state machine of the specific messages, but also established controls over which data can be transmitted across messages. This may not be particularly obvious, but higher-level state leak across out-of-sequence messages is also a particularly dangerous source of bugs in the handling of network protocols.

Now, to confirm everything that we have discussed in the chapter till now, let's work through a more complete example covering an end-to-end usage of the interpreter.

Working through an example

So far, I have been working on simplified examples and on a minimal version of the HTTP protocol. Now, it is time to test the interpreter in a real use case while still targeting a protocol that falls within the limitations of the programming language.

A good example for this is SMTP, the protocol that underpins email infrastructure on the internet, because it has a wider variety of states than plain HTTP. In SMTP, there are specific states that are preserved across various messages, and the interpreter needs to be able to convey those states.

Understanding SMTP

I won't go into a full explanation of the protocol, but by the end of this section, you should have a firm grasp on how it works. Let me start with a diagram that describes the different states in the protocol:

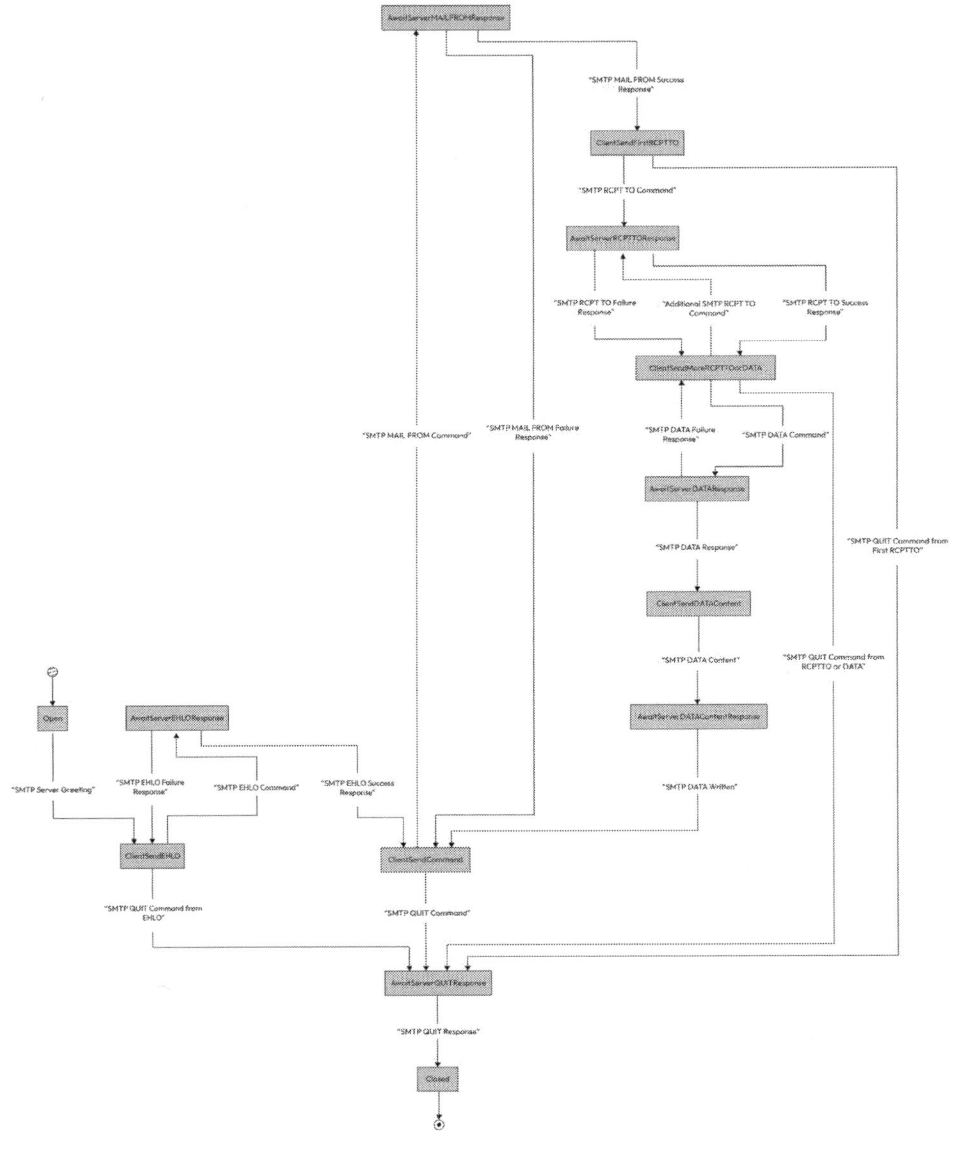

Figure 17.1: State machine diagram for SMTP
(This image is for visualization purpose only. Check the graphic bundle for a high-resolution version.)

I will do a brief description of the diagram. The states are represented by the boxes, and the transitions are represented by the arrows. These will map directly to the concepts in the programming language.

The protocol starts from the `Open` state, followed by the server sending a greeting message, which is responded to by the client. If the server recognizes the client, the protocol lands in the client command loop, which allows sending messages by using the `MAIL FROM` command. If the server accepts the sender, the protocol enters another loop, where the client will use the `RCPT TO` command to indicate the recipients of the message. Once all the recipients are indicated, the `DATA` command initiates the contents of the email, which are finished by a sequence of `CRLF`, followed by a dot, followed by another `CRLF` sequence, which then returns to the main command loop.

There is a specific thing I want to highlight on how the SMTP protocol works: if you follow the diagram, you will notice that there are a few cases where the states are in a cycle. The first loop begins at the `ClientSendCommand` state. This state comes after the client identification, which means that the context for all the messages in the loop that includes the `ClientSendCommand` state occurs in the context of that same client session.

Likewise, there is a loop that starts after the `AwaitServerRCPTTOResponse` state, where the client may send multiple recipient addresses for the same message, and the server is meant to accumulate those addresses until the client finally sends a `DATA` command, which will ultimately take the state back to `ClientSendCommand`.

The reason I'm highlighting this is that it shows how SMTP maintains and resets state information: while the data about the client domain, introduced in the `EHLO` message, must be preserved across all subsequent messages, the information gathered between `MAIL FROM` and the end of the `DATA` command needs to be discarded when the state returns to `ClientSendCommand`.

Expressing SMTP in the DSL

With that, I can now work through the code that expresses SMTP in our DSL. Let's start with the greeting the server sends when the connection is first established:

```
message "SMTP Server Greeting" {
    when: Open;
    then: ClientSendEHLO;
    agent: Server;
    data: {
        code_tens:
```

```
          int<encoding=AsciiInt, unsigned=True, bits=8>;
        msg:
          str<encoding=Ascii7Bit, sizing=Dynamic,
          max_length=1024>;
    }
    parts {
        tokens { "2" code_tens " " msg }
        terminator { "\r\n" }
    }
}
```

It is worth noting that I encoded the *hundreds* digit in the protocol to encode success and failure messages. Since success or failure results in different transitions in the state machine, setting it explicitly this way allows the interpreter itself to handle those transitions.

After that, we have the client submitting the `EHLO` message, which describes the client domain:

```
message "SMTP EHLO Command" {
    when: ClientSendEHLO;
    then: AwaitServerEHLOResponse;
    agent: Client;
    data: {
        client_domain:
          str<encoding=Ascii7Bit, sizing=Dynamic,
          max_length=256>;
    }
    parts {
        tokens { "EHLO " client_domain }
        terminator { "\r\n" }
    }
}
```

At this point, the server may refuse the client, sending it back to the `ClientSendEHLO` state:

```
message "SMTP EHLO Failure Response" {
    when: AwaitServerEHLOResponse;
    then: ClientSendEHLO;
    agent: Server;
    data: {
        code_tens:
```

```
            int<encoding=AsciiInt, unsigned=True, bits=8>;
        msg:
            str<encoding=Ascii7Bit, sizing=Dynamic,
            max_length=1024>;
    }
    parts {
        tokens { "5" code_tens }
        terminator { " " }
        tokens { msg }
        terminator { "\r\n" }
    }
}
```

Similarly, I encode the *hundreds* digit here so that the protocol description indicates the meaning in a way that influences the state machine. That means a client using this language would not need to handle that manually.

I will not cover all the error cases, since they all look very similar. Let me now look at the success path:

```
message "SMTP EHLO Success Response" {
    when: AwaitServerEHLOResponse;
    then: ClientSendCommand;
    agent: Server;
    data: {
        client_domain:
            str<encoding=Ascii7Bit, sizing=Dynamic,
            max_length=256>;
        code_tens:
            int<encoding=AsciiInt, unsigned=True, bits=8>;
        msg:
            str<encoding=Ascii7Bit, sizing=Dynamic,
            max_length=1024>;
    }
    parts {
        tokens { "2" code_tens }
        terminator { " " }
        tokens { msg }
        terminator { "\r\n" }
```

```
    }
}
```

The thing to note here is the fact that we have a data member for `client_domain` that is not actually in this message, but that indicates what information we need to preserve across messages. This illustrates how the protocol description itself encodes which information should be preserved across the transitions.

At this point, the protocol enters the `ClientSendCommand` state, where you have a loop of commands between the client and the server, which allows a client to send multiple messages in a single connection. For all of these commands, the same `client_domain` must be preserved.

The main command is the `MAIL FROM` command:

```
message "SMTP MAIL FROM Command" {
    when: ClientSendCommand;
    then: AwaitServerMAILFROMResponse;
    agent: Client;
    data: {
        client_domain:
          str<encoding=Ascii7Bit, sizing=Dynamic,
          max_length=256>;
        sender:
          str<encoding=Ascii7Bit, sizing=Dynamic,
          max_length=320>;
    }
    parts {
        tokens { "MAIL FROM:<" sender ">" }
        terminator { "\r\n" }
    }
}
```

As before, `client_domain` is preserved through this transition, even if it is not in the message. The message describes the sender of the message, which the server will either accept or reject. The following transition shows the success case:

```
message "SMTP MAIL FROM Success Response" {
    when: AwaitServerMAILFROMResponse;
    then: ClientSendFirstRCPTTO;
    agent: Server;
```

```
    data: {
        client_domain:
          str<encoding=Ascii7Bit, sizing=Dynamic,
          max_length=256>;
        sender:
          str<encoding=Ascii7Bit, sizing=Dynamic,
          max_length=320>;
        code_tens:
          int<encoding=AsciiInt, unsigned=True, bits=8>;
        msg:
          str<encoding=Ascii7Bit, sizing=Dynamic,
          max_length=1024>;
    }
    parts {
        tokens { "2" code_tens }
        terminator { " " }
        tokens { msg }
        terminator { "\r\n" }
    }
}
```

You can see the pattern now: this transition accumulates both `client_domain` and `sender`. You can also notice that the target state is `ClientSendFirstRCPTTO`. The reason for this is that we need the state machine to be deterministic about when the `DATA` command is acceptable, which is only after the first `RCPT TO` command, since there must be at least one recipient:

```
message "SMTP RCPT TO Command" {
    when: ClientSendFirstRCPTTO;
    then: AwaitServerRCPTTOResponse;
    agent: Client;
    data: {
        client_domain:
          str<encoding=Ascii7Bit, sizing=Dynamic,
          max_length=256>;
        sender:
          str<encoding=Ascii7Bit, sizing=Dynamic,
          max_length=320>;
        recipient:
```

```
        str<encoding=Ascii7Bit, sizing=Dynamic,
        max_length=320>;
    }
    parts {
        tokens { "RCPT TO:<" recipient ">" }
        terminator { "\r\n" }
    }
}
```

The response to the first `RCPT TO` command will then lead to a state that allows the server to accumulate the recipients:

```
message "SMTP RCPT TO Success Response" {
    when: AwaitServerRCPTTOResponse;
    then: ClientSendMoreRCPTTOorDATA;
    agent: Server;
    data: {
        client_domain:
          str<encoding=Ascii7Bit, sizing=Dynamic,
          max_length=256>;
        sender:
          str<encoding=Ascii7Bit, sizing=Dynamic,
          max_length=320>;
        recipient_list:
          array<element_type=
           str<encoding=Ascii7Bit,
           sizing=Dynamic, max_length=32768>>;
        code_tens:
         int<encoding=AsciiInt, unsigned=True, bits=8>;
        msg:
         str<encoding=Ascii7Bit, sizing=Dynamic,
         max_length=1024>;
    }
    parts {
        tokens { "2" code_tens }
        terminator { " " }
        tokens { msg }
        terminator { "\r\n" }
```

```
    }
}
```

And now I introduce a new data member—`recipient_list`—that is never a direct part of any message. It allows the server to accumulate the recipients sent by the client. The target state now allows the client to either send additional recipients or go to the `DATA` section.

Since the additional `RCPT TO` message looks very similar, I'll skip it and go straight to the point where the user sends the `DATA` command:

```
message "SMTP DATA Command" {
    when: ClientSendMoreRCPTTOorDATA;
    then: AwaitServerDATAResponse;
    agent: Client;
    data: {
        client_domain:
          str<encoding=Ascii7Bit, sizing=Dynamic,
          max_length=256>;
        sender:
          str<encoding=Ascii7Bit, sizing=Dynamic,
          max_length=320>;
        recipient_list:
          array<element_type=
            str<encoding=Ascii7Bit, sizing=Dynamic,
            max_length=32768>>;
    }
    parts {
        tokens { "DATA" }
        terminator { "\r\n" }
    }
}
```

This makes it clear that when the client issues the `DATA` command, the entire set of data already belongs in the state machine. The server then responds that the client is permitted to send the data, and the client will send the entire contents of the email:

```
message "SMTP DATA Content" {
    when: ClientSendDATAContent;
    then: AwaitServerDATAContentResponse;
    agent: Client;
```

```
    data: {
        client_domain:
          str<encoding=Ascii7Bit, sizing=Dynamic,
          max_length=256>;
        sender:
          str<encoding=Ascii7Bit, sizing=Dynamic,
          max_length=320>;
        recipient_list:
          array<element_type=
            str<encoding=Ascii7Bit, sizing=Dynamic,
            max_length=32768>>;
        content:
          str<encoding=Ascii7Bit, sizing=Dynamic,
          max_length=65536>;
    }
    parts {
        tokens { content }
        terminator { "\r\n.\r\n" }
    }
}
```

This finally gets us to the point where the server has the entire structured data for processing an arriving email, and it can actually implement handling it. If the server accepts the message, then the state goes back to `ClientSendCommand`, preserving only `client_domain` and discarding all the additional data that was accumulated in the other states.

I didn't cover every message in the protocol, since a lot of them didn't add a lot of context on how the language is used. Now, we can go to actually implementing the usage of the code.

Implementing an SMTP server

In both *Chapter 12, Running and Testing Language Operators,* and *Chapter 16, Generating: Turning an Abstract Syntax Tree into Instructions,* I mentioned that I had implemented tests using an integration with a specific I/O library. As I get to this point, it becomes clear that a user of this interpreter would benefit from being able to reuse this integration themselves. To support that, I added a new library to the project, integrating the various parts of the interpreter with the machinery of the `libuv` library.

As this integration is not part of the interpreter code itself, and it is mostly about how `libuv` itself works, I won't get into the details of that implementation here. I will also leave it as an exercise for you to consider what other integrations would look like. You can see the code for the entire integration with `libuv` in pull request #49 (`https://github.com/PacktPublishing/Building-Programming-Language-Interpreters/pull/49`).

Now, I can focus on the implementation of the server itself. I'll start from the outside and move into each of the details, starting with the `main()` function.

The first step is loading the interpreted program:

```
auto maybe_program = smtpserver::load_interpreted_program();
if (!maybe_program.has_value()) {
  std::cerr
    << "Failed to load the interpreted program."
    << std::endl;
  return 1;
}
```

Then, the `libuv` loop can be started, and I also initialize the work queue that will be used by the `libuv` integration to start the actual server process:

```
// Set up libuv loop and async work queue.
uv_loop_t *loop = uv_default_loop();
networkprotocoldsl_uv::AsyncWorkQueue async_queue(loop);
```

Then, we can let `libuv` run in a background thread:

```
// Start the libuv loop in a separate thread.
std::thread io_thread([&]() { uv_run(loop, UV_RUN_DEFAULT); });
```

Here, we run the server. I will cover the `main_server` function later:

```
std::span<const char *>
 args(argv, static_cast<size_t>(argc));
smtpserver::main_server(args, *maybe_program, async_queue);
```

And finally, once the server exits, we can unwind everything and leave the process:

```
async_queue.shutdown().wait();
io_thread.join();
return 0;
```

Now, let's get deeper into the `load_interpreted_program` function that returns the interpreted program:

```
std::string source_code = std::string(
#ifndef SMTP_NETWORKPROTOCOLDSL_LITERAL
#error "SMTP_NETWORKPROTOCOLDSL_LITERAL not defined"
#endif
#include SMTP_NETWORKPROTOCOLDSL_LITERAL
);
return
networkprotocoldsl::InterpretedProgram::
  generate_server_from_source(source_code);
```

This function performs all the steps: lexing, parsing, analyzing, generating the operation tree, and returning an interpreted program. These are all the steps we have covered in recent chapters. For simplicity, I decided to load the source code as string literals using the preprocessor. This does have the drawback of the complexity of having to generate the string literals to be loaded in the code, but it simplifies the runtime as the program won't have to load that resource later.

Now, let me step into the `main_server` function. I will not go through the setting up of the application, with argument parsing and loading of configuration. The code uses the CLI11 library to parse the command-line arguments and populate a `ServerConfiguration` struct:

```
struct ServerConfiguration {
  std::string server_name;
  std::unordered_map<std::string,
      std::unordered_set<std::string>>
      valid_recipients;
  std::unordered_map<std::string,
      std::unordered_set<std::string>>
      blocked_senders;
  std::unordered_set<std::string> blocked_client_domains;
  std::string maildir;
  std::string bind_ip;
  int bind_port;
};
```

This is, of course, not a production-ready SMTP server, but I did want to make it as real as possible, so I wanted to implement something that actually behaved correctly.

Let me focus on the code for the server itself. First, it converts the server configuration into a set of server callbacks:

```
// Get the server callbacks.
auto server_callbacks = get_server_callbacks(config);
```

I will return to the `get_server_callbacks` function later, but for now, let me continue on the overall shape of the server, which uses the `libuv` adapter via `async_queue`:

```
// Create server wrapper and start the server.
networkprotocoldsl_uv::LibuvServerWrapper
   server_wrapper(program, server_callbacks, async_queue);
```

And with that, we can actually bind the server to the configured port, and make sure the binding was successful:

```
auto bind_future =
  server_wrapper.start(config.bind_ip, config.bind_port);
bind_future.wait();
auto bind_result = bind_future.get();
if (std::holds_alternative<std::string>(bind_result)) {
    std::cerr
        << "Bind failed: "
        << std::get<std::string>(bind_result)
        << std::endl;
    return std::nullopt;
}
```

At this point, we know the server is bound and waiting for connections, so I just set up a condition variable that gets triggered by a `SIGINT` signal to finally tell the server to stop:

```
// Setup signal handling for SIGINT.
std::signal(SIGINT, signal_handler);
std::cerr
 << "Server is running; press Ctrl+C to stop." << std::endl;
{
  std::unique_lock<std::mutex> lock(signal_mtx);
  signal_cv.wait(lock, [] { return stop_signal_received; });
}
std::cerr << "Stopping server... " << std::flush;
server_wrapper.stop();
```

Once the signal is received, the `main_server` function returns to `main()`, which unwinds `libuv` and exits the process.

Implementing callbacks

Now, I can finally get to the part where the callbacks are defined. Since this is an implementation of the server, I only need to specify callbacks for the states in which the server is the agent. Let me start with the `get_server_callbacks` function:

```
networkprotocoldsl::InterpreterRunner::callback_map
get_server_callbacks(const ServerConfiguration &config) {
  return InterpreterRunner::callback_map{
      {"Open",
       [&config](const std::vector<Value> &args) -> Value {
         return onOpen(config, args);
       }},
      {"AwaitServerEHLOResponse",
       [&config](const std::vector<Value> &args) -> Value {
         return onAwaitServerEHLOResponse(config, args);
       }},
      {"AwaitServerMAILFROMResponse",
       [&config](const std::vector<Value> &args) -> Value {
         return onAwaitServerMAILFROMResponse(config, args);
       }},
      {"AwaitServerRCPTTOResponse",
       [&config](const std::vector<Value> &args) -> Value {
         return onAwaitServerRCPTTOResponse(config, args);
       }},
      {"AwaitServerDATAResponse",
       [&config](const std::vector<Value> &args) -> Value {
         return onAwaitServerDATAResponse(config, args);
       }},
      {"AwaitServerDATAContentResponse",
       [&config](const std::vector<Value> &args) -> Value {
         return onAwaitServerDATAContentResponse(
                    config, args);
       }},
      {"AwaitServerQUITResponse",
       [&config](const std::vector<Value> &args) -> Value {
```

```
          return onAwaitServerQUITResponse(config, args);
        }},
       {"Closed",
        [&config](const std::vector<Value> &args) -> Value {
          return onClosed(config, args);
        }}};
}
```

Here, I use a lambda capture to close over the `config` argument, which will then be passed to each of the callbacks. And that's the only state those callbacks will have access to, ensuring that the only data available to each state is the one that flows through the state machine.

I won't go over every one of those callbacks, but I'll walk through a few representative ones to illustrate the point. Let's start with the callback handling the `EHLO` response:

```
static Value
onAwaitServerEHLOResponse(const ServerConfiguration &config,
                          const std::vector<Value> &args) {
  // Extract the data dictionary from the incoming message.
  value::Dictionary dict =
      std::get<value::Dictionary>(args[0]);
  auto client_domain_member =
      dict.members->at("client_domain");
  std::string client_domain =
      *std::get<value::Octets>(client_domain_member).data;
  if (config.blocked_client_domains.find(client_domain) !=
       config.blocked_client_domains.end()) {
    return value::DynamicList{
    {_o("SMTP EHLO Failure Response"),
     value::Dictionary{
       {{"client_domain", client_domain_member},
        {"code_tens", 55},
        {"msg", _o("Bad client, go away!")}}}}}};
  }
  return value::DynamicList{
      {_o("SMTP EHLO Success Response"),
       value::Dictionary{
         {{"client_domain", client_domain_member},
          {"code_tens", 50},
```

```
            {"msg", _o("Hello, pleased to meet you")}}}}};
}
```

In this case, the server will check whether the client domain is in a list of blocked domains, and if so, instructs the protocol to take the "`SMTP EHLO Failure Response`" transition; otherwise, it proceeds with the "`SMTP EHLO Success Response`" transition. The data that should be included in that transition is then forwarded accordingly by the callback through its output dictionary. The _o function is a simple wrapper that returns `value::Octets` by taking `const char*` as input; it makes the code a lot easier to read.

For a final illustration of the implementation, let me walk you through the callback that actually writes down the email into `maildir`. I will go through it one section at a time, starting with extracting the context from the incoming dictionary:

```
value::Dictionary dict = std::get<value::Dictionary>(args[0]);
auto client_domain = dict.members->at("client_domain");
auto sender = dict.members->at("sender");
auto recipient_list =
 std::get<value::DynamicList>(
    dict.members->at("recipient_list"));
auto content =
 *std::get<value::Octets>(
   dict.members->at("content")).data;
```

It's important to note that it is safe to use `std::get` directly here, because the data is actually correctly typed as it flows through the state transitions. It may still be interesting to include runtime assertions for your developer builds to ensure that, but for the purposes of this exercise, I wanted to focus on the specifics of the SMTP server. And at this point, all the data required to actually record the incoming emails is available.

I will not cover the details of how the `maildir` files get written, since there's nothing particular to the interpreter there, so let me skip to the end:

```
return value::DynamicList{
    {_o("SMTP DATA Written"),
     value::Dictionary{
        {{"client_domain", client_domain},
         {"code_tens", 50},
         {"msg", _o("Message accepted for delivery")}}}}};
```

And since this transition will lead back to the state where the client can send another command, the output dictionary goes back to including only `client_domain`, ensuring that no additional data from the previous states leaks through to it.

You can see the entire code for the example SMTP server in pull request #50 (`https://github.com/PacktPublishing/Building-Programming-Language-Interpreters/pull/50`).

Finally, to prove that everything works, I'll launch the server and deliver a message via telnet:

```
$ telnet localhost 8080
Trying 127.0.0.1...
Connected to localhost.
Escape character is '^]'.
220 Welcome to the SMTP server
EHLO mydomain.com
250 Hello, pleased to meet you
MAIL FROM:<ruoso@test.com>
250 Sender OK
RCPT TO:<user1@example.com>
250 Recipient OK
RCPT TO:<user2@example.com>
250 Recipient OK
DATA
354 Start mail input; end with <CRLF>.<CRLF>
From: ruoso@test.com
To: user1@example.com
Subject: Test

This is a test email.


.
250 Message accepted for delivery
QUIT
221 Closing connection, goodbye
Connection closed by foreign host.
```

With this, I have an end-to-end demonstration of the interpreter working with a fairly complex network protocol, where the code that I had to write in the native language remains completely abstracted from the network communication, interacting only with the interpreter's transitions and data structures.

My goal with this section has been to help you navigate evaluating your own interpreter. The important point is finding a use case that actually demonstrates how your programming language and interpreter are able to deliver a value that would be harder to deliver in the native language.

If you are building a general-purpose language, there are plenty of exercises that can be used to evaluate how your language provides benefits for specific types of exercises and how the specific trade-offs you chose result in a better experience for the user.

In the next section, I will come to the conclusion of this overall exercise and reflect on the results.

Was it worth it?

Before we can talk about whether the effort was worth it or not, it's important to think about the costs involved. Of course, not all of them can be measured, but I did spend a significant amount of time in the design phase. That being said, the **source lines of code (SLOC)** count is not a completely unreasonable metric to consider.

Using the **sloccount** tool, here's the summary for how many lines of code were used on the various parts of the project:

Lines of code	Directory
6,329	`src/networkprotocoldsl`
653	`src/networkprotocoldsl_uv`
2,850	`tests/`
408	`Examples/`

Table 17.1: Source lines of code across the project

Of course, this is far from a complete interpreter, and there would still be a significant amount of work to do before this can be considered production quality. But I, personally, was actually expecting it to require a lot more code before achieving this first release.

I think being able to reason about each part of the problem as I have been doing throughout this journey has allowed me to develop fairly well-constructed components that ended up fitting together without many surprises in the end.

My main goal with guiding you through that journey was, in part, to demystify just how complex building an interpreter can be, and I hope that I was able to convey that it is more accessible than you may have thought before.

My secondary goal was to showcase how the latest features of the C++ language have made it significantly more interesting to solve these kinds of complex problems, and I hope that I have been able to inspire you to do a deeper dive into those features, as that is likely to benefit you in other areas as well.

If this had been actual infrastructure for a product, it would be a lot more straightforward to decide whether the investment made sense. For example, if you are in the game development space, you might see the opportunity of offering artists better tools to integrate content into your games.

I do have a confession to make, which is that this idea of a DSL for describing network protocols has been on my mind for the past 20 years, although it never fit into any of the projects that I was working on until now, and maybe that puts me at a bias that this was definitely worth the effort. I guess I will see whether more people agree with this interest of mine, so I guess I'll see you in pull requests.

Summary

When evaluating the results, it's always important to go back to the original goals that you set when starting the project. Some of those goals will have survived till the end, while other goals will have become requirements for a future version.

Finding the balance between your initial goals and the scope of an MVP is hard. That's why it helps to have a precise description of what it is that you consider a true test of success. This forms the acceptance criteria. In that sense, developing a new programming language and interpreter is not that different from other software development projects.

One thing that is different, though, is the fact that a new programming language and a new interpreter can only be proven by trying to use them in new scenarios that you hadn't exercised before, and seeing how they perform end to end. That way, you will have a very concrete idea of how useful they are.

At the end of the day, the economic value of building a new programming language and a new interpreter will depend a lot on the context and requires a careful cost–benefit analysis, as with any other project. That being said, I hope this journey has shown you that the cost may not be as high as you thought.

18

Unlock Your Exclusive Benefits

Your copy of this book includes the following exclusive benefits:

- Next-gen Packt Reader
- DRM-free PDF/ePub downloads

Follow the guide below to unlock them. The process takes only a few minutes and needs to be completed once.

Unlock this Book's Free Benefits in 3 Easy Steps

Step 1

Keep your purchase invoice ready for *Step 3*. If you have a physical copy, scan it using your phone and save it as a PDF, JPG, or PNG.

For more help on finding your invoice, visit `https://www.packtpub.com/unlock-benefits/help`.

> **Note:** If you bought this book directly from Packt, no invoice is required. After *Step 2*, you can access your exclusive content right away.

Step 2

Scan the QR code or go to `packtpub.com/unlock`.

On the page that opens (similar to *Figure 18.1* on desktop), search for this book by name and select the correct edition.

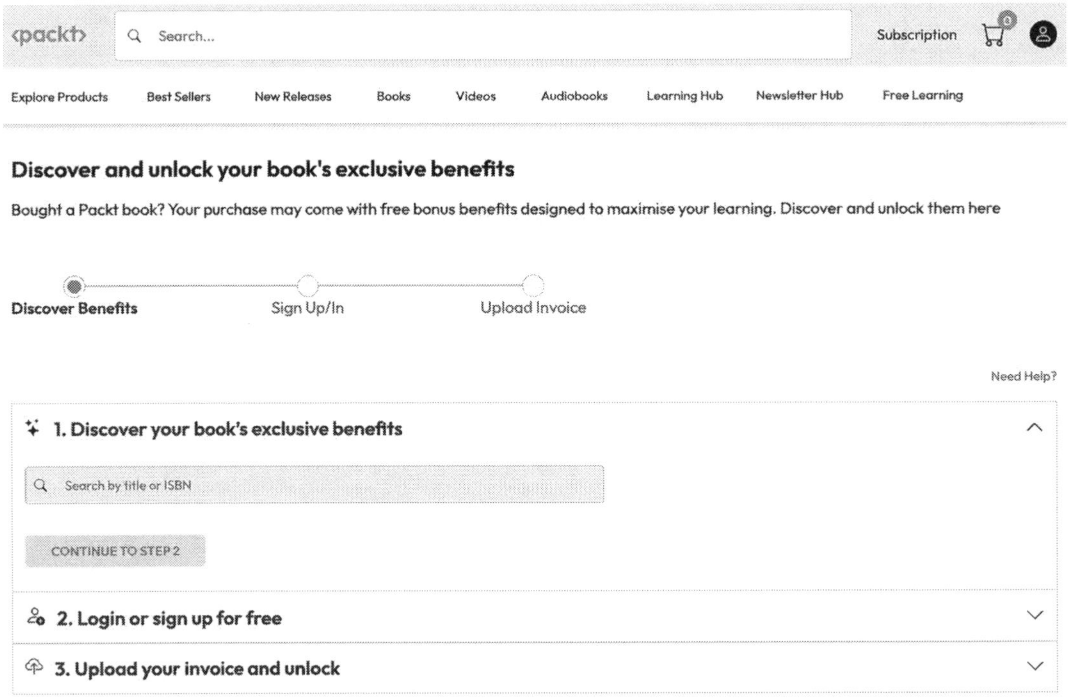

Figure 18.1: Packt unlock landing page on desktop

Step 3

After selecting your book, sign in to your Packt account or create one for free. Then upload your invoice (PDF, PNG, or JPG, up to 10 MB). Follow the on-screen instructions to finish the process.

Need help?

If you get stuck and need help, visit `https://www.packtpub.com/unlock-benefits/help` for a detailed FAQ on how to find your invoices and more. This QR code will take you to the help page.

Note: If you are still facing issues, reach out to `customercare@packt.com`.

packtpub.com

Subscribe to our online digital library for full access to over 7,000 books and videos, as well as industry leading tools to help you plan your personal development and advance your career. For more information, please visit our website.

Why subscribe?

- Spend less time learning and more time coding with practical eBooks and Videos from over 4,000 industry professionals
- Improve your learning with Skill Plans built especially for you
- Get a free eBook or video every month
- Fully searchable for easy access to vital information
- Copy and paste, print, and bookmark content

At www.packtpub.com, you can also read a collection of free technical articles, sign up for a range of free newsletters, and receive exclusive discounts and offers on Packt books and eBooks.

Other Books You May Enjoy

If you enjoyed this book, you may be interested in these other books by Packt:

LLVM Code Generation

Quentin Colombet

ISBN: 9781835462577

- Understand essential compiler concepts, such as SSA, dominance, and ABI
- Build and extend LLVM backends for creating custom compiler features
- Optimize code by manipulating LLVM's Intermediate Representation
- Contribute effectively to LLVM open-source projects and development
- Develop debugging skills for LLVM optimizations and passes
- Grasp how encoding and (dis)assembling work in the context of compilers
- Utilize LLVM's TableGen DSL for creating custom compiler models

The C++ Programmer's Mindset

Sam Morley

ISBN: 9781835888438

- Apply computational thinking to complex C++ problems
- Break problems into components using abstraction
- Use algorithms and data structures effectively in C++
- Design modular and reusable C++ code
- Analyze and improve algorithmic performance
- Parse, transform, and interpret data in multiple formats
- Scale up with concurrency, GPUs, and profiling tools

Packt is searching for authors like you

If you're interested in becoming an author for Packt, please visit `authors.packt.com` and apply today. We have worked with thousands of developers and tech professionals, just like you, to help them share their insight with the global tech community. You can make a general application, apply for a specific hot topic that we are recruiting an author for, or submit your own idea.

Share your thoughts

Now you've finished *Building Programming Language Interpreters*, we'd love to hear your thoughts! Scan the QR code below to go straight to the Amazon review page for this book and share your feedback or leave a review on the site that you purchased it from.

`https://packt.link/r/1837638071`

Your review is important to us and the tech community and will help us make sure we're delivering excellent quality content.

Subscribe to Deep Engineering

Join thousands of developers and architects who want to understand how software is changing, deepen their expertise, and build systems that last.

Deep Engineering is a weekly expert-led newsletter for experienced practitioners, featuring original analysis, technical interviews, and curated insights on architecture, system design, and modern programming practice.

Scan the QR or visit the link to subscribe for free.

`https://packt.link/deep-engineering-newsletter`

Index

A

B

C

H

I

J

L

M

N

O

P

R

S

Made in United States
Orlando, FL
04 November 2026

90201655R00205